NOT IN A TUSCAN VILLA

DURING A YEAR IN ITALY, A NEW JERSEY COUPLE DISCOVERS THE TRUE *DOLCE VITA* WHEN THEY TRADE ROSE-COLORED GLASSES FOR 3 Ds

JOHN AND NANCY PETRALIA

Cover design by Toby Schmidt Meyer
Published in the United States by Chartiers Creek Press, LLC
Copyright © John and Nancy Petralia, 2013 All rights reserved.

ISBN-10: 0615762530
EAN-13: 9780615762531

BEFORE ITALY

What you get by achieving your goals is not as important as what you become by achieving your goals.

HENRY DAVID THOREAU

BEFORE ITALY. LIKE BC, BCE, OR AD, IT'S THE NAME I GIVE TO THE period in my life before our year in Italy—April 2009 to March 2010—the year that changed our lives.

Before Italy, Nancy and I dreamed of living *La Dolce Vita*. It was something we both wanted to do—you know, sometime in the future.

Nancy's my wife. Before Italy, I would serve Nancy coffee in the morning. Now, along with a wake-up kiss, she gets a frothy cappuccino. No, I don't have one of those big fancy chrome-finished machines with an array of handles, spouts, and nozzles that only professional baristas can operate properly. Instead, Nancy gets a squirt of coffee—brewed from Starbuck's beans—topped, not with steamed milk, but with skim milk whipped with a little battery-powered mixer we bought at IKEA.

Don't misunderstand. Save for a few specialties like grilling, coffee, and sandwiches, I leave most of the food preparation to Nancy. I'm the full-blooded Sicilian. She's a perfect Scots-Irish blend. But when it comes to cooking, Nancy is thoroughly Italian.

Before Italy, we cooked authentic Italian dishes. We still do. Except now we know there are two kinds of polenta—yellow and white. With fish, we prefer the latter because of its lighter, subtler flavor. Our cupboard also contains salt from Cervia, Sicily, and Sardinia, a variety of milling peppers, three or four different types of anchovies, tuna in jars, and three Italian rices including a black variety called *Venere Riso Nero*. No, it's not infused with squid ink. *Riso Nero* is naturally black rice, crunchy and delicious. Nancy frequently serves it with seafood, especially shellfish. Delicious.

Like me, Nancy has lived most of her life in the Philadelphia area. When we both retired in 2001, we moved full-time into what used to be our second home. Located on Long Beach Island (LBI), a barrier island 65 miles east of Philadelphia off the coast of New Jersey, our house is a short walk from the beach.

Before Italy, Nancy and I would take long walks on the beach. With ocean accompaniment, her voice is like music. I've always enjoyed listening to the sound of her voice. Now, I also like listening to what she's saying.

Before Italy, I followed the Philadelphia Phillies. During our year in Italy, however, I became an obsessed fan. Whether we were in our apartment or in a hotel, the first thing I did in the morning was switch on my computer to check scores, batting averages, and injuries. When he came to visit, my brother Robert fed my obsession with various Phillies paraphernalia including a red and white Phillies cap.

Ball caps, especially ones emblazoned with Yankees logos, are certainly not uncommon in Italy. At tourist sites, you can find street vendors selling assorted fake Yankees shirts and caps—often in weird color combinations. I tease my American friends going to Europe that if they want to blend in with the locals, they should wear tight jeans, soccer shoes and a Yankees cap, preferably a purple one with green letters.

Before Italy, I thought America's best days were behind us. I admired President Obama personally, but I saw his inexperience and ultraliberalism as only helping to accelerate our downward trajectory. While in Italy, interacting with Italians and other Europeans, I started to understand why Italians still see

America as a land of opportunity, and why President Obama has become the embodiment of hope to young people everywhere.

Before Italy, I had not yet formulated my "Theory of Imperfection," which states that you can get the most wonderful outcomes—an incredible meal, a great story, a superior investment portfolio, and even a stronger country—from seemingly imperfect components. The secret is in the blending.

Before Italy, I didn't know that Italian-Americans had fought in every American war, including the War of Independence and the Civil War. At one point, Lincoln considered making Italian hero, General Giuseppe Garibaldi, head of the Army of the Potomac. The persistence of slavery in the Union in 1861 queered the deal. Although Garibaldi never got to swap his trademark red shirt for a blue coat, thousands of his brave troops fought to rid America of slavery. One ex-red-shirt, General Luigi Palma di Cesnola, was awarded the U. S. Congressional Medal of Honor. By WWII, hundreds of thousands of Italian-Americans were serving in our armed services. Some were to die on the very same beaches where their parents and grandparents had once huddled in hopeful prayer before boarding ships heading to America.

Before Italy, I occasionally used my bike for exercise. It's one of those multispeed, sleek English racers—fenderless, with hand brakes, skinny tires, and sloping handlebars that forced my head into my crotch. In Parma, we rode creaky old Holland-style bikes—fenders, one speed, upright handle bars, padded seat, bell, light, and a huge shopping basket. We used them constantly, for commuting to the train, sightseeing, joy riding, shopping, and picnicking in distant parks.

Before Italy, I kept my wallet in my pants pockets. While in Bologna, a deft, infant-toting gypsy lifted it. Thanks to fast thinking, quick action, and a threatening stance—all by Nancy—I got my wallet back. On my bike in Parma, I realized I could not stop change from falling out of my pants pockets. The solution: a man-bag. I bought it at a local flea-market. Small and black with a cross-body strap, I found it handy for carrying currency, passports, train tickets, and change. Yes, it does match my soccer shoes. And, yes, I do use it in the States, even in New Jersey. (You talkin' to me?)

Before Italy, I could only read in English. Now, with a dictionary and grammar book by my side, I regularly read articles and books—even some of our book club selections—in Italian. Admittedly, it's a struggle, but reading, for me, is the best way to decipher the vagaries of the seemingly incomprehensible Italian verb forms, especially the subjunctive. If you want to avoid the subjunctive, never start a sentence with "if."

If I had to give just one reason why anyone would want to learn to read, write, and speak Italian, it would be so that you might one day experience the thrill that Nancy and I did when we sat one warm, fall evening at an outdoor café enjoying a *spritz* with new friends—a bestselling Italian author and his fiancée—discussing his important new book, all in Italian.

Before Italy, I could not write a letter in Italian. Now, I use my laptop to hunt and peck e-mails and even letters in acceptable Italian. Curiously, when I compose in English, I do so mostly in long hand. I suppose it's some sort of muscle memory thing that drives my two different modes of composition. I learned English on paper. But I learned to write Italian in the computer age.

English is my mother tongue, sort of. When I was a child, my parents spoke a Sicilian dialect, with a little English thrown in. Reluctant immigrants, they left sunny Sicily in part to seek a better life in America. My parents loved their adopted country for many reasons but mostly for the advantages America gave their four boys, all born in Philadelphia. In their minds, however, Sicily was home.

Before Italy, Nancy and I contemplated making Sicily our base of operation for our *Dolce Vita* year. But it was too removed from the art and culture of Rome, Florence and Venice. After considerable research, we chose Bologna. On paper, Bologna seemed perfect—medium sized, centrally located, with a great university and good food. Unfortunately, it proved to be a terrible mistake.

Before Italy, I knew little about socialized medicine. Although I am retired and on Medicare, philosophically I did not like the idea of universal healthcare. Hospitalized twice in Italy, I learned first-hand what it's like to be a patient in a foreign country. While I don't recommend getting sick to prove the point, I will tell you unashamedly that my encounters, bolstered by some solid research, sold me on universal healthcare. I have no doubt that if adopted in America, the Italian preventive-medicine approach to healthcare would not only help our economy but it would also increase our lifespans.

Oh, I know about Italy's national debt problem. But you can't blame it on their healthcare program. The fact is, Italy's debt as percent of GNP is about the same as ours. Both countries have governments that spend more than they take in. Italy's debt differs from ours in two important ways, however. First, most of Italy's debt is owed to their fellow citizens, not to China. Second, Italian government spending (funded by taxes and debt) provides, in addition to other services, *free* higher education as well as universal healthcare. In America, we over-indebted individuals pay for both.

Before Italy, we were active members of our little beach community. While in Italy, we discovered that almost all towns, even little ones like my namesake Petralia, in Sicily, put major emphasis on reducing their dependency on fossil fuels. Moreover, for Italians it's important to bury utility wires. Since our return home, we have become activists—environmental ones.

Before Italy, I was content to look back on my life's achievements. Now, I just want to look forward.

The Dream Realized

Cannot see contents of nut until shell is cracked.

Charlie Chan

The taxi deposits John and me and our heaps of luggage on the wet sidewalk in front of the apartment building where we had arranged to live. We recognize it immediately from the photos Gemma had sent. Renting on the internet, we'd taken the extra precaution of meeting our landlady in New York, and she immediately charmed us. Now, standing in the cold April drizzle with our eight suitcases, I blow my nose while John rings the bell under her name. Within moments a woman opens the door and embraces us. Elvira, Gemma's mother, is tiny, dressed in smart low heels, a brown wool skirt and heather jacket, a grey and brown scarf around her neck. Behind her, a sweater-clad young man in his 20s grins, shouts *Ciao*, grabs two suitcases and heads back inside. Together we move everything from the street to the elevator and then up to the second floor.

The apartment looks just like the internet photos—a little sparse. The antique sofa, which had given me pause when I saw it in the living room photo, is more worn than I'd expected. But I'd already figured on purchasing some pillows to brighten things up. I've even planned on making covers for the ladderback chairs at the dining table. Squirreled away somewhere in my luggage are several rolls of iron-on seam tape and velcro for just that purpose.

Elvira and Gino, Gemma's brother, are already in an animated Italian chat with John. We leave the pile of suitcases in the hallway, and Elvira shows us around the apartment explaining how to operate the washing machine and where the vacuum cleaner is stored. She speaks no English, so I'm doing my best to follow her off-hand directions. The "well-equipped" kitchen Gemma promised is actually early-dorm-room. Pointing it out, Elvira thinks I'll be pleased with the American-style drip coffeemaker (probably left over from the last tenants) rather than a traditional Italian one. She had bought everything I'd inquired about—cutting board, kitchen knives, an ironing board—but the quality is bare minimum. Taking credit for her thoroughness, she points out the two new plastic mixing bowls and a rectangular glass baking dish.

Down the hallway we finally see beyond the corners of the bedrooms shown in the photos (all of which were strategically angled and didn't show much) and discover that the beds are from IKEA. They're very low with thin, flat mattresses. At least there's a pretty duvet on the master bed. When Elriva and I start to make it, however, the sheets don't fit. The towels are old, thin as a dish rag and rough as carpet. I'm more than a little disappointed. I was hoping for a bit more comfort (even luxury) for our $2400 a month.

After the tour Elvira gets down to business. Quite a piece of work that woman! No broad smiles and reassurances like her daughter. She's firm and a little haughty. "Everything is to be paid in cash. I'll collect the rent and the utilities in person every month."

John has on his diplomatic face, "The utilities are included in the rent," he tells her. But she's standing firm that they aren't.

Thankfully we brought a copy of our lease. Although it's clear on this point, she isn't convinced until John whips out his cellphone and calls Gemma. Yes, we're right and Elvira backs down. Telephone and internet are another matter though. We asked several times to have them working when we arrived but it hasn't been done. "You can easily sign up for them yourself," Elvira tells us in a matter-of-fact, dismissive tone.

Gino, more empathetic than his mother, promises to come the next day with his car and take us grocery shopping and then to order the phone and internet service. We agree that the rent, TV, and internet expenses will be paid in cash to Elvira on the fifth of the month. Her "welcome" assignment completed, she slips on her coat and the two of them depart.

After nearly twenty hours of travel, schlepping everything we'll need for a year, we can't wait to relax. John plunks down on the vintage sofa and broken springs push back. "This thing is horrible." He bounces down the seven foot length. "There isn't a comfortable spot on it."

I try it out too. "You're right. We can't sit on this. We'll have to ask her to replace it. In the meantime, we've got these little upholstered seats. They're okay." Armless and narrow, they sit about 18 inches above the floor. Next to the other furniture, they look like kiddie chairs.

"Not for me. I've got to have a place to *rest*," he says, flopping heavily into the black vinyl chair. "This isn't so great either." Injured when he was young, John's back has been a lifelong problem.

"Before you get too comfortable," I tease heading for the suitcases, "we should get a few things unpacked. At least the essentials. I think our underwear and sweaters are in the bag with the blue tag. I'll get my tote bag unloaded. We're both running on adrenaline, so we might as well take advantage of it. We'll crash soon enough."

We decide to put all the still-packed luggage in the small, third bedroom that faces the street. I plan to set this room up as an office so we can keep all our electronics, books, and travel paraphernalia out of the modest living-dining room.

The only photo we'd seen of this third bedroom was of an alcove with a daybed that had looked passable. There's also an old wooden desk, some cheap mismatched chairs of wood and metal, and a few bookshelves mounted on two walls at just the right height to crack your skull. Along the back wall is a doubled-up metal frame of another single bed—ugly and useless. There's also a large freestanding clothes closet. Inside the room's door, a plastic sticker is affixed to the lower panel. When I pull it off there's a big hole.

I'm sure the hassle of traveling has made me cranky, but the whole place feels shabby. Nothing anywhere in the apartment matches. I guess I'd watched too much HGTV and read too many Martha Stewart magazines back home. My dream of an Italian home was like the simple but elegant hotel rooms we stayed in and the *agriturismo*, a farm B&B, we visited 15 years ago. Spotless, with lace-trimmed linens ironed smooth as marble. I think about my New Jersey home with it's sleek, modern Italian furnishings. We aren't wealthy. We have plenty of IKEA finds, but we treasure good clean design. Do I have to live like a student at age 61? Okay, I tell myself, don't obsess about this. You're resourceful. You can manage this. It'll just take a little time and imagination.

"Let's go for a walk," John suggests. "We've unpacked enough. It's time to work the travel kinks out of our bodies."

"Great. I'm ready for a little Bologna scenery."

We head downstairs, dash across the wet road, and slowly walk under the portico, passing dog walkers and people toting groceries along with their dripping umbrellas. I can't help peering at them. These are our Italian neighbors. We pass office storefronts, some *alimentari*, vegetable stands, and a few tiny restaurants. We stop at the open door of a fishmonger and inhale a bit of sea air wafting from the fresh catch. Across the street, a wave of wisteria tumbles over a wall toward the sidewalk. There's so much to take in.

About half a mile away, the portico ends across from the Saragozza Gate and we pause in the drizzle. Guarding the old part of the city, it's one of twelve gates that were once the only entrances to the walled town. The gate looks like a tiny castle itself with a high arched entrance topped by an overhang with small elegant arches supporting it's tiled roof. A portico is attached to each side, and next to each of them are round turrets with crown-like tops. Two lions, on high columns, guard the front of the gate.

"Isn't that great," I say, admiring its typical Bologna style. This ancient city is our home now—so different from America.

Before I can start walking again John says, "It would be fun to go on into town now, but I'm *tired*, and it's still raining. Let's head back."

On our return walk, we discover an *enoteca*, an Italian wine bar that serves "small plates." When we enter, we're the only patrons. There's a waiter and a bartender and we quickly learn they're the owners. Alberto *con capelli*, with hair, I dub him this for his long grey ponytail, and Alberto *senza capelli*, balding, are friendly and tolerant of my halting Italian speech. Telling them that it's our first day here and that it's my birthday, we settle in with our wine at a table in the next room where a band is setting up. It's jazz night—four pieces and a singer. Minutes later Alberto *con* appears at our table with a large plate laden with paper-thin slices of mortadella, prosciutto, salami, and big hunks of Parmiggiano-Reggiano.

"*Buon compleano,*" he smiles. Happy birthday.

I'm deeply touched by this unexpected gesture. The Albertos have made us feel welcome in this city. There will be challenges but I decide in that moment that life here will be more about the people we meet and befriend than any inconveniences we experience.

Not long afterwards, the band begins then stops. They tell us they're just warming up and that the show will start at 10:30 or 11:00. But by 10:00 we're too sleepy to stay any longer. We bid *buona notte* to the band and the two Albertos, walk home, and crawl into our low, creaky bed.

"Well, here we are," John says, pulling the ill-fitting blankets up over his shoulders. With the shutters drawn tight, the room is completely dark. Outside we can still hear the street traffic whizzing by.

"I still can't believe it. That was a really nice thing the Albertos did. It made my birthday for me. That, and moving here." It's cold in the apartment and I snuggle closer to John. "I still can't get over not having to go through Customs."

I'd read that Italian Customs were really tough, so I followed every direction explicitly and packed our medicines and vitamins in more than a dozen, separate, plastic bags making our carry-on extra bulky. To get around the weight allowance, we'd filled our coat pockets with converters, chargers, a router, and other heavy electronics. For the entire trip we felt like barbell smugglers. Exhausted, we arrived in Bologna, followed the crowd through the airport, and wound up at the taxi stand. No Customs at all.

I feel his arm tighten around me and I say, "I was really worried about you being your usual macho self. Lugging all those suitcases around without letting me help. We need to take it easy for a bit now. Rest up for the year ahead."

"Well, tomorrow we'll get our internet ordered. Until we get it, we'll have to find some other way to communicate with the folks at home. I don't want them to worry about us." He squeezes me closer. "Now it's time for sleepy. Happy Birthday. I love my Baby."

"I love you too."

It began with his birthday gift.

A first-generation American, John heard his parents talking to each other in their Sicilian dialect all their lives. But, like most immigrants of the 1930s, they were determined that their sons be *American*. No Italian talk from the boys. Years of listening, however, had given John a capacious vocabulary and good understanding of Italian. His grammar, though, was far from perfect. How often I'd heard him say he wanted to improve it and become fluent. So, on his 65th birthday, I had given him advanced Italian lessons at the nearby LBI Foundation for the Arts and Sciences.

Before long John had talked me into taking a beginner class, and I was surprised how much I enjoyed it. Italian is a difficult language—think ten ways to say "the." But slowly, it was sinking in. Our instructor, Rita Kostopolous, fostered what she considered her *famiglia italiano* through group dinners, movies, shopping excursions, and any excuse for a celebration. As our language confidence and circle of Italian-speaking friends grew, though, John and I realized that weekly classes were not going to make us fluent. To do that, we'd need an immersion experience. Increasingly, our conversations turned to our next visit to Italy.

"Wouldn't it be wonderful to stay for more than just a vacation?" we'd say wistfully, our eyes drifting off into visions of Venetian canals, Pompeii's ruins, and tiny trattorias. Once, we'd dreamed of spending a year in four countries, chasing the sun and warmth around the globe. Now we focused more and more on Italy.

"What we should do," John said one evening, "is pick a place and stay there for three or four months. Get to know the people and practice our Italian."

Like many Americans, the thought of living in romantic Italy was my ultimate fantasy. I envisioned old ladies in black dresses haunting the markets, chic women in high heels clicking their way down cobblestone streets, men gathering around an outside table playing cards or simply jabbering loudly together, tenor arias soaring from open windows, ancient ruins and slick modern furnishings, and, of course, the world's most wonderful food—one of my passions.

I may be Irish by birth, but I'm Italian by marriage and cuisine. I love to cook and entertain, and over the years I'd found myself more and more drawn to Mediterranean dishes. John's mother, whom unfortunately I never met, was a great cook, and my husband prides himself on his discriminating palate. At the end of a meal, he sometimes leans over and tells me, "A level *seven!*" Don't ask. The scale will always be his personal secret. But it's a high compliment.

"If we were to go," I said to John one evening, "I'd like to stay longer. In three months, we'll barely get settled before it would be time to leave."

"Maybe six months would be better," he replied, nodding slowly. Like the two fig trees we'd planted in our yard, our idea began to take root. Before long, like our budding trees, we too were reaching higher.

We talked about Italy constantly. Where would we live? What would we want to see and do? It may be only the size of Arizona, but Italy shoehorns more history and art into its boot than most of Europe and America combined. In our country, exploring our nation's oldest historical sites might entail a drive from Boston to Washington, D.C., with a stop in Philadelphia. In Italy, one trips over Roman ruins in almost every small town, and 700-year-old architecture is considered new. In our language class the occasional visitor from Italy told of less visited locales and unique customs found in many towns. These types of experiences, we decided, and the chances they would give us to interact with the locals and improve our language skills, that's the *real* Italy we wanted.

"If we're going to go," I said a few months later, "I want to spend a year. I want to experience everything the Italians do—all the seasons, the holidays, the festivals. And, I want to visit Sicily, to see where your family is from."

Yes, but *doing* it. How would we go about that? We aren't youngsters; we're both in our sixties. We'd traveled a good bit, been to Italy a few times, but never for more than a couple weeks. The thought of moving our entire lives across the ocean, living in another language, and dealing with foreign customs and systems was exhilarating—and daunting. This would take serious planning. And, just what would it cost to live our dream? We knew that being in one of the popular tourist cities would be fabulous, but it would also be expensive. Could we find someplace with good access, but not the high costs? We started searching the internet for ideas.

"Look at this place," John called one evening. "Doesn't it look great?" He was pointing at a rustic grey stone building with red shutters on the windows. Just to the left of the doorway sprouted a clump of yellow flowers, and in one of the windows you could see a white lace curtain blowing.

"Wow, yeah, it's adorable!. Where is it?"

"Outside a little village in Umbria."

"How far is the village?"

"It says just a kilometer." That's about two-thirds of a mile.

"And what's in the village? Let's Google Earth it." Hmmm. Not a lot there. And these photos have six inches of snow!

"There's supposed to be a bus into Orvieto. That's a good-sized town and you can pick up the train there."

We talked it over. There wouldn't be any car. Renting one would be impossibly expensive, so we'd have to walk. Let's imagine this...walk into the village...in the summer heat...in the winter snow...and then back again carrying all our supplies. If we needed more than basics, it would be a bus trip. We'd look for something else.

Slowly, we defined the criteria for our ideal city: a mid-size town off the tourist track so we'll have a better chance to practice our Italian; good transportation so we can travel without a car, and things we can do without advanced language skills. For each potential town we grabbed tour books, searched travel magazines and online reviews, and checked out Google photos. Does it look it hilly? What is the weather like throughout the year? Just where *is* the train station? How often do the trains run? How long does it take to get to...?

Meanwhile, John's grammar was improving and I'd grasped the present, present-perfect, imperfect, and future tenses. Sticky notes with Italian names covered all my kitchen foods and utensils. Opening a cupboard, John rolled his eyes and he groaned. But I'd progressed to the Intermediate class! Rita regaled us with funny stories *in italinao*. Our group went to a Catholic mass where John's classmate celebrated in Italian. We watched Italian films *Il Postino, Pane e Tulipi*, and *Ciao Professore* with the class and *La Dolce Vita* and *The Bicycle Thief* on our own. One afternoon John and I took the class on a tour of Philly's Italian market district and then to Franco's—for dinner with the singing patrons. With each experience, the pull toward Italy grew stronger.

"We need to *say* it," John announced one day. "Once we've told people, we can't turn back." Indeed, that had worked for us before. A few years ago we told people we were going to publish a book about the ecology of our island. Saying it helped us line up volunteers to write, edit, and illustrate *The Island Blue Pages*. And so, we started telling people about our Italian dream.

"We're going to live in Italy for a year," we'd say to family, friends, and neighbors. There. It was out in the world. We couldn't turn back, chicken out, give up. Otherwise we'll be just boasters and frauds. Now we *had* to go.

"You are! Why?" they'd ask.

"It's our dream. We want to live like Italians, experience Italy they way they do, not as tourists. And we want to improve our language skills. Become fluent."

"Where are you going to live?"

"We don't know yet. We have a lot to figure out. But we're *doing* it."

"Oh, I'd *love* to do that," the usual gushing reply. "Are you renting a villa?"

A villa! You've got be kidding. Fabulous idea for a week or two. Five bedrooms out in the countryside with a pool and a view of vine-covered hillsides. Olive oil from the owners' crop, wine from their cellars. Cost no object—it's just for a fortnight. Reality, actually *living* someplace, where you have to do your own toilet paper shopping, where you can't hire a cook or go to a restaurant for every meal, where you have to locate a hairdresser and maybe buy a new pair of boots or an umbrella, or find your way to a truffle festival, that's altogether *different*.

Just after the "we're going to live in Italy" line, we'd started adding, "Why don't you come and visit." So now we needed to look for a place with *two* bedrooms. And two baths—our one American-style concession.

14

We narrowed the search to someplace along the north-south train line. Much of what we wanted to see is north of Rome, so we cut the search off there. We could always travel to the southern areas. Rome and Florence were beyond our pocketbook, but perhaps Montevarchi or any one of dozens of other smaller cities might work. Todi, touted somewhere as the "most livable Italian city" was too remote. You couldn't get there without a car. Milan and Venice were too far west and east respectively.

"Bologna." John said one night. "I was there once, maybe 25 years ago. They've got these porticos, covered walkways, along all the streets. You can go just about anywhere in the city under them. And it's the switching center for the southern train line to Milan and Venice. All the trains go through there."

Compared to the traditional tourist cities, Bologna gets little coverage in the tour books. Rick Steves doesn't even mention it. We figured we'd have a better chance of finding non-English-speaking residents. Sounded good, but we needed to check it out. Google was our Oracle of Delphi.

Bologna was big enough (population 300,000) to have everything we needed. It's home to the first university in the world and has an excellent medical school. We could check off healthcare access. The old city retains much of its walls and medieval feel. Music seemed to be one of its attributes. I found lots of concert listings. Unlike Orvieto and many other charming towns that perch high on a hilltop, Bologna's old city nestles at the foot of its hills.

While John searched for apartments, I discovered that the Bologna Center, a part of John's Hopkins International School of Business, has a fantastic speaker program. Held in English, the lectures are *open to the public*. We like the stimulation of attending college classes, so this seemed perfect.

"Now," John said slowly, his eyes narrowing in thought, " we have to figure out how we can afford to do it."

This would be no small matter. As the saying goes, everything comes down to time and money. Time was no problem. We could go whenever we wanted. We'd have to see about the money. We aren't wealthy, but we do have one valuable asset. Our home is on the Jersey shore. In summer, our island's population swells from barely 9000 to more than 150,000. Many summer residents return to the family beach house. But many others rent a house. This could be the way to finance our trip. Once, when it was just our summer getaway, renting our place would have been an easy decision. Now, it's our *home*. All our personal stuff is here. The closets are full. The drawers are packed. Our artwork, though not particularly valuable, is cherished, much of it made by local artists and friends. And the house has five bedrooms, so it's likely there would be a big crowd staying. We contacted a few local rental agents for advice.

"Any rental from a listing," said one of the top agents, "is going to bring in at least ten or twelve people. Maybe more." I imagined wet bathing suits and sandy feet flopping on my sleek Italian furniture, and toy cars careening over my new dining table. "If you want to have just a couple here, you're better off renting it yourself."

In July we tacked a note on our tennis club's bulletin board about rental for the next summer. We spread the word among our friends: anyone with friends or family who wanted a place for the season, send them our way. I broached the subject with some summer residents at the local pottery studio. No takers. In late August a couple came to see the house. They seemed pleased, but decided to remain in Florida. Our prospects were dwindling.

Meanwhile, we started working on getting visas. Any visit to Italy that exceeds 90 days requires one. In the past, people would just leave the country for a few days then re-enter for another 90 day period, but the government had cracked down and this wasn't possible anymore. According to the Italian embassy website, there was an Italian consulate in Philadelphia where we could go to apply. I downloaded the forms and instructions. Just one problem. We needed to have a place of residence in our destination city. Back to the apartment search.

Unlike in America, there's no real estate multi-list in Italy. We were having an awful time locating anything for rent. Searching online brought up sites for villas, holiday homes and other short-term rentals, and two-room student housing. Family-type housing just wasn't there. Through one of our classmates we met a local woman who, it turned out, is from Bologna and keeps an apartment where she spends a few months each year.

"Italian rentals are handled by local agents within the city," she told us over lunch. "You have to go to each one to find out their listings. It's not like here."

"How do we find them? I'm having no luck online."

"Very few agencies are on the internet. The best thing to do would be to go there and check it out yourselves. You can visit the local agencies and see what they have, see what areas of the city you like." Unfortunately, a preview trip wasn't in the budget. Fortunately, she made a generous offer. "I'm going in about ten days. I can see if there are any agencies near my place." We thanked her and parted hopefully.

For months we spent several hours daily searching the web. At bedtime my eyes burned, and John's head throbbed. Maybe it was because of the warnings he'd read about online scams that prey on uninitiated Americans looking to rent abroad. While perusing some listings one afternoon, John noticed the same photo for apartments in three different areas of the city. The exact same photo. Kind of like finding the photo of your ideal mate on match.com...in Charleston, St. Louis, and Salt Lake City. Scratch them. While we found a Craig's List for Italy, it was scanty, especially for rentals. We checked VBRO.com for owner rentals—with no luck. Searching SabbaticalExchange.com for university listings, all we found were tiny grad-student type garrets.

The lady from Bologna failed to contact us. When we finally reached her, she said she wasn't able to find anything. "I guess I can understand," I told John. "If I only had a few weeks in my home city, I wouldn't be spending much time looking for apartments for someone I hardly knew." But this was a disappointment.

Then one day John called me over to his PC. "This looks pretty nice. Three bedrooms, two baths, nice looking building." The Craig's List entry had just a couple of photos, but they looked promising. We sent off an email to the owner.

It was now September and we still had no tenant. If we couldn't rent our place next summer we'd have to postpone our trip for an entire year. Then, around midmonth, the phone rang.

"You know Toby and Ed?" our friend Pat said. Of course we did. John had known them both for years. "They're looking for a house for next summer. The one they've been renting was just sold. I'll have them give you a call."

Two days later they came to look around. Toby, an artist and designer, loved the place. Ed loves what Toby loves. And they were both crazy about the location, just two minutes from the tennis courts.

"We'd like to rent to a couple, not a big crowd." John told them. "It would be great to have people we know, like you guys, in our home."

"It's just the two of us—maybe our grandkids on some weekends." Toby said. "You know we'll take good care of it. If you have any special people for cleaning or odd jobs, we'd like to use them." And so, we made a deal. Not nearly as much money as we could have made if we'd rented to a crowd on a weekly basis. But peace of mind, and matter, was worth more than extra money.

Our budget set, now we got serious about finding an apartment. We'd had a return email from the woman who owned the Bologna place. She sent a few more photos, but they didn't show much. She said it was rented to tenants who would be leaving at the end of November. She promised us better pictures then. In the meantime, she sent a floorplan. It looked almost perfect. A decent sized living-dining area and an eat-in kitchen. Two bedrooms, each with a convenient bath. A small bedroom where we could put our computers and printer. The price was at the top of our budget, but there was plenty of room for company, and it wasn't far from the city center. Navigating on foot would be no problem.

John continued to worry about the scam stories. The owner wanted us to wire two months rent, plus another two as security deposit. What if this wasn't what it appeared? Somewhere in her conversation, we learned she lived in New York. *That's just two hours away.* How about we meet for lunch and talk it over? And so, one morning in October we headed for Otto, Mario Batali's trattoria in Tribeca.

When the woman and her boyfriend arrived, they could have been from Central Casting. She was stunning, tall and slender with long, thick, waves of dark hair caressing her cheeks and shoulders. He was handsome with a shy smile and close-cropped curly brown hair. Dressed with casual elegance, they were both charming. And we were smitten—with them and the promise of the Bologna lifestyle. After an avalanche of recommendations and advice, we closed the deal over lunch. When we left, it was *baci, baci,* kisses on both cheeks. Our chatter on the way home was laced with excitement. *We were moving to ITALY!*

Gino arrives at noon the next day and drives us to a huge shopping area a few kilometers outside of town. First we go to Media World for cellphones, a TV upgrade and internet service. After purchasing two modest phones, we head to SKY, the satellite TV provider. A package that will give us access to international channels and news plus non-soccer sports will cost around $130 a month. But, because we aren't citizens, there's *una problema*. Only the property owner can order the service. What a crazy system! After some discussion we put the service in Gino's name, then pay for the installation and first month with our credit card. The clerk tells us it'll be done in about ten days. Next stop, the Fast Web counter for internet service. But there's no clerk available. Now this is a store about the size of a Super Walmart. It offers TVs, computers, washers, air conditioners, video games, household appliances, phone service from three providers, TV service, and internet access. So why is there only one clerk who can handle Fast Web? And he's not here today. "This is Italy," Gino explains with a shrug.

After lunch at a nearby *ristorante* we head to the supermarket for grocery staples. By the time we're finished, Gino's Ford Fiesta is packed to the roof. Back home again, we spend the rest of the day cleaning out from the old tenant and unpacking. Many people asked us about how we'd pack for a year. We brought all our electronics, prescriptions, rain gear, a bath pillow, blow-up hangers for drying clothes, and stain remover. Who knew the most valuable thing would be...the ShamWows..clothes wringer, bath mat, table cover, cleaning rag, and computer wrap. *Sono magnifico,* they're wonderful.

Two days after our arrival, we decide to find the *Questura*. When we got our visas, the embassy stressed that when we arrived in Italy, we would have eight days to apply for the *Permesso di Soggiorno*, a residency permit which allows us to stay for an extended period of time. The embassy's instructions were to go to the police station, called a *Questura*, to apply. Easy enough, we'll just ask a policeman. We find a pair of them walking the portico and ask them where the *Questura* is, so we can get our *permesso*.

"No, you need to go to the post office, not the *Questura*," one of them says. Okay, the instruction from the embassy was wrong. And it's after noon now, the *postale* is closed. The *permesso* will have to wait—but not for long.

"You're not sad, are you?" John says. It's 9:30 on our third night here, and I'm soaking in the bathtub. "I don't want you to be sad." My travel head cold has really taken hold, and I'm trying to steam my head open before turning in.

We've had a pretty good day. Finally found our way to Piazza Maggiore—the city's main square. About the size of Times Square, the several dozen people passing through were barely noticeable. There was no motor traffic but rather small groups of people, several dog walkers, and shoppers with their bags and packages. White granite lines divided the piazza's enormous stone-paved center into huge squares of red and grey. In front of the *duomo*, cathedral, kids were settled on the steps. Bordering two sides were block-long red buildings with decorative arch-shaped windows. Crimson banners hung just below the huge second story windows of one and Italian flags waved above the columned entrance of another. In one of the wide exits, a bronze King Neptune stood guard atop a fountain. Nearby, a chubby man in a jacquard clown suit and a red nose was filling helium balloons.

We walked past him onto Via Independenzia, the main shopping street. Under its broad, high porticos we ogled clothing and shoe stores, sniffed the aroma of fresh-baked pizzas, and squeezed past clusters of tiny tables in front of every restaurant, careful not to disturb the patrons. The Saturday throng bustled by—groups of lively college kids, strolling families pushing carriages, and couples arm in arm. Everyone eyed the shops but few were buyers.

We were trying to find a WiFi spot. Out of touch since we left America, John was anxious to check on a situation back home and to send an important email. So he'd been carrying his laptop and all our paperwork in his backpack. The PC is old and heavy, and it was clearly a strain. Everyone we asked sent us to rent-by-the-minute internet businesses. At the first one we realized we couldn't use our own machine, so that option was out.

I was sneezing and blowing into tissues all day, so about 3:30 we stopped in the Swine Bar—yep, that's its name. We ate in its cozy enclosed, heated outdoor area, which looks like a swanky living room. White sofas and low tables, warm wooden cupboards, and a few dining tables surrounded us. A big wood-burning stove filled the space with toasty scents and baked the chill off our bodies. We lingered over salads and bruschetta, then headed back through the cold.

Approaching Piazza Maggiore again, we discovered the *Bibliotecca*, city library, tucked under an archway of the government building. Inside we learned we could get free WiFi access for three hours a day, but only in the building and surrounding area. We'd have to come in every few days.

"It'll keep us off the computer and enjoying Italy," I said with a laugh.

The woman at the desk spoke excellent English and quickly got John set up. He sent off his email and we walked slowly home. At the entrance of an ancient *salumeria*, we stopped to admire the neat array of cheeses in the window. The air was thick with the aroma of long-aged hams, which dangled from most of the ceiling. We bought lemons, a big hunk of cheese, and a quarter of a prosciutto ham, all for the equivalent of $35. Macerated figs tempted us, but we left them for another day. The friendly proprietor, his head and shoulders just visible above a cooler piled with cheeses, was pleased when I offered up my own carry bag. "*Complementi, senora.*"

All day we'd been talking about the apartment. "How do you feel about staying here?" John asked over our dinner of cheese and prosciutto. "Should we look for something else?"

"The space is great. But not one of those chairs is comfortable, and the bed's lumpy. With only that dim ceiling light, I can't see a thing here in the kitchen. And it all feels so ragged." I hated to be so negative but a year's a long time.

He licked the oil from the olives off his fingers. "We did see photos, you know."

"Yeah, but only partials and not that many." I put another piece of the cheese in my mouth—a piquant explosion. "And photos are deceiving. It's just a lot shabbier than I thought it would be. Gemma's so elegant. I can't imagine her living here."

"It does seem incongruous. Maybe she stays with her folks when she comes. Hand me another piece of that bread please."

"Even before we left, I figured I'd buy some things to perk this place up, pillows and stuff." I piled a piece of the prosciutto and cheese on my slice. "Maybe a rug would help, and..."

"Hey, we don't want to refurnish the place. How about Monday we'll hit the rental agencies in the area?"

"Okay, sounds like a good idea. At least we can see what's out there."

"In the meantime," John said, as he refilled my glass, "we can make a list and call Gemma to tell her our concerns. We'll ask her to consider what she can do, talk to her mom and Gino, and let us know."

"That's a good plan."

Am I sad? No, just feeling punk. John's concern is endearing. He wants it all to be just like we dreamed. Back home our lives were full of distractions. Here it's just the two of us. We share our ideas and opinions, try not to bicker, and kiss a lot more than usual. We get lost together, share a snack together, and discover together. Fighting through the challenges together actually feels good.

BALANCING ACT

Any idiot can face a crisis - it's day to day living that wears you out.

ANTON CHEKHOV

I DON'T KNOW WHY OR HOW IT HAPPENS BUT SOMETIMES WHEN I LEARN A
new word, I can't stop myself from using it, even incorrectly.

Yesterday, my word was *squilibrato*. It means unbalanced, out of equilibrium.
To me it sounds like what it means, *squilibrato*. I love saying it. *Squilibrato. Squilibrato.
Squilibrato.*

I find endless uses for it, mostly pejorative. While crossing a street, a driver
who nearly hits us becomes a stinkin' *squilibrato*. A car that is parked on the
sidewalk—not an uncommon sight in Bologna—was obviously put there by a
half-assed *squilibrato*. The neighbor who ignored our Hello could best be described
as an arrogant *squilibrato*. The Italian Consulate in Philadelphia is manned by so
many *squilibrati*. Oh, by the way, in Italian, the plural of a word ending in "o" is
almost always formed by changing the "o" to "i." So it is that the immigration
police here in Bologna are at various times officious *squilibrati*, tedious *squilibrati*,
or, my favorite, god-damned *squilibrati*—depending on the *situazione*.

To be fair, my barbed use of Italian words is not restricted to strangers. After having too much wine with dinner, I have to admit that I become
more than a bit *squilibrato*. To get a laugh out of Nancy, I call her a *squilibratina*,

23

a completely made up word that could be the diminutive form of *squilibrato*. Fortunately, my obsessive episodes with a new word usually last only a day or two. During that time, the word becomes a mantra akin to the "om" in Herman Hesse's *Siddhartha*.

Today, my mantra is *disponibile*. It means available as in free, accessible, handy, or helpful. When I call the satellite TV company to ask about our TV hookup, I learn that Sky is not available in our building. "It is not *disponibile*" is the response to my question. But our landlady told us it would be *disponibile*, I say. I try to explain that the *disponibilità*, availability, of TV and Fast Web is important to us. We'd like to watch CNN and we must have access to the internet. "What does it take to make it *disponibile*?" I ask. When none of his responses satisfy me, I ask if his supervisor is *disponibile*? His response, "*Il capo non è disponibile.*" At that point, I'm convinced I'm dealing with a total *squilibrato*, so I give up, at least for the *momento*.

I know my fixation on isolated words paints me a bit bizarre. I neither defend nor hide my condition, or as they say in Italy, my *condizione*. Which brings me to another of my word obsessions: derivatives, as in many English words are *derived* from Italian. The words "moment," "situation," "pejorative," "bizarre," "diminutive," "condition," and "equilibrium," for example, all derive from Italian words, which is to say they are a form of *derivato*, derivative, which itself is derived from the word *derivare*, to derive. I am no expert, but my guess is half of all English words come from Italian.

What can be more American than blue jeans? Here's the derivation. Early jeans were made from a blue canvas that came from Genoa. In America, Blu Genoa became blue gen, as in: Hey Luigi, send me a shipment of some of that new-fangled blue gen stuff. The pants that Levi Strauss made from blu gen morphed (from *morfologia*) into blue jeans. *Comprendere?* Ditto for words like *descrivere*, describe, *presentazione*, presentation, and *foto*, photo.

Incidentally, ditto comes from the Italian, *detto* meaning said. Here in Bologna, to be emphatic, they like to say "*Detto, fatto.*" Said and done. As in, that will be last word on this subject, period, full-stop, point, *punto*. I've heard Italians also use *punto* dismissively in argument, *argumento*, as in I'll give you that point but let's get real, *realità*. This last point allows me to *segue*, or as they say in Italian, *segue*, to another variation on my word fixation: double-meanings.

The thing that can really throw me is when an Italian word does not mean what it sounds like. Very annoying. Two examples of these false friends are *fattoria* and *golf*. The former sounds like it should mean factory; instead it means farm. Golf, one of many English words imported into Italian, has a double-meaning. It does indeed refer to the game; I'm okay with that. But, *golf* also is what Italians call a pullover sweater. Go figure, *figura*.

In Italy, double-entendres are not that unusual. One of my favorite Italian characters is *Benvenuto Cellini*, the great 16th century goldsmith. His *autobiografia* can be found on many Great Books lists, *liste*. *Benvenuto*, a common Italian name, also means welcome, as in well come, as in *ben*, good, *venuto*, arrival. Frankly, I had never put the two roots together until a few days ago when I saw a sign in English, German, and Italian saying: Welcome, *Willkommen*, *Benvenuto*. Click. The light bulb in my head went on, at which point my mantra, from the word *mantenere* meaning to maintain, became *benvenuto* this and *benvenuto* that. It's a really nice word to say, particularly out loud. *Benvenuto!* But, believe me, if you walk the streets of Bologna screaming *benvenuto, benvenuto, benvenuto*, as I did, people are bound to think you're more than a bit *bizzarro* which is to say *squilibrato*. Which, come to think of it, might be the reason our neighbor ignored my Hello.

It's a Different System

The Promised Land always lies on the other side of a Wilderness.

HAVELOCK ELLIS

"I'VE *GOT* TO GET THESE STITCHES OUT," I SAY ON OUR FIFTH DAY IN ITALY. I'd had some minor surgery just before we left New Jersey, and the doctor had explained that because the cut was on my nose, I needed to be sure to have the stitches removed within ten days. Today is the ninth day.

"We'll look for a doctor's office when we go out today," John answers. We need to go to the post office first for our *permesso* papers. It's only a few blocks away.

The clerk is pleasant, but says we need to go to the main office, so we walk another mile or so to the *Postale.* Inside, the large space is packed with people. Near the door a yellow and blue machine dispenses tickets. It seems everywhere we go we have to take a number. Peering at the pictured selections, we try to discern which one we need, then choose what looks like an envelope and push the button. A printed slip, marked C127, emerges from the machine.

Long rows of chairs are set up near the front of the room. "The sign says they're on C95. Guess we should try to find a vacant seat," John says.

While we wait, we try to figure out the system. There are four kinds of lines. One is for *documenti*, documents. This looks like where people pay their bills. Another is for packages. A third is for stamps. The fourth seems to be for general purposes. The lines advance like the spring thaw, but everyone appears to be patient. We wait close to a half hour before our number comes up. At the counter a surly clerk tosses a large envelope at us with no explanation then turns to call another customer. Inside we find a stack of papers that we decide to leave for when we get back to the apartment.

Outside again, we head for a doctor's clinic we'd seen from the cab the day we arrived. Thankfully it's not far. Opening the office door, we find a small waiting room with about 25 people seated in the few chairs or leaning along the walls. We don't see any reception counter—not even a door. "We could be here all day," John says.

"We don't even know if this is the right kind of doc. We could wait all that time and still get turned away."

"I think we should go to a hospital."

Normally, I'd think this was serious overkill, but here in Italy, where we don't know the system, it seems a logical choice. "Let's get coffee first," I say.

Seated at a nearby *bar*, we watch several men step up to the counter for their *caffe`*. The barista serves it accompanied by a shot glass of clear liquid that gets downed after the hot brew. "What do you think that is?" I ask John. "Are these guys drinking *grappa* this early in the morning? How can they go to work?"

"Who knows. They've got some funny customs here. Maybe a good shot in the morning is how they start their day. I remember my mother making *spatude* for us before school. Egg yolk, sugar, coffee, and Madiera. Just the thing for a six-year-old." Turning to the barista, John asks, *"Dove prendiamo il bus per l'ospedale?"* Where do we take the bus to the hospital? She tells us the stop is just across the street. After I've spooned the last foam from my cappuccino cup, we catch the number 37 to *Ospedale Maggiore*.

The hospital is an enormous complex—modern, with a busy entrance. At the information desk, we're directed to the ER—around the side. There's a waiting area with some chairs far, far down the broad hallway, but to see the triage nurse we have to get in a line at this end of the room. A monitor overhead tracks this hospital with several others in the city for pending cases, designated as white, green, yellow, or red. We assume we're a green one—the wait almost three hours. "At least the line is pretty short," John observes. "I wonder why it takes so long." Eventually we find out.

Around the corner is the real ER entrance where the ambulances come in. Just like in the States, anyone coming in there preempts our line. But, there's just *one* triage nurse who handles everyone. In this whole big hospital, can't they find another nurse to work here and speed things up?

The line moves with the speed of an IV drip. In front of us is a young man from north Africa who's got a slip to get a physical. Beyond him are three young women, one of whom is nauseous. A construction worker is holding his hand, which is wrapped in a bloody cloth. Everyone is shifting from one foot to the other, rocking slowly back and forth, and looking around the room for anything of interest to pass the time. No TV or magazines, just a large clock whose hands tick, tick, tick in tiny jerks. When our turn finally comes, the nurse is professional and efficient.

"I just need to get these stitches removed." I show her the note I have from my American doctor with the date it needs to be done by—translated by an Italian speaker in his office to be sure it's clear. "Do you have a nurse who could do it?"

"You should see our nose specialist." She smiles and hands us some paperwork to take to another floor. When I suggest that's not necessary, she insists.

"Well, they sure are thorough," I say to John. "We'd never bother a specialist with this."

A volunteer escort takes us to the floor where we're to go to room number eight. But, every door has two sets of numbers—red and white, and, of course, there are two door number eights. A patient takes pity on us wandering from door to door. "Just sit over here and wait. They'll come out and call you," he says.

It isn't long before we're escorted into the doctor's office. He's a beefy man, in his forties, seated behind an empty table. I hand him my paperwork and the note from back home, and John explains why we're here. "She needs to get the stitches out today," he says.

"I'm back here on Friday. Come in then," says the doctor without even glancing at my nose. Friday! It's Tuesday. That's three more days. They're supposed to come out today or tomorrow at the latest.

"Can't you do it *now*?" I plead.

"Friday. Come back Friday," he says shoving the papers across the table. "Take these back to the ER to schedule the appointment." He turns to a conversation with his assistant—his back, our final answer.

Bewildered, we head back downstairs and get in the triage line once again. It's now mid-afternoon and the line is moving a bit faster. Except for the people who, like us, are turning in paperwork, everyone is pretty patient. We stand another 45 minutes waiting to hand our papers to the triage nurse and schedule my appointment. "Can we go directly to his office on Friday, or do we have to come here?" I ask her.

"You need to come here, then we'll send you upstairs." Oh, great. We better come early.

I keep remembering my doctor's warning. "If it's on the face, you need to get those stitches out on time or the skin will grow over them and they'll have to be dug out." That thought makes me quiver. So back in our apartment, John calls Elvira. Is there some doctor nearby who she thinks could help us?

"I have an appointment myself tomorrow morning. Why doesn't Nancy come with me. I'll pick her up at 9:30." I'm grateful and very relieved. We should have thought of this earlier.

Now we pull out the papers we got at the *postale*. There are half a dozen complicated forms, all in unintelligible Italian. This doesn't seem right but we're too tired to worry about it—and tuck them away before going to bed.

The next morning, I'm alone in the car with Elvira proudly chatting in Italian as she drives out of the city, up into the hills, past lovely homes, to a modern office building. The doctor speaks a few words of English, but the note from my doctor is all he needs. Within five minutes, he's snipped the black stitches and I'm finished. I look normal again. And I don't have to worry about that pompous, burly man digging away at my face. "Thank you so much," I say, "please let me pay you."

"No, no. It's not necessary," he says, waving his hands.

"Please. I insist," I say, handing him a 20-euro note. "Please."

He nods modestly. *"Molto grazie."* Thank you very much.

I thank Elvira profusely when she drops me off. Maybe she's warming up to us a bit. Or maybe I just feel a little more comfortable. Over risotto with porcini mushrooms that evening, John and I reflect on our healthcare encounter. "What a system. All that waiting, and waiting, and the paperwork," I say.

"Yes, but it's not that different from our own ERs. And here *everyone* gets treated."

"What a difference when I finally got to Elvira's doctor. Of course, she had an appointment, so we got right in. But her doctor was a lot nicer than that nose guy at the hospital."

"I think a lot of people have their own personal doctors. It gives them a leg-up on the system."

But here's what I really don't understand. When you go to the post office, you take a number, have a seat, and wait for the lighted sign and bell to signal you to a counter. When you go to the hospital, you just get in line and *wait*. We stood more than two hours to go 20 feet. Why can't you take a number and sit down *there*? Let's see: sick people...stamps...sick people...bill payments. *Sono confuso.* I'm confused.

We decide the papers we got at the post office are wrong, and I check my notes. We need to go to the *central* police station, a different *questura*, for the *permesso*. Because we still have no internet connection, the next day we load my Macbook Pro into John's backpack with our thick packet of residency papers. We walk to town and find the main *Questura*, but again, it's not the right place. They say we have to go to Immigration—on the outskirts of town.

First we go back to the library to check our email, where the nice lady signs me up for WiFi. John has a message from Gemma that Elvira will come tomorrow with a new chair. Good news. But the sofa stays. She won't do anything about it. It's just going to take up our living space for a year.

We find a bus and head in the direction of Immigration. The neighborhood street signs are confusing. After walking for half an hour we finally find the place. A *huge* crowd is milling around outside. Everyone has a number. John goes inside to ask: no more numbers today. At the information booth, a kind policeman says, "We're finished for today. You'll have to come back tomorrow morning. Be here by 7:30 to get a number." John's shoulders are sagging and his face looks strained.

"How about giving me the backpack?" I say. "You could use a rest."

"I'm fine," he says, shifting it on his shoulders. "Let's find the bus stop."

At 7:30 that evening we meet Daniele, a local real estate agent, who'll show us a modern apartment. Like many Italian men, he's of medium height and slim with large, warm eyes. He's dressed impeccably. Under his suit jacket is a padded vest that can zip to his neck. (I've noticed this very practical Italian fashion on others.) His shoes are soft leather and beautifully polished. He shows us photos of a newly remodeled apartment with a shiny red kitchen, new appliances, and a magazine-worthy bedroom. When we visit it, it's beautiful, but miniscule. The 40 square meters it contains are about the size of our current bedroom and bath.

"It's way too small," I say with a sigh, looking around after Daniele unlocks the street-level door.

"But it's really nice," John replies. I can hear the disappointment in his voice.

"Pretty, yes, but we'd kill each other in a week." Only the bedroom is what we consider standard size. One tiny room is for lounging, cooking, eating, and watching TV. And being right on the street is worrisome. "So what else have you got, Daniele?" Not much it seems, but he promises to call in a day or so.

We're up at 6:30 and out by 7:15 the next morning. After two bus rides, we arrive at the Immigration office at 7:45 to get in line. It's already a half-block long and the gate won't open until 8:00.

Some people ignore the line and push right up to the entrance gate. Others shove back or curse. When the gate opens, a man passes out numbers based on your type of request. We get number twelve for window number one. Not bad, but though the window opens at 8:30, by 10:00 they're only on number five. We eat the snack we've brought and go up the street for coffee. Back thirty minutes later, we find they're on number ten. Commandeering one of the few benches in the courtyard, we feed pigeons and watch a couple of African girls playing on the stair rail. Dozens of bored people wander aimlessly outside or circle the few interior seats like hungry birds. Around us are Eastern Europeans, Africans, Muslim women in headscarves, rowdy children, and crying babies. No WASPy faces save mine. "I guess we shouldn't be surprised," I say, "considering what happened with our visas."

We had applied for a 13-month visa—our lease year plus a bit of a cushion. The website said the Philadelphia Consulate was open Monday, Wednesday, and Friday from 9:00 until noon. On a Wednesday morning we headed to the city—in a monsoon. The normal two-hour drive took nearly three. When John pulled up in front of the building on Washington Square, it was 11:40. I hopped out and he drove off to find a parking spot.

In the lobby, I signed in at the security desk, then took the elevator upstairs. Room 1026 had a decidedly unfriendly, massive steel door and a camera trained on the threshold. I pressed the button, *buzzzzzz*, and a disembodied female voice asked what I wanted. I told her I'd come for a visa and the lock clicked open. The modest room I entered had five service windows. Four were for Italian citizens' business, the fifth was for visas. I signed in and took a seat. A few minutes later, John joined me.

Next to us was a striking brunette in a fur coat I was coveting. She was in her mid-thirties and, when her name was called, she handled the woman behind the glass with confidence and grace.

"Where are you going?" I asked when she returned to her seat.

"I've got a program in Florence starting next week," she replied with a slight accent. "I'm an opera singer. I'll be there about three weeks."

John leaned forward. "We love opera," he said with enthusiasm. "Are you doing anything later in the year. We won't be going to Italy until April, but we'd love to come to a performance."

"Not any more in Italy this year."

"Sounds like you do a lot of traveling." I said.

"Oh, yes. I travel quite a bit. It's much easier now that I'm an American citizen. I'm Cuban, you see. When I first started working I always had trouble with my Cuban passport. I'd get pulled aside and delayed all the time. Now that I have an American passport, it's much better."

The door buzzer sounded. Behind two-inch thick glass, the woman glanced at a tiny television screen, then said into a microphone, "We're closed."

Even through the thick glass we could hear the tinny voice. "But it's only 12:05."

"We're closed. Come back Friday."

"We drove all the way from Maryland," the voice pleaded. "The rain was horrible and traffic was jammed up all along the highway. We got here as fast as we could."

"Come back Friday." She shuts off the microphone.

As we continued chatting with our opera friend, a bearded young man about college age was edging nervously toward the window. When his name was called and he got his passport back, his shoulders relaxed and he headed for the door, then stopped and turned back to the window.

"The date for my entry is wrong." I could hear the alarm in his voice.

The woman behind the glass barely looked up. "No problem."

His eyes squinted and his eyebrows knitted. "But it says the seventh and my plane gets in on the sixth." He was standing in the middle of the room, arms waving for emphasis.

"It's not a problem," was her flat reply.

"But I've had problems before. I got stopped at the airport and asked a ton of questions. They may not let me in."

The woman behind the window sighed in annoyance. "You won't have any problem."

He pushed his fingers through the dark wavy hair surrounding his olive complexion. "How can you be sure? Look at me. I look like an Arab."

It's the opera singer who replied. "You won't have any problem. You're an American. I've gone in and out of there a lot. Italy won't hassle an American. But," she teased, "it wouldn't hurt to shave."

Relieved, he smiled at her. "I do plan to shave. Thanks." And he headed for the door.

At last we made our trip to the service window. The woman behind the glass looked to be in her fifties. She wore a deep-cut v-neck sweater, a gold pendant over her ample bosom. Her shoulder length, dark brown hair fell forward as she scrutinized our application. "You want a visa for over a *year*?"

"Yes," I answered a little startled.

She stared out at us. "What kind of job do you have?" Her tone was challenging.

John said quietly, "We're retired. We just want to spend a year living in Italy."

Rolling her eyes slightly she turned in her chair and called in Italian into the room behind her. "Marco, these people want to move to Italy for a year... just to *live* there." It seemed quite a comical idea. Marco appeared and looked at our application.

"You just want to go to visit?" he asked, grinning through the glass.

"Yes, that's what we want to do," I answered.

"We want to improve our Italian," John added. The two of them chuckled together then Marco returned to the other room.

"Where are you staying?" she asked. Our comical mission seemed to have softened her now.

"In Bologna. Here's a copy of our lease." I passed the papers through the slot.

"We need proof of funds to cover a year's expenses."

"I printed a copy of our checking and savings statement yesterday. And here are copies of our other financial resources."

She checked it over. "I'll need your medical insurance too."

"I've got that right here."

She spent a few minutes paging through everything. "You know you need to get a *Permesso di Soggiorno* when you arrive. You need to apply for it within eight days. As for the visas, we have to contact Rome to issue them. They're closed now, so you can either come back in a few days or we'll mail the documents to your home."

"It's a long drive," John said. "Mail is fine."

"So your bill for the total will be $169.47." John handed her four fifty-dollar bills. "We can't make any change," she said. "You need the exact amount."

"You're kidding," he answered.

"Maybe you can find change somewhere outside," she offered.

I rummaged through my wallet. "I have sixteen dollars and...thirty-three cents." John added a few ones. "We're still fourteen cents short."

Across the room a man called, "Here. I've got some change you can have."

"Thank you *so* much," I said as he added his change to ours. "Okay, we've got it."

Everything now perfectly in order, she gave us a receipt. "You should carry a copy of all your paperwork with you for Customs inspection," she added before we departed. "And you'll need to show it again for the *Permesso*."

Nine days later a package arrived from the embassy. Delighted, we pulled our newly updated passports from the envelope.

"Look, here it is. My official Italian visa," I said admiring the new addition to my passport.

"There's just one thing," John replied, squinting at his page. "They're for exactly one year. No thirteenth month."

"What? How can that have happened?" I confirmed that mine too was shorter than our request. "I wanted that last month to travel south. Do you think we can do something about it?"

He gave an Italian shrug. "We'll just do our traveling during the year. And if we stay a few days extra, what'll they do? Throw us out of the country?"

Now waiting in the crowded Bologna courtyard, I pull out of my recollection and glance at the screen again. "Look! It's number twelve," I say pointing. It's nearly 1:00.

On the door to where transactions take place, a sign reads *chuiso la porta*, close the door. I push it open. Inside it's stuffy and crowded, with no air circulating—that single door, the only way in or out. A Sengalese family of seven is in front of us, the children twisting and pulling with fatigue. The agent looks up from his paperwork and suggests we wait outside until our turn. Another thirty minutes and we're recalled. The agent disappears with our passports for ten minutes, then asks us to step into the hallway outside.

He's speaking entirely in Italian. "I'm sorry, but you're in the wrong place," he says. "What you have to do is go to the post office, show them your papers and get a kit. Fill it out and mail it in. Then, after two months you can return here, and get fingerprinted to obtain the *Permesso*." I feel like a drowning man who's just been tossed an anchor.

John's back stiffens and his eyes narrow. "We're tourists, and *old*, and we can't *deal* with all this. We aren't immigrants! We don't want a job. All we want to do is live here for a year and *spend money!*" His voice is rising with each declaration. When he gets to the money part he's shouting.

The agent takes a step backward but is otherwise unruffled. "*Un momento*," he says with a nod and disappears into an office. A few minutes later he returns with a pretty blonde, about thirty, who speaks perfect English. Her name is Shiela. Instead of an agent's uniform, she's wearing a pale blue sweater over a tailored skirt and blouse.

"Are you planning to visit anywhere besides Italy?" she asks.

"Of course," I say, relieved to be in my native tongue.

"Well, you have the wrong visas. These are good only to *stay* in Italy: you can't travel throughout Europe. If you leave, you won't be able to get back in."

"What?" A personal visit to the embassy and they gave us the wrong visas?

John's reached the end of his Sicilian rope. "That's *it*," he shouts. "We're not *doing* this anymore." He moves a step closer and looks straight at her, a half-smile now on his face. In a quiet voice he says, "Isn't there something you can do to help us?"

Returning the smile, Sheila gently touches my arm. "Wait here," she says. In about ten minutes she's back with a new to-do list for us. "Buy a special stamp at the *tabaccheria* shop," she says. It's for some kind of tax. "Buy a form at *any* post office. Bring those and your other papers back to me. You don't need to wait in line, just come after 8:30. We'll process your application and I'll fix your visa problem."

Just that and we're done? Wow, thank you, Sheila.

To celebrate, we decide to get lunch at MoMBo, Bologna's modern art museum. The main exhibit is Giorgio Morendi (1890-1964), considered Italy's greatest still-life painter, who was born in Bologna. We conclude he was a really boring guy. He painted the same few grey-brown bottles, boxes, and pitchers his whole life. (I thought artists were supposed to evolve.) Some of the other exhibits are amusing, some challenging, others pretty weird. That's modern art—not my favorite.

On the way home, we find a *tabacchi* shop and purchase our special stamps. The post offices are closed now, so we'll buy our form tomorrow.

Today, Good Friday, we get an email from Gemma saying it will be difficult, if not impossible, to get either satellite TV or internet access in the apartment. Before we signed the lease, she told us it would be no problem. And we've already paid nearly $200 for the TV hookup...in Gino's name. What'll we do now?

Frustrated, we load both computers in the backpack and trudge the eight blocks to a little electronics store we visited yesterday. Piero, our new best friend, sells us a USB stick for satellite access to the internet. A mere $179. We hope this will solve the problem.

"My legs are killing me," I say when we finish the transaction. We've walked miles and miles in the past week, much of it lugging heavy bags of one kind or another.

"I need to sit," John groans. He's been complaining of feeling weak the last couple days. There must be a shortage of chairs in Italy, because the only place we can ever find one is in a restaurant—or sometimes in the post office. Piero suggests a little pizzeria down the street. After an early dinner, we start home. As John walks, he's constantly opening and closing his hands.

"What's wrong?" I ask.

"My hands are cramping up. And I feel dizzy."

He's dizzy? Not good. "Lean on me," I say taking his arm. "We'll walk nice and slowly." I'm concerned about the distance, but we manage and finally unlock the apartment door.

"We need to find a doctor," I tell him while grabbing the phone book. His agreement sends my worry antennae up further. We call every cardiologist in the book, but no one answers. One has a long and complicated message that we can't understand. Then I remember seeing a doctor's office along the portico not too far from the apartment. "Stay still," I say, pulling on my coat. "I'll be right back."

Normally, I'm a fast walker but my muscles strain from my half-jog pace. Running is only possible in short spurts. About three blocks away I find the office. It appears to be closed. I struggle to read the instructions posted on the door, frustrated by my poor vocabulary. Suddenly from behind me, a man excuses himself and simply pushes the door open. It isn't closed! Now I just need to speak to a doctor. I'm pacing around the room when the man speaks to me...in English.

"You look worried. Can I help?"

I explain our recent arrival, my husband's dizziness and cramping, and our search for a cardiologist.

"This doctor is an endocrinologist," he says. "He's not going to be any help. Easter weekend is one of the biggest holidays in the country. Everyone takes a long weekend, so I'm not surprised you can't locate a doctor. But, if your husband still feels bad after 8:00, there's an evening emergency service that you can call. They'll come to your apartment. If you go to the pharmacy a few stores down, you can get a brochure with the information about it."

I remember now. Gemma had given us some emergency numbers: fire, police, ambulance. She hadn't said anything about the hours though. With many *molto grazies*, I leave my Good Samaritan and hurry back toward the apartment, looking for the green cross that signs a pharmacy. As the door swings open I let go a relieved sigh.

When I get back home, John is in bed huddled in all the blankets—looking gray. He says he's feeling really woozy. There's no fever, but his hands are still cramping and he has chest pain. He says he's afraid to close his eyes.

My own chest tightens with anxiety. What'll I *do* if something happens to him? I can just about get around the supermarket on my own. And how will I manage to help him? Okay, think. We need a *doctor*. John's cousin Donna back in Philly is a crackerjack doc. I grab his cell and hit the speed dial. No answer. Five hours difference, she's probably not home yet. Then I think to call our LBI neighbor Bill Halperin, another physician.

When I get him on the phone, he sounds awful. "What's wrong?" I ask.

"You didn't get my email," he answers in a hollow voice. "Are you sitting down?"

Over the next 15 minutes he tells me how his wife, my dear friend Rhoda, who had been in California speaking at a conference, had stepped off the plane looking terrible. He drove her to the nearest hospital and dropped her off at the ER where she walked inside. He went to park the car. By the time he got back, she had crashed and, despite hours of attempts, she never revived.

Rhoda gone? My wonderful friend and tennis buddy, who swam every day and biked miles every afternoon. Gone? The most generous person I know, who taught me to knit, and supports not just all the local businesses but half a dozen struggling students too. Bill says it was some kind of incredibly aggressive leukemia and, given the inevitable outcome, he was glad she didn't have to suffer. I want to wrap my arms around his sturdy shoulders and give his bearded cheek a kiss. The phone line's never felt this long.

Gently, and with apology, I tell him about John and ask what to do. Boom! He goes right into physician mode. "Go to the hospital. Now." We agree I won't tell John the Rhoda news yet.

I call the number in the brochure and an ambulance arrives within five minutes. Two attendants clamor out of the elevator and through my open door. Speaking to John in Italian, they quickly take his blood pressure and do an EKG.

"Why did you wait until 11:00 to call?" one of them asks me. *That* I understand and it sounds like an accusation.

"I called every doctor in the book. No one answers. We've been here *one week*. I didn't know *what* to do. His chest pains *started* tonight."

A few minutes later we're helping John into the ambulance. A smile is pasted on my face as I squeeze his hand, but my heart is racing. After the experience we had there a few days ago, we're not looking forward to a return to the hospital— and the ER lines—but at midnight, we are the only ones coming in.

The nurse speaks quietly and confidently. She does another EKG, then insists that John stay. A doctor will arrive shortly she says. While he lies in another room, an attendant comes over to me. "There's a bed over here," she says softly. "You can lie down while he waits to see the doctor."

"*Grazie. Grazie tante,*" I say wearily.

I can't rest much but it does feel good to lie down. I can see the room where John is from my position and keep watch for the doctor. Thoughts of Rhoda keep interrupting my vigil. She was the last person I expected to lose. I think of poor Bill and wish I could do something like make some calls or a dinner for him and his sons. It would be as much about healing me as it would be for them. But here I am 3000 miles away—feeling helpless.

Around 4:00, they take us to the cardiac ward, a room with about 20 beds, most of them filled. Two attendants help John into one and draw the curtain around us. There's just enough room for a night stand and an uncomfortable chair.

"I don't want you to go home now," John says. "It's too dangerous. Wait until morning." He's still worrying about me in this unfamiliar city.

"You try to sleep. I'll be fine in this chair." I lean my head over onto the edge of the mattress and close my eyes. My brow is throbbing and I'm trying not to panic. They seem competent here, I tell myself. He'll be okay, I tell myself. My neck is stiff from leaning on the bed, and the snores and nighttime noises of the patients keep both of us awake. About 6:00 I gather my things, give John a soft kiss, and take a taxi home.

In our cold apartment, I crawl into bed with every skimpy blanket available wishing my mom were still alive. She knew how to comfort people—how to make them feel safe. My mind is skipping from one problem to another and back again. We've got insurance here, but if he's got a heart issue I want to be *home*. Our island house is rented though, so where would we go? Stop. He's going to be fine. This apartment, though, he'll never last here. His back will be killing him. It's not the comforting place I want for him. And it certainly doesn't feel like home.

Just let him be okay, please. Just let him be okay.

DREAM BECOMES NIGHTMARE

All the world's a stage, and all the men and women merely players: they have their exits and their entrances; and one man in his time plays many parts, his acts being seven ages.

WILLIAM SHAKESPEARE

THE BEDS ON EITHER SIDE OF ME ARE OCCUPIED BY MEN WHO DO NOTHING but sleep. I envy them. My night was restless. I'm afraid to sleep. When I close my eyes, I have this sensation of falling into a deep well, a black hole. I'm afraid, if I fall asleep, I'll never wake up. Anyway, there's too much light. The room smells like shit. Why am I so dizzy? What the hell are they doing to me? Have I had a heart attack?

It's morning. I'm in Hospital Maggiore. I've been up all night. All the patients are men. So are the nurses. Everything is blurry.

I can see that I'm hooked to two monitors and an IV. An old man in bed across the room spent most of the night crying, cursing, and messing the bed. At least, he was understandable. Screams coming from the guy in the corner bed are some kind of African gibberish. Best I can discern, I'm in a ward with maybe 20 beds, ten on each side of the room. I can't tell if they're all occupied but it feels crowded. It's noisy. My vision is partially obscured by the bed curtain to my right. It must be capable of going all around the bed, but I don't want to screw with their system. When I used my papier mâché urinal during the night, I didn't bother to pull the curtain.

If there's a bathroom, they have it well hidden. My night stand holds a bedpan and a fresh urinal, both made of papier mâché. I peed twice during the night so I know how weird they feel. Disposable. It makes sense, I suppose. But I'm certain I'd crush the bedpan were I to sit on it.

The old guy across the room must be incontinent. Two burly nurses in their late thirties were in during the night to change his bed sheets. I watched with one eye closed. What else did I have to do?

First, they rolled him over onto an adjacent bed. They quickly gathered the soiled bed sheets into a neat bundle. As one carried the sheets away, the other washed him down. He never stopped screaming obscenities. The noise didn't seem to bother the other patients. I was awake anyway. In two minutes, the old man had fresh sheets and a clean body. Ten minutes later, amazingly, the two nurses were back, laughing at him and themselves, to repeat the process. Again, I watched.

Someone is speaking to me. *"John William, lei capisce Italiano?"* He's asking me if I speak Italian. I explain that I can understand well enough but I would do better if I had my glasses to *see* what he's saying. I'm not sure he gets the humor but my comment does initiate a frantic pat down of my night table. The blur hands me my glasses.

Relieved to be able to clearly see my inquisitors—there are two of them—I force a smile and say *"se avessi saputo che voi siete qui, avrei studiato italiano piu."* If I knew I'd be here, I would have studied Italian more. I get a smile from both.

The speaker is Marco Bruniello, M.D. His name is prominently displayed on an overly large plastic badge. He tells me he is my cardiologist. Why do I have a cardiologist? The other man identifies himself as an *infermiere*, a male nurse. He's also wearing a badge but I don't catch his name. I can't get past that word... *cardiologiste*.

While I'm completely focused on Bruniello, I find it curious that the two men look so similar. They're about the same age, both have light brown hair, glasses, and are dressed in long white lab coats. They're there to double team me…with questions. How old am I? What medications do I take? Do I have chest pains? Can I lift my head, follow the finger, look down, look up, wiggle my right foot, grab his hand?

The inquisition, all in Italian, lasts ten minutes. At the end, Dr. Bruniello says, "Mr. William, we think you are suffering from a sinus infection that has infected your inner ear, causing the dizziness. We don't think you have had a heart attack but we want to do more tests. Meanwhile, I suggest you rest. Okay, Mr. William?" Instead of answering, I tell him my name is John William Petralia. Something must have been lost in the translation.

"No problem, Mr. William," Bruniello says in English. He then shows me my chart. It clearly says Petralia, John William. *Shit, everything is so confusing.* I try to stay calm. "No problem," I say. I'm too tired to argue. Maybe I can sleep.

Four hours later, I awake to Nancy's smiling face. She's holding my hand. The curtain is now fully closed. We are alone. I like it that way. The look on her face is one of relief. It says I'm going to be okay. She tells me that she spoke with Dr. Bruniello. I have to stay at least one more night. Even though tomorrow is Easter, she tells me that the doctor will be in to see me in the morning, most likely to release me. He wants me to rest. I squeeze her hand.

"How do you feel?" she says. "Be honest."

"I feel like shit. This place is awful. There are people screaming all night. It stinks. They keep calling me John William. Have they put me in a loony bin? This wasn't on my bucket list. This was supposed to be a dream vacation. I have to go."

"Go where?"

"I have to go to the bathroom. I'm not using that stupid bedpan."

Nancy quickly springs into action. First she confirms that the nearest bathroom is in the hall outside. Then she comes back with a nurse. He smiles and says "Hello, John William." Speaking in broken Italian, I explain what I want. Can we unhook the monitors so I can use the bathroom?

Surprisingly, he says, in English, "No problem." And without getting anyone's permission, he unhooks the two monitors and the IV.

With Nancy's help—I'm still dizzy—I maneuver through the room, into the hall, and turn left into the unisex visitor's bathroom.

Time was that I had three claims to fame. I never mowed a lawn, never been to Disney World, and never saw The Sound of Music. I could now add one more. I've never yet taken a shit in a papier mâché bedpan.

DAY BY DAY

An unhurried sense of time is in itself a form of wealth.

ON EASTER SUNDAY AFTERNOON WE LEAVE THE HOSPITAL TOGETHER. AFTER a slow walk into Piazza Maggiore, we settle at one of the outdoor bars to watch the crowds. Kids are chasing each other, shrieking with laughter, and playing with balloon animals made by the jacquard-suited clown who sits by the library. An impromptu jazz band has set up in the middle of the square, which draws a small foot-tapping crowd. Under the portico that borders the square, a mime in head-to-toe white poses statue-like on a pedestal, shifting only when someone offers a donation. Multigeneration families drift through the piazza pushing baby carriages, elders leaning on younger arms. On our walk home, we stroll by the fancy storefronts of Via de` Pignattari as part of evening *passaggiata*.

That evening I'm chopping vegetables to toss with our pasta when John comes into the kitchen. "How about a glass of wine and a little toast to my being in your bed again?"

"With your choice of *two* private bathrooms."

He wraps his arms around my waist, presses hard and kisses the back of my neck. "Now I can squeeze you all I want."

I'm so relieved he's feeling better—and that we're together again. Even though the hospital staff seemed competent, I felt excluded. They wouldn't even let me be with him during the doctor's exam. No visitors allowed, not even a wife.

John pours a local Lambrusco and offers me a glass.

"*Salute,*" I say, clicking his. To your health. "Thank goodness it wasn't something really serious. I don't know what I would have done." I lean in to kiss his cheek and add a tease. "At least *you* can understand what people are saying around here."

"Things haven't exactly worked out like we thought," he says. "The apartment, the city, and now this."

"No. It's not what we expected it would be. But it's only been two weeks."

He gives me a serious look. "Do you want to go home?"

Go home? "Do *you*? You're the one with the health issue. If you'd feel better at home, we should go back."

"No, no, I'm feeling better. And the care here was good. That's not it."

I give his hand a soft caress. "Well, if you're okay, I don't think we should give up. But is something else bothering you?"

"We planned this for so long and it's our dream. I want it to *be* a dream for you."

"It is...It will be." I click his glass again. "You know what you always say, 'it's not where you are but who you're with.'"

"Right." The worried look is gone. "When we find a better place to live it'll make a lot of difference."

"In the meantime, we can explore more options around here." I turn back to the cutting board. "Now, give me a hand with dinner."

A few days later, all our documents in hand, we catch a bus over to Immigration to see Shiela. She smiles, emerging from her office.

"*Buongiorno.*" She takes our paperwork and looks it over. "Fine, everything is here. You'll need to go into the processing room," she says opening the *chuiso* door.

What a place! It's eight feet by 20 with no ventilation. About 40 sweaty adults and half a dozen cranky children are crammed together. It smells like a gym locker. Behind the thick glass wall over the counter, crisp-looking agents work in a spacious room with the windows open. If you could put your nose on the counter, you might get a whiff of fresh air from the pass-through.

While we wait John is starting to fume. Then our names are called. Thanks to Sheila, we've jumped the line. An agent checks, stamps, staples, copies, stamps, clips, stamps, and returns our documents, then sends us to another agent at the opposite end of the room—to have our thumbs printed. Once more we jump the line. When we exit the smelly sardine can, Shiela is waiting. "One more step to go," she tells us. We have to get more fingerprints at the police station downtown.

At the original *Questura* in town, they again tell us we're not in the right place. Fingerprints are taken at the *Politzia Scientifica*, a few streets away. There the waiting room is cold and uncomfortable, but at least you can breathe. On the wall, a giant crucifix looks down in sympathy. We wait about 30 minutes and then get "printed": all ten fingers, both palms, and a full handprint. Just to live here and spend money! I wonder what they do with criminals and terrorists?

Sheila had said we could go back to her in about a month to get our *Permesso* and new visas. We say our prayers.

Our Italian lives move at a different pace. The kitchen clock is the only one in our apartment, so I don't know the time when I wake up. If the shutters are closed, the room is totally dark—just a crack of sunlight comes through to let you know it's there. Time to roll over? Time to get up? Whatever. For the first time in our lives, time doesn't seem to matter. For the first time, we're really living in the present, not worrying about what we haven't done yet or who we have to meet. It's just, well, time to do something we want. Our American life has dissolved into this foreign one.

Days are consumed with explorations and curiosities and adjustment to a new lifestyle. We haven't figured out the shop hours yet. Some open early, close midday, and reopen. Others stay open all day. Some open late and remain so. A few open only in the evenings.

Restaurants are a puzzle. If we get there too early, they *may* let us order a drink and wait for the opening. Or they may tell us to come back at the appropriate time and nudge us toward the door. Snack places seem to be open most of the day. Bars too. Every place has days off, and there's no rhyme nor reason to the schedule. Figuring it out is part of the fun.

"Want to walk into the Center today? See if we can find that place Gemma told us about—the wine place where you bring your own food?" John's eager to visit this local haunt, so today, that's our goal.

The people we pass under the portico keep their focus straight ahead. I smile or nod but no one returns my greeting. It makes me reluctant to say even *buongiorno*, good morning. "I know we look different," I say, conscious of my fair skin and blonde hair, "but why doesn't anyone even *smile?*"

"We knew northern Italy was more reserved," John answers. "Maybe it's because Bologna has so *many* foreigners. The Italians have gotten used to ignoring them."

As we walk along we make mental notes of the stores we want to visit later. Many of the doorways have their metal shutters drawn down to the pavement. Even the signage is covered, so it's impossible to know what's behind them. Graffiti covers the walls, the metal doors, and the pillars along the portico. It reminds me of an ugly city ghetto, and I'm sad there's so little respect for these ancient walls. We pause by a storefront revealed between its shuttered neighbors.

"We have to remember *this* place!" I say. "Look at that doorway. Everything looks so different when those big, metal shutters are up." Well-patinaed wood frames the display window and glass door. Across the entry, a worn bar carved from a tree branch beacons your hand to push inside. "Look at the hinges and those big rings at the bottom of the window. This place is *old.*"

Over the storefront hangs a wooden sign—*Salumeria Formaggeria*. Salami and cheese. Scores of different cheeses are stacked artistically in the window. Behind them, salami and prosciutto hang from the ceiling. Even though it's early morning, we're tempted to duck inside for a hunk of the freshly cut Parmigiano. "Maybe on the way home," John says.

We pass a young man strolling patiently arm in arm with a woman who must be his grandmother. We've seen them a few times before. Walking with their owners, big dogs and small stop along the wall to lift a leg or leave a deposit. Few people pick up after their pets here. And protected by the porticos, rain never washes the walkways so a strong odor permeates the pavement. In front of several doorways, we see white powder scattered over the sidewalk and assume it's to absorb the pungent smell.

At the ATM in front of a bank, John makes a withdrawal while I watch a customer enter the bank. He pushes a button next to a heavy, glass, single-person capsule that is the doorway. The curved wall slides open and when he steps inside the tiny space, it closes behind him. *Beam me up, Scottie!* He waits for an employee to buzz open the other side of the capsule to let him in. To exit, it's the reverse. Nobody could break in with that crazy entry system, but if you're claustrophobic I guess you won't have a bank account.

A few steps away from the ATM, a gypsy woman is seated in her usual spot; the pallid little boy beside her is looking off into space. *"Che peccata."* What a shame, says John. "That kid should be in school, not hanging out all day begging with his mother. He looks sick too." There are lots of gypsies here. Perhaps that's one of the reasons people have learned to ignore strangers. A block later, I note another regular in front of the florist shop, where the sweet aroma of fresh-cut flowers fills the air.

"This woman doesn't beg," I say. Thirty-something and well-groomed, in a simple dress and shawl, she offers a daily newspaper to us as we pass.

"Grazie," says John, handing her a coin. "You'd think the shop owner would want to hire her." She's nicely dressed, always here, and pleasant. She even smiles.

We pass through Porta Saragozza, cross the tiny park where old folks gather on benches near the Padre Pio statue, and turn toward the city Center walking under another covered walkway. These medieval streets are narrow, cars can't speed through them as they do on the wider straightaway outside our apartment. But motorbikes and Vespas still do. *Varoom!* Two fly by us, ridden by young women in short skirts, high heels, and bike helmets.

We wind our way to Piazza Maggiore and cross to the the other side where the daily market is just a block beyond the elegant stores. No shuttered store-fronts here. Spilling into the pedestrian street are tables loaded with a painter's pallet of fresh produce. Grapefruit-sized fennel bulbs, varieties of greens I've never seen before, purple-green artichokes, long pods of peas, tiny eggplants, and orange zucchini flowers. At the fishmongers, dozens of bright-eyed, color-ful species are laid out on ice. I peer at the bulbous octopus, prawns, and tiny brown clams—mentally planning a future meal.

"Let's get some bread and prosciutto for lunch, maybe a little cheese," John says stepping into a bakery. We stop in three stores for our purchases and restrain ourselves from buying more than we can carry. Like other women at the market, I drop it all into one of the roll-up carry bags I always have in my purse.

"Now we've just got to find that little wine place," I say as we turn the corner. After three trips up and down the tiny street, we can't find the wine bar. Giving up, we ask two old men who are talking together where it is.

"*Stiamo cercando una vecchia enoteca,*" John says. We're looking for an old *enoteca.*

"It's in the middle of the block," says one in Italian, pointing back the way we came. "Look for the word *vino* over the doorway."

The word is in minuscule letters over a nondescript white painted doorway. No wonder we passed it. Inside, the graying walls are hung with ancient draw-ings and cartoons. The room must be 400 years old. Long tables, dented with age, stretch down its length, and small groups are seated here and there enjoy-ing food from white paper wrappings—salami and cheeses, fresh fruit, roasted chicken, and pizza slices. I take a seat along the wall and John goes to buy wine at the bar up front, returning with two glasses of red. At a table in the alcove, we catch a snippet of English, but otherwise we hear only Italian. Eventually we venture a conversation with some nearby Italian girls.

"We're studying at the University," one tells us in her native tongue. Bologna's is the world's first university, started in 1088. Today there are several here. Nearly 80,000 students flood the city during the school year.

"I'll be graduating with my law degree in a few weeks," the other says.

"Oh, so you'll be a lawyer."

"No, no. Most Italian students study the law for their baccalaureate program. To be a lawyer, you have to get another degree and pass a test."

Returning to the market, we buy several things for our dinner, then head back home, our purchases weighing us down. "I want to stop at that great *salumeria*," I say already tasting the musky cheeses in my mind. But all the metal shutters along the portico are drawn down again, and we can't even locate it. Disappointed, we continue back to the apartment.

When I look up at the clock as I'm starting supper, I see it's after 7:00. Other nights it might be 8:30 when we eat. Nothing marks time for us. There's no evening news to watch and no sunset we can see from our windows, which are shuttered now against the cold and noise. Tomorrow we'll wander somewhere else. Walking tires us but leads to unexpected discoveries.

We find a tiny art gallery in a converted church and an interior shopping space lined with ceiling frescos. We visit San Stefano's seven churches and the monthly antiques market. Laughing with the crowd, we watch the antics of a famed comedian as he films a commercial in one of the squares. In a tiny chapel, we hear a concert played on ancient harpsichords—their notes echoing as they must have done centuries ago. On Via degli Orefici we find Venchi, a tiny *gelateria* with lemon and strawberry *granita* that cools the near 100-degree days. On Via Nosadella we discover a wonderful bakery where the women make honey-laced risotto cake and crunchy cookies as delicate as dried leaves.

We get to know the city bus routes saving miles on our soles. When we want to explore another part of the town, we hop a bus, city map in hand, and travel the entire route making note of the landmarks to get our bearings, then ride again just for fun. It's a cheap sightseeing tour.

In May the *Giro di Italia*, the Italian bike championship, goes right down our street. We try to catch sight of Lance Armstrong as the riders fly past on their way to the final steep climb to San Luca on the hilltop high above us. Following them, we start our own ascent on the stairs under the portico that weaves up, up, and up the mountain, but after maybe a thousand steps we can't go on. Locals with children and even old men and women pass us for the celebration at the summit, but we go back to watch it on TV. Years of walking has given them stamina we don't have.

A much slower parade follows the same path when the Virgin of San Luca's icon is carried up the hill in the annual pageant. A thousand years ago, as the story goes, there was a terrible drought. The townspeople carried the icon down to the Saragozza Gate, praying for relief. When the icon reached the gate, she cried...and it began to rain. Every year since, thousands of singing townsfolk follow behind the priests and city dignitaries as they escort the icon back to her home.

As we get to know the city and her rhythms, we begin to feel we're living here—not just visiting. Despite the problems, Italy is starting to be home. Late at night, after a long day of walking and an Aleve, we snuggle under the coverlet. "A pretty good day," I say, moving closer.

"And tomorrow. What'll we do?"

"I don't know. It doesn't matter. We've got lots of time. Let's see how we feel in the morning." After a few moments I ask, "What did you like best about today?"

"Just being with you," he says.

"Me too. *Ti amo.*" I love you.

The History Lesson

Living is dreaming. Only in the grave are there no dreams.

UNION ARMY GENERAL LEW WALLACE, AUTHOR OF BEN HUR

SPEAKING IN ITALIAN, GIULIANO EXPLAINS HOW THE MANY-SPOUTED fountain of Neptune, installed in 1563, is a new embellishment to the original Roman wellspring. The water system that feeds it goes back to Roman times. Nancy, reading from her guidebook, adds in English "The larger-than-life bronze statue was designed by Sicilian architect Tommaso Laureti and executed by Flemish sculptor Giambologna."

In Italian, I ask, "Flemish, with a name like Giambologna?"

Giuliano responds in Italian. "Giambologna was a sort of nickname. His real name was Jean de Boulogne. Medici's court where he worked dubbed him Giambologna." I, in turn, explain Giuliano's answer to Nancy in English. With these sorts of roundtrip conversations, we all get to improve our language skills in a fashion that completely nullifies anything you could characterize as an uncomfortable moment of silence.

We first met Giuliano and his wife Teresa through Bologna's Johns Hopkins Center. An English language teacher at the school told us about a local man, Giuliano, looking to practice his English. I called him and we arranged a meeting.

At the Center's little coffee bar, we cobbled together our arrangement. He would help us with our Italian if we would "occasionally" speak English to him. Perfect. Our next meeting was to be in the middle of Piazza Maggiore, Bologna's main square, where we would implement Giuliano's plan: he and Teresa would give us a walking tour; we'd all get to know each other and practice our language skills. Despite the fact that Teresa speaks virtually no English, Giuliano's plan works beautifully. Like me, Giuliano is a retired business owner, a traveler, and a seeker. My senior by only five days, over the course of our year in Italy, I would learn much more from him than just Italian.

The fountain is our last stop of the day. That morning, we met Giuliano and Teresa in front of the Palazzo del Comune, the town hall. Built in the 13th and 14th centuries, its beautiful bell tower with a carillon clock stands as a testimony to three major art works: a terracotta Madonna by Nicolò dell'Arca, a bronze statue of Pope Gregory XIII, and two eagles carved in red marble from Verona, attributed to Michelangelo. We know from guidebooks that the interior of the building is also very beautiful, but because it was undergoing repairs, we did not get to go in. Maybe next time.

From the town hall, we walk across the piazza to the Palazzo dell' Archiginnasio, the original location of the University of Bologna. Founded in 1088, it is home to 700,000 books, codices, and rare manuscripts. Today, the university is spread throughout the city. Up until the 16th century, the Archiginnasio campus was the only one. Inside, more than 7,000 coats of arms of both the Italian and foreign students who attended the university during the 16th to the 17th centuries are displayed. Famous for its medical school, the structure also houses the *Teatro Anatomico*, Anatomy Theatre. Built entirely of wood, including panels, benches, and statues of famous doctors, it houses two nearly life-size figures carved by Ercole Lelli. They depict the sinewy human anatomy of a man and a woman—without skin.

Noteworthy alumni of the university include the greatest names of Italian literature including, Dante, Petrarch, and Boccaccio. Noted foreigners such as Archbishop Thomas Becket and astrophysicist Nicholas Copernicus graced the halls. Luigi Galvani, who discovered biological electricity, and Guglielmo Marconi, the pioneer of radio technology, taught here.

The University of Bologna remains one of the most respected and dynamic post-secondary educational institutions in Italy. And to this day, Bologna is still very much a university town. The city's population swells from 300,000 to more than 400,000 whenever classes are in session. Locals like to blame the city's overabundance of graffiti on *stranieri*—foreigners.

The imposing two-story Palazzo has 30 arches around the portico's interior courtyard. The first floor is primarily administrative offices. The second story, accessed by two large staircases, is comprised of what were ten separate classrooms, one for each subject. The rooms now house books and manuscripts. There are also two lecture halls, one at each end of the floor—one for artists, now the reading room of the library, and one for Human Rights. Incredibly, in the hall leading to the library, we spot a crest dated 1543, belonging to a student from Peru. Imagine, only 51 years after Columbus discovered America, students from the new world were already doing a semester abroad.

Thanks to our "tour guides," we are allowed access to a room containing ancient manuscripts. Seated at a large oak table, a pleasant looking gray-haired woman dressed in a white lab coat, white gloves, and a monocle is inspecting a book nearly a meter square in size. She allows us to look over her shoulder. Studying the text intently, she is careful not to touch the pages. She turns to me and explains, "You are inches from a manuscript dating back to 1155." The best I could muster is, "Wow."

By her look, I can tell she is not impressed with my reaction. I stare harder. Emerging from faded scribbling, I discern the Latin word *libertas*, freedom. Trying to compensate for my previous ineptitude, I point and utter *In libris libertas*. In books there is freedom.

White-gloves again turns to me without removing her monocle, stares at me like a Cyclops, nods politely, and whispers *punto*, point. It's one of those expressions that Italians use in a variety of ways. *Punto*. Depending on the inflection, it can mean "now, that's a great point." It can also be dismissive. *Punto* as in: "You've made a point; it's a very small point; a truly insignificant point; now shut up." This *punto* was definitely the latter.

From the Palazzo dell' Archiginnasio, we walk north several blocks to the main shopping district along Via Independenza, where we stop to admire a grand statue depicting Giuseppe Garibaldi on horseback at the battle of Calatafimi in Sicily, 15th May 1860. On the base of the statue is the inscription: *Qui si fa l'Italia o si muore.* Here we make Italy or we'll die. It refers to the war of unification, the *Risorgimento*, literally, the awakening. In 1860, while America was breaking apart, Italy was being reassembled.

Before the Risorgimento, what we now call Italy was a crazy quilt of regions controlled variously by Spain, Austria, France, Greece, the Moors, and, perhaps most prominent, the Holy Roman Catholic Church. Unification of these disparate parts into a single entity was achieved largely by a series of battles over three decades. It was Giuseppe Garibaldi who led the revolution in Sicily, bringing about the collapse of the Bourbon monarchy, the retreat of the Austrian empire, the overthrow of the Papal States, and the creation of the Italian nation. At one point the Pope put a large bounty on Garibaldi's head, but not one Italian betrayed him.

Born on the 4th of July in 1807 and inspired by America's revolutionary vigor, he was destined to become a freedom fighter. In 1833, Merchant Marine Captain Garibaldi joined *La Giovine Italia*, Young Italy, a group committed to freeing Italian provinces from Austrian and Papal domination. Sentenced to death in absentia by a Genoese Court for participating in a mutiny against the Piemontese navy, Garibaldi fled to France and then to South America, where he fought with the Rio Grande do Sul separatists in Brazil. He then traveled to Uruguay, where he married a local Indian woman. Instead of honeymooning, the newlyweds led local freedom fighters against Argentine imperialism. It was in these battles that he mastered the art of guerrilla warfare. Clad in red gaucho shirts, he and his followers swept to victories at the battles of Cerro and Sant'Antonio. In 1846, his forces secured Uruguay's freedom and made Garibaldi a hero throughout South America. Upon their triumphant return to Italy, Garibaldi's "Red Shirts" became the military force behind the unification movement.

In 1860 General Garibaldi led a military expedition from Genoa to aid a Sicilian rebellion. The Red Shirts easily took the island and, crossing onto the mainland, took Naples by early September. Like General Mark Clark in WWII, Garibaldi desperately wanted to proceed directly to Rome where the pope was protected by French troops. But Victor Emmanuel II, king of Sardinia and subsequently of Sicily and Naples as well (thanks to Garibaldi's victories), decided that French help would be needed to complete the unification of Italy. So he called off Garibaldi's advance. With no more immediate battles to fight, Garibaldi retired to his home in Sardinia.

It would not to be long before Garibaldi received an enticing invitation from an ardent admirer in North America. It was the summer of 1861 and the Union was in big trouble. Starting with the battle of Bull Run in July, the South was winning battle after battle, and it appeared that Washington, D.C. might soon be occupied by Confederate troops. Abraham Lincoln needed help. None of his generals seemed capable of moving against the Confederate Army. General George McClellan certainly was not the answer. Constantly overestimating the strength of the enemy, he was slow to engage. Lincoln finally suspended him from command on March 11, 1862. The president wanted and needed a general who would fight. Garibaldi, the very definition of aggression, seemed tailor-made for the job. Horace Greeley, editor of the *New York Tribune*, published an open letter to Lincoln urging him to enlist the services of Garibaldi.

To an embattled Union, Giuseppe Garibaldi seemed a smart choice. An abolitionist, a proven warrior, and an avowed Lincoln admirer, Garibaldi had lived in New York before his South American expeditions. He was looking for a reason to return. Through the American consul in Italy, James W. Quiggle, the minister to Belgium, Henry Shelton Sanford, and George Perkins Marsh, the first American minister to the new Kingdom of Italy, several different diplomatic correspondences traveled between Washington, D.C. and Caprera, the Sardinian isle where Garibaldi lived.

A key sticking point, however, was the issue of slavery. When Garibaldi and his wife were fighting for a free Uruguay, they specifically recruited liberated runaway slaves. These men proved invaluable in battles against the forces of former Uruguayan president Manuel Oribe and Buenos Aires governor Juan Manual Rosas. Garibaldi admired the fighting spirit and bravery of these Black men whom he referred to as his Sword of Freedom. Yes, Garibaldi would fight for Lincoln, but only if the President agreed to emancipate all slaves in the North and allow Garibaldi to recruit them for his army.

For Lincoln, who was trying to hold together a fragile Union—one that included five slave states—the timing for emancipation was not right. He had won the presidency—in a four-way race—with only 40 percent of the popular vote. The Republican mantra in 1860 and 1861 was to "restrict the expansion of slavery into the federal territories of the West," not abolish it. Indeed, while negotiating with Garibaldi, Lincoln was assuring slaveholders in the Union's border states that he would uphold the Constitution and the Fugitive Slave Law. Moreover, Lincoln had given no indication that he was ready for the races to live together as equals. During the Lincoln/ Douglas debates, he had said, "I am not nor ever have been in favor of bringing about in any way the social and political equality of the white and black races...I will say in addition that there is a physical difference between races which I believe will for ever forbid the two races living together on terms of social and political equality." In 1860, Garibaldi's demands were a deal killer.

Ironically, as the American war progressed, both the circumstances of battle and Lincoln's views quickly evolved. Escaped slaves from South Carolina and the lower Mississippi Valley were crossing over into the North by the thousands. Many wanted to join the Union Army. They wanted to fight for freedom. Although a 1792 Federal law prohibited Blacks from serving in the military, the increasing number of escaped slaves, coupled with the declining number of white volunteers, pushed generals into reconsidering the ban.

Union generals John Fremont in Missouri and David Hunter in South Carolina issued proclamations in their respective military regions that allowed escaped slaves to serve. While these generals were *officially* reprimanded by their superiors, the practice continued unofficially. As Garibaldi predicted, the freed slaves made a huge difference. On September 22, 1862, Lincoln issued his own Emancipation Proclamation, freeing all slaves in the Confederacy (but not in the Union). Eventually, 180,000 black soldiers, 10 percent of the Union Army, were organized into 166 all-black regiments. Nearly 40,000 black soldiers gave their lives over the course of the war. Sixteen black soldiers received the Medal of Honor. And, Lincoln would become known as The Great Emancipator, a name given him by none other than Giuseppe Garibaldi.

In August 6, 1863, still unhappy with the progress of Italy's unification, Garibaldi wrote directly to President Lincoln:

"In the midst of your titanic struggle, permit me, as another among the free children of Columbus, to send you a word of greeting and admiration for the great work you have begun. Posterity will call you the Great Emancipator, a more enviable title than any crown could be, and greater than any merely mundane treasure. You are a true heir of the teaching given us by Christ and by John Brown. If an entire race of human beings, subjugated into slavery by human egoism, has been restored to human dignity, to civilization and human love, this is by your doing and at the price of the most noble lives in America.

It is America, the same country that taught liberty to our forefathers, which now opens another solemn epoch of human progress. And while your tremendous courage astonishes the world, we are sadly reminded how this old Europe, which also can boast a great cause of liberty to fight for, has not found the mind or heart to equal you."

Ever the revolutionary, in 1863 Garibaldi raised another army to march on Rome. He was shot in the foot and captured by Federal troops loyal to King Emmanuel II. His career as a soldier over, he retired to Caprera.

Although Garibaldi never did get to trade his red shirt for a blue coat, many Red Shirts did take part in our Civil War. The Garibaldi Guard was the nickname of the 39th New York Infantry, a regiment of Italian-Americans recruited mostly from New York City under the auspices of Francesco Casale and other Italian leaders in the North. Most of the members of this regiment were men who had fought under Garibaldi. Four Red Shirts became Union generals, including General Luigi Palma di Cesnola, who received the Medal of Honor; later, he became the first director of New York's Metropolitan Museum of Art.

All told, an estimated 10,000 Italians fought in the Civil War—for both the Union and the Confederacy. Ironically, as General U.S. Grant began to achieve success in key battles, his Italian troops dubbed him Victor, in honor of King Victor Emmanuele II of Italy. The nickname was to spread along with his fame.

Back at the Fountain of Neptune, Nancy notices some graffiti scrawled on the north wall of the town hall. Sprayed in foot high letters, it reads *"Qui si fa l'Italia* **russo** *o si muore"* Here we make a red Italy, or we will die. As she figures out what it says, Nancy points, laughs, and quips *"Oggi, c'e troppa libertà."* Today, there is too much liberty. Now we're all laughing.

A month ago, Nancy and I would not have understood the significance of *"Qui si fa L'Italia,"* even if we could have deciphered the words. Now it speaks volumes to us. Context is meaning. We are living our dream.

Thank you, Giuliano and Teresa, *Grazie.* Thanks for the tour, the chance to practice our Italian, and the history lesson.

FINDING FRIENDS

Fan the sinking flame of hilarity with the wing of friendship; and pass the rosy wine.

CHARLES DICKENS

AFTER A MONTH, ONE THING IS BECOMING CLEAR. MASTERING ITALIAN IS not going to be easy. John's got a big leg up on me, and he does most of the talking when we meet someone. Comprehension is my problem. When someone responds to me, it's like a blast of sound with a few recognizable syllables. I can't sort them out. Usually I stand with my eyes rolled up in my head, trying to parse the sounds again—to see if I can get the gist while the speaker gapes at me. This doesn't make for conversation.

We aren't finding a lot of speaking opportunities either. Other than conversations with merchants and bureaucrats, it's hard to get folks to talk with us. And I'm especially hesitant. If we're going to improve our Italian we'll have to find another way.

This afternoon we're heading for our first visit to the Bologna Center at Johns Hopkins International School of Business. The Center has already been a big help to me—in planning our trip here. I used the brochure they give to students to find out what things we should bring from America—like a year's worth of our prescriptions, over-the-counter meds, and vitamins. The brochure said OTC drugs and essentials like dental floss are expensive here.

The school only offers graduate programs taught in English. Visiting speakers from around the world come in every few weeks and the school opens the talks to the public. The chance to hear great minds was one of Bologna's big draws. Today Richard Portes from the London School of Business will be speaking.

The building is modern but its red brick facade fits well with the surrounding old Italian structures. Inside there's a large, bright library and café on the first floor. Lectures are in the fourth floor penthouse. At the rear of the lecture room with its sleek, modern furniture is a balcony overlooking the city. Over the treetops and red-tiled roofs we can see the town's famous Two Towers in one direction and green, rolling hills in another.

Dr. Portes speaks about an hour then takes questions from the 50 or so students and faculty, and John asks a question as well. On our way out we talk with two of the Center's professors. No, they say, they hardly ever get attendees who aren't students, but we're welcome.

Downstairs we browse the library, apply for a library card, and stop for a soda before leaving. Along one wall of the café is a long bulletin board with notices and personal notes. "Maybe there are some other events we could come to," I say to John as I head over for a look. Among the postings about student housing, tutors, and services, we find a posting by Nicola who wants to trade Italian conversation for English practice.

"That could be great for us," John says. "A Italian grad student who would help us with our conversation skills. Take down the information and we'll contact her."

That evening I compose an email to Nicola. We figure it's better coming from me as she might be wary of meeting up with an old American guy. I explain that we're in our sixties and live in town. We get an enthusiastic reply with an invitation to meet for coffee at the Neri bakery along Via Saragozza, and I send off a description so she'll recognize us.

Walking along the portico a few days later we can't help but speculate. "I bet she'll be pretty," John says begging a reaction.

"They're *all* pretty," I answer.

We're approaching the bakery when a handsome young man steps up to us. He's holding a black motorcycle helmet and wearing gold-framed aviator sunglasses. "Ciao, amici," he says reaching out a hand. "I'm Nicola."

A *man*? We thought when the name ends with an "a" it's feminine. Now it's my turn to smile. Nicola is handsome, a young Tom Cruise. Lessons with him will be fun!

Over coffee we tell him about ourselves and our Italy adventure, chatting in a mixture of English and Italian. His English is good and he has a warm, engaging way. A 27-year-old law graduate, he spent a year living in Chicago—to perfect his English—and has an American girlfriend. He's crazy about Chicago and would like to go back, or possibly to Australia, while he's still young and free. We tell him about the problems we have with our apartment and that we'd like to find something else. At the end of our conversation he offers to walk back and look at it.

"The price is a little high," he says as he looks around. "But it's not too bad for all this space. Why do you *want* so much space? This is enough for a whole family."

"It's an American thing. We'll have a lot of friends visiting us through the year, so we wanted two bedrooms and two baths. With these beds though, I think they might find it a pretty uncomfortable stay," John says.

"And I figured I'd make the third small bedroom into an office, but that's not going to be possible. The computers and printer need the bigger type of electric plug, and there's no outlet in there of the right kind. So I have to keep everything on this little table in the hallway and that room is pretty much useless," I tell him.

Before he leaves we set a time for a next conversation and "Nik" invites us to *La Vespata*, an annual gathering of Vespa owners. He's organized it for Bologna's club. "We gather in Piazza San Dominica, then spend the day touring the countryside together. You don't have to go on the ride. But there will be hundreds of Vespas there," he says. "Old ones, new ones. My dad will be there with his vintage model."

"Sounds like fun," John says as we send him on his way. "We'll be sure to check it out."

Two weeks later we arrive in Piazza San Dominica on a Sunday morning to find it clogged with at least a hundred people huddled around old and new Vespas. Named for the wasp, these two-wheelers, introduced in Italy in 1947, are still the quintessential vehicle for buzzing the streets. Painted every conceivable color, they've appeared in movies and iconic photographs ever since.

"Just like in that movie, *Roman Holiday*," John quips as we wander through the crowd.

"Check out that girl with the wild blond hair. She's almost as cute as Audrey Hepburn."

He wanders over to a yellow-and-white-striped model. I've discovered a red one from the 50s or 60s that's covered with stickers from all over Europe. It reminds me of old steamer trunks that showed off all the owner's voyages. Vespa's bright colors and scooter design appeal to me. They seem safer than a motorbike, and prettier too.

"There's Nik," John says pointing across the piazza. "Let's go say hello." We find our young friend sporting a navy neckerchief and *La Vespata* T-shirt.

"You came!" he shouts over the crowd, his face spreading into a grin. Shouldering his way through, he gives us both *baci* on each cheek. Handing John an official *2009 Vespata* sticker—which I'm sure will end up on our car—he takes us to meet his dad who poses with his silver 1960 model. While Nik finishes getting everyone organized, we circle the piazza admiring the rows of vehicles. Before long, the motors start buzzing and a swarm of Crayola colors circles the piazza then whiz off to the countryside leaving us to walk home.

Conversation with Nik is fun, but he works in San Marino during the week so the time we can get together is limited. We need a more structured learning experience. In early June we start two weeks of classes at Madrelingua, a local language school. The owners, Stefi and Daniel, are professional and upbeat. After an evaluation, we're placed in different classrooms. I'm glad. I'll learn more at my own level.

There are just two others in my group—Miriam, a pretty Slovakian blonde with beautiful eyes, who's moved here recently and Tony, a Cypriot who lives in London but has taken time off to decide whether he wants to move to Italy.

They both speak excellent English and we hit it off immediately. With a couple years of Italian already, I've got a leg up on them, but it's apparent how much I don't know. Even though the teachers are really good, the classroom rule, *solemente in italiano*, makes it hard for us to understand them sometimes. The three of us puzzle things out together, and the exercises and assignments, which are fun, help us get to know each other. Every day at 11:30, the whole school takes a break. All the classes walk together to a tiny *bar* where everyone orders espresso and we have a chance to converse with other students and teachers...*in italiano*.

There's an easy camaraderie among the international students. Each week one of the teachers arranges a voluntary dinner at a local restaurant, and we explore some of the city sights with others. There's a wine tasting and evening cocktails at the Swine Bar. Students come from all over the globe, and John and I enjoy learning about their lives and what's brought them to Italy. We bond easily over our shared frustrations with *italiano*. After two months of talking mostly to each other, conversation with other people is a treat.

I especially like Tony and Miriam. We hang out after class sometimes, grab lunch occasionally, or just stroll the streets together. We arrange a dinner together at a jazz club so we can meet Miriam's Bologna boyfriend Giuseppe. Charming and obviously smitten with her, he's easily welcomed into our little circle. I'm so happy to have *friends* here.

Full-time classes are expensive so at the end of the two weeks, we depart Madrelingua. We stay in touch with the teachers and several of the students, however, stopping by the *bar* sometimes for the 11:30 coffee session. Miriam, Tony, and I get together on a regular basis and we introduce Nik to Tony. Making friends, even non-Italian ones, helps us feel more at home here. We're moving from observers to participants in the local scene.

I find I don't miss my life back in the States. There's so much to learn here—how to navigate the buses, uses for the funny-looking local produce, and where to buy things in a country without superstores on every corner. I'm even mastering Italian online resources. Because holding a conversation in Italian is so hard, I feel really proud of my progress. When I manage an exchange with the ladies in the bakery about the ingredients of the *torta di riso* and leave laughing with them about a little joke, I feel like an Olympic medalist. At the bus stop one morning, I manage to chat with a woman about the signs posted next to the schedule. She tells me that the date and times of the frequent transit strikes are always announced on flyers so people can plan. It's a crazy system and a *lingua difficile*, but I'm beginning to understand it. A little.

MINORITY VIEW

One change always leaves the way open for the establishment of others.

NICCOLO MACHIAVELLI

IT'S THAT TIME AGAIN. I NEED A HAIRCUT. MY APPOINTMENT AT THE BARBER is at 11:00. I'm ten minutes early, highly unusual for Italy. The receptionist tells me to have a seat. My hairdresser Marco is not quite ready for me. It gives me time to read my current book club assignment, *Other Voices, Other Rooms* by Truman Capote. I'm three-quarters of the way through the novel. It's an interesting book. I want to finish it. But the cover of a Vogue magazine sitting on the table in front of me has diverted my attention. No, I say. I'm not going to pick you up. I'm busy. I want to finish this book. I don't want to look at Vogue. Stop distracting me.

I give in. I pick it up. Vogue Italy, the July 2008 issue. Who knew there was an Italian Vogue?

The cover displays a group of nine or ten beautiful models, all black women. Okay, I'll bite. What's this about? Inside, there are great pictures, but only of black women. Even in the ads. Everything is written in Italian but these are not Italian women. I could understand if this were, say, Nigerian Vogue. But why are there only black women?

Marco's ready for me. Tall, thin, young, handsome, shy, and very effeminate, he's full of smiles. This is the third time I've been to this shop. The first time, Myrsa, a cute Romanian girl, was my barber. Last time, I got Marco. This time, instead of taking potluck, I specifically asked for Marco because he cuts my hair the way Johnny Romano, my Sicilian barber in Philadelphia, used to. Johnny was from my mother's hometown of Acireale near Catania. Come to think of it, all my barbers, from the day I got my first haircut, have been Sicilians. Marco is not. He's from Bologna. But he knows how to cut hair like a Sicilian. Myrsa gave me more of what I call a box cut. To me it looked too middle-American or even perhaps eastern-European—not Italian. Marco tapers the back the way I think a man's hair should be cut.

"*Come primo.*" Like before. I'm actually happy that Marco speaks no English. It gives me a chance to practice my Italian. When I remind him to taper the back he gives me a look as if to say, Is there any other way to cut a man's hair? We're in sync.

I point to the Vogue that I left on the table. "Yes, I've seen it," he says. "Interesting, eh?"

"What do you make of it?" I ask.

His response is quick and to the point. "That issue of Vogue is really very Italian. You know, Italians love controversy. Vogue is simply giving us what we want. Did you have time to read the editorial? I shake my head, No.

"Vogue wants to make a point. Several years ago, black models were all the rage. Today, not so much. So, this all-black issue is Vogue's way of reminding us, as well as themselves, that black is still beautiful."

This is getting pretty complex. I understand what he is saying, but I don't quite know how to formulate an intelligent response. Instead, I just blurt out: "Naomi Cambell. Tyra Banks. Iman."

"*Punto*", he says, telling me that is indeed the point.

"Yes. We know them. But name some current black models. Name one." I can't.

"Punto. There are none. Fashion changes. The fashion today is for very pale, very white, very blond." He picks up a loose-leaf folder filled with clippings—photos of models and starlets. "Notice that in some cases, even the eyelashes are blond. Actually white. Hair blond. Lashes blond. White skin. It's called a white-out look. Two of my regulars have the look."

I think to myself: they must look like ghosts. Who knew this was the fashion? I like to keep up with what's happening but I have not seen this white-out look on the streets—in Italy or in the States. Then again, Marco and I travel in different circles.

"Black is not completely out," he says. "They still use black models. But, it's not unusual to see black models with blond Afros or straight, blond hair like Beyonce."

"Ahhh," I say. "Works for me."

"Yes," he says. "But, notice. None of the black models is this special issue has blond or white hair. They're all brunettes."

I'm beginning to catch on. Vogue is championing a minority that Vogue itself has been guilty of restricting, not out of malice but as slaves to fashion. Eye-catching. Different. Provocative. I like it.

I thank Marco for helping me see beyond the cover. My brain is going a mile a minute. What about President Obama? Our first black president. Does Marco view him as some sort of fashion statement, a fad? Instead, I ask about Truman Capote.

"Marco, have you read anything by Truman Capote?" His steely stare is all the answer I need.

I try to explain the reason for my question. "You see, I'm reading this book by Capote." I show it to him. "It's vaguely autobiographical. It takes place in the American South in the late forties. It features an effeminate boy of twelve, struggling with his sexuality, seeking to find his place in the world."

"Sounds very interesting, Mr. John," he says. "Do you want some gel or shall I keep it dry?"

"Huh?"

"Your hair. With or without gel?"

"Oh. Oh. No gel. Thanks, Marco. And thanks for the perspective on the Vogue."

The treatment of minorities in Italy is something Nancy and I are trying to understand. On the one hand, there are certainly plenty of foreigners in Italy—including us. We cannot help notice the number of foreign voices on the local buses. During rush hour, Russian, Polish, Romanian, and African languages seem even more dominant than Italian. Walking the streets, we'd noticed a fair number of biracial couples and lots of cute dark babies with blond curly hair. At the outdoor markets, there are always groups of tall African men selling knockoffs. No, thank you, I don't want a "Yankee" cap or a "Gucci" handbag.

In any restaurant anywhere in Italy, the chances of a Pakistani or an African approaching to sell you a rose for your lady is 100 percent. (Nancy noted that one such rose I bought her lasted two weeks.) As for gays and lesbians, there are plenty of indications that, if not accepted, they are out there. We'd been to an art gallery in Bologna where the sign over the ticket booth let you know that all proceeds went to support the local gay/lesbian alliance.

In *Il Resto del Carlino*, the Bologna newspaper, I read that some Italian towns have been trying to pass ordinances limiting the number of pizza-kabab stores. As best I could understand, the ordinances would allow any number of pizzerias, and any number of kabab vendors, but there would be a moratorium on adding places known as pizza-kabab establishments. Why? The locals in Palermo, Assisi, Urbino, and Capri seem to have a problem with the combination: Pizza-Kabab. Crazy? I have to admit, it made little sense to me until I met Mike and Helmuth.

We encountered these two businessmen in the lounge of our hotel in Rome. Dressed neatly in sports jackets and ties, they were having an animated but pleasant conversation in English. While sipping our late afternoon prosecco, I could not really overhear what they were discussing but I did hear the younger one mention New Jersey. From his accent, my guess was Hoboken or Jersey City. Wait. I know what you're thinking. This guy is really full of himself if he thinks he can tell one Jersey accent from another. (You talkin' to me?) Think what you like. But I can tell you that North Jersey is a suburb of New York, whereas South Jersey is an extension of Philadelphia. Anyway, I know a North Jersey accent when I hear one.

The other gentleman spoke with a slight German accent. To be unobtrusive—translate that as we were eavesdropping—Nancy and I spoke to each other in Italian. Unfortunately, my Phillies cap sitting on the chair next to me blew my cover. The younger man turned to us, pointed to my cap and said, "Americans. Philadelphia?"

"Yes, originally," I said. "We're from New Jersey now. Long Beach Island."

"Oh, how about that. I'm from Jersey, too. Anyway, used to be. I now live in the City."

I learned long ago that when someone from Northern New Jersey says they live in the City, they don't mean Jersey City. They mean New York City. If someone from South Jersey is going into Philadelphia, they do not say, I'm going into the City, they say I'm going into Philly. See the difference?

"Lucky you," Nancy says. "Great town. We just love New York."

We all introduce ourselves. The young, handsome Jersey guy is Mike. Helmuth is from Zurich, Switzerland. An elegant chap in his late fifties, his English is perfect. They are in Rome for a trade show. Heavy Equipment. I mention Caterpillar. They laugh. No, they're not with Cat. But their company, based in Switzerland, sells to Cat and lots of other big players in the business.

Mike says, "I'd be interested in your view on the subject we're discussing."

"Sure. Fire away," I say.

Mike explains that he and Helmuth are having a friendly debate over a recent law passed in Switzerland outlawing the construction of minarets. According to the law, Muslims can have mosques but their mosques cannot have minarets. Nancy and I had read about the new law. To us, it was like saying you can build a church as long as it has no steeple. Helmuth approves of the law. Mike thinks it's racist and xenophobic. "What do you two think?"

OMG. What the hell have we gotten ourselves into? Nancy, the smart one, smiles at me as if to say John was talking about this just the other day. Mike then adds, "Look, John, do you think people in New Jersey would have a problem with any sort of place of worship? Could you imagine a law outlawing minarets?"

"Honestly, no," I say. "I think most of the people I know would not object. Anyway, our constitution protects the freedom to practice the religion of your choice."

Helmuth turns to me and smiles. "John, Nancy, you are Americans. You have a beautiful country and a wonderful heritage built upon liberty and freedom. Mike knows how much I love America. I lived in Chicago for five years. My youngest daughter was born there. Technically, she's an American citizen."

"How many languages does she speak?" I ask.

"All my children—I have three—speak German, Italian, French, and English. My oldest, a boy, is in medical school. The second is a girl; she's an engineer. And the youngest is studying biochemistry."

Somehow, I knew he was going to say something like that. I have two Swiss friends, Maria and Irma. Both speak several languages. I think I asked the question just so he would confirm what I already knew. I'm trying so hard to master Italian, and seemingly all the Swiss are like Roger Federer—cool and facile with languages.

"Very impressive," I say. "Most Americans don't even have a second language."

"Yes," he says. "But you do have Da Bears."

We all laugh. Da Bears.

"I still follow them," he says. "I like many things American. Da Bears. Obama. The Grand Canyon. New York. Broadway. Seinfeld. America is a great country. But so is Switzerland."

I can't argue with him. What's not to like about Switzerland? The countryside is gorgeous. The cities are clean and efficient. I've never been an accomplished skier but I have enjoyed skiing in parts of Switzerland. A few years ago, on a business trip, I even managed a glorious weekend skiing at the Badrutt's Palace Hotel in St. Moritz. Very posh. I have always found the Swiss to have a sort of understated competence. In Basel, when I mistakenly drove the wrong way up a one-way street, a patrolman at the other end stopped me, motioned me to lower the window, questioned me, and then dismissed me with a shrug and a wave of his arm that said: You are too dumb for me to bother with; get out of my sight.

On a trolley car in Zurich, there was a foot-wide sign over the conductor that read *nicht sprechen mit der wagenfurher*, don't speak with the trolley conductor. To me it meant: This is Switzerland. If you don't know where you're going, you should not be using our trains. I never forgot that sign. To this day, when I'm writing or otherwise don't want to be disturbed, I'll shout out to Nancy, *nicht sprechen mit der wagenfurher*. To which she'll invariably answer with another of my favorite bits of German that I made the mistake of teaching her: Don't be a *hosenschietze*, shit-pants.

I tell Helmuth about the trolley sign. He laughs and confirms that indeed there used to be such signs—but no longer. "Too many foreigners nowadays. They can't read the sign."

Now we're all laughing. Then Helmuth shifts gears. "In Switzerland, there is no talk of building an electrified fence on our borders to keep immigrants out." Ouch. Helmuth knows how to deliver a line. This is not the first time he's had to defend his turf against a few holier-than-thou Americans.

He goes on. "It's not about restricting people; it's a question of balance. We don't mind change, but we want it to come gradually, manageably. We are also a melting pot, but ours is on slow simmer. When visitors come to Switzerland, they have certain expectations. They want to find Switzerland not Mecca. Tourism is one of our major industries. Our skyline in Zurich, where I live, is a part of who we are. It's part of our brand, just like Coke, IBM, and Cat are brands. Switzerland is also a brand, a brand that needs to be protected. Just as Coke will go to court to protect its brands, we in Switzerland have used the courts to protect our identity. North Africans want to come to Switzerland because in Switzerland they can have a better life. Part of the reason we can absorb these people is our affluence, and some of that is because of tourism. Do you understand?"

I'm thinking to myself, how much of this is purely aesthetic? Americans come to Italy expecting all the restaurants to have red and white checked table-cloths. When they find white tablecloths instead, they don't go home. Would we stop coming to Italy because there are too many pizza-kabab vendors? The more I think about it, the more I believe there's more style here than substance.

Cripes, wearing a veil in France is verboten. You'd think that if any nation could accept a different style of fashion, it would be the center of haute couture. On the other hand, there's Geno's Steaks in South Philly where Joey Vento wouldn't serve you a stupid cheesesteak unless you ordered it in English.

It strikes me that wherever minorities bump up against majorities, the minority might be acceptable for a while, even fashionable, like the Black models in Italian Vogue. There really is a tendency to revert to the mean.

Maybe it's because Nancy and I recently read a book about the Comanches, *Empire of the Summer Moon*, that Native Americans are on my mind. I say, "In America, the Comanche were once the most feared race on the face of the earth. But the white man beat them by destroying the buffalo. Eventually, they were pacified. Translate that as starved to death. They became a minority. Now, save for a few casino owners and bit movie actors, there are not many Native Americans around. Nobody lives in fear of the Comanche nowadays."

Now everyone is looking at me like I'm a total nut case. And, I'm thinking, why the hell did I bring up Native Americans? "Here's my point. It's never good to be a minority. When I'm in the minority, I'd better be smart enough to keep a low profile."

"So you're telling me if I come down to Philly to see the Giants play the Eagles, I'd better not wear my Giants cap," Mike says with a grin. His comment gets us all laughing again. We've resolved nothing, but somehow the fact that perfect strangers can discuss these sensitive subjects with good humor buoys my spirits.

An hour later, Nancy and I are in a mass of people in front of the Trevi Fountain. Nancy, holding a single rose, gives me a big smile and says, "The guidebooks say this is one of the highest pickpocket zones in all of Italy." It's her diplomatic way of telling me I should take off my Phillies cap, lower my profile. I get the message. I roll up the hat, and put it in my backpack.

"I can do with a snack, " I say. "Getting hungry?"

"*Si, Signore.*"

"Okay. Let's go over to that place near the Spanish Steps. What's your pleasure, pizza or kabab?"

LOOKING FOR A WINNER

Appreciation is a wonderful thing: It makes what is excellent in others belong to us as well.

VOLTAIRE

BACK IN OUR APARTMENT AFTER A JUNE AFTERNOON CONCERT IN THE Center, we head for the wine bottle and a not-so-soft chair. "This was supposed to be our ideal city," I say as we ruminate again about our situation. "The food's wonderful and there seems to be a lot of music, but otherwise I'm not crazy about living in Bologna."

What looked good on paper has quickly disintegrated with the friction of real life. A different apartment would help, but there's an edgy, gritty feel to the city that makes us hesitant. Rather than giving protection, the porticos close in on us—like long empty tunnels. The train service is excellent. But all we can think about is getting out of town. Is this the Italy experience we want for a year?

"Maybe we need to rethink what's important to us," John replies.

"Okay, so what are we really looking for?"

"All this walking is killing me. Even taking buses, we're still hiking around most of the city. I'm sure some of our frustration comes from being so worn out." He's jabbing a pillow, scrunching around in the chair to find a comfortable position. "Transportation is more important than we thought. That's gotta be high on our list."

I have a sore back too. I try not to buy too much when we're shopping, but when we hit the Saragozza Gate and there's still half a mile left to get home, I'm dragging. It's painful to admit I'm not as fit as I used to be.

"Maybe we should get a scooter," he says. Probably a red one like Gregory Peck and Audrey Hepburn rode in *Roman Holiday*. Is he crazy? Dozens of them buzz off en masse at each traffic signal, zigging and zagging around cars and pedestrians. We'd be roadkill in no time.

"And the people," I say with a sigh. "We've made a few friends, but the neighborhood folks aren't very friendly." We know the Vitalis and Nik and made friends at school, but we can't manage any casual connections. I'd like to get to know the people in our building. But the woman across the hall hurries to slam her door whenever we see her. A few days ago the couple downstairs nearly knocked me over—without so much as a *scusi*. I know the "gregarious Italian" is a southern image, but I thought I'd be able to befriend more than dogs in the north. Maybe we'll find other friendly people here, just not in our building. Anyway, we're going to Modena day after tomorrow. Maybe people there will be different.

Twenty kilometers to the northwest, Modena is pink and white. Porticos line the main streets and there's no graffiti on the walls. Bicycles glide the streets. "It feels much lighter here," I say after we've walked for a while. "These pastels are so different from Bologna's dark buildings. And I love all the bikes. No zipping motorcycles either. Everything seems restrained, more refined."

"We know from lunch that the food is just as good. Let's see if we can locate their market."

Peering over our tourist map, we're bickering about which direction to go when from behind us a woman's voice says in English, "Can I help you find something?" She's blond, thirty-something, and very pregnant. The man with her is a bit taller, dressed in jeans, a crisp, white shirt open at the neck, and a blue jacket. They're both smiling.

"We're looking for the market," I say, returning her smile.

"It's just a few streets away," she says and points out the directions. They're Italian and live in Modena. Later, when we meet them again in the marketplace, they offer some help in finding an apartment. They have a friend in the business.

"Maybe Modena will be the ideal city," John says on the train back to Bologna. " I want to come back and explore it more. We'll see if their friend can come up with some place to live."

Modena, Pavarotti's hometown, has opera, another check-off for our perfect locale, and a wide tree-lined boulevard where the ancient city walls once stood. Inside this ring road, the old town is small enough to walk comfortably, and even easier to ride around. But finding an apartment in the Center proves impossible, so we keep looking.

Ferrara is the next possibility we consider. There's a tattered copy of Lonely Planet's *Italy* in our apartment. About the thickness of a brick, this tour book lists information about even the smallest cities and we check it often for things to do.

"I found something I think you'd enjoy," John says one day late in April. "It's a horse race called a *palio* in Ferrara. I think we can get there on the train."

He knows I've loved horses since I was little. In my late twenties I even owned my dream horse, a gray Arabian. I've always been a sucker for gray horses. It wasn't a good match. We were both too green, and, after he tossed me halfway across the practice, ring we parted company. But I never pass up an opportunity to see a horse show or race. "That sounds wonderful. When is it?"

"Ferrara has costumed events for the entire month of May, but the race is the final event on the 31st. Plenty of time to figure out the logistics."

At the end of May, we board a train towards Venice and in 30 minutes arrive in Ferrara. Taking a bus into the Center where there's an old castle and museum, we aren't prepared for how lovely the city is. Unlike Bologna's old town where everything is close together, several of Ferrara's medieval streets are wide. An enormous brick castle sits inside a real moat. A huge clock on one of its four towers faces the main piazza.

Crossing the drawbridge, we start our tour from the classic courtyard where pillared arches supporting a wall on one side are echoed by dark red brick arches set into the surrounding walls. Originally built for defensive purposes in 1385 by Duke Nicolo II d'Este, Castle Estense eventually became the family home. Each successive duke renovated it. The simple brick and white plaster interior has ornamental ceiling frescos and a well-curated exhibit of the castle's history. It's dramatically lit. Big mirrors slanted on a 45-degree angle in the center of the rooms reflect the ceiling frescos. What a novel idea. No twisting your neck stiff trying to see them. When we emerge atop a terrace on one corner of the fortress, we find an orangery and city views revealed through decorative holes cut in the thick castle walls. "Hey, I'll bet those old dukes did a lot of spying on the townsfolk from up here," John calls as he peers down on the piazza below.

"Now it would be a fabulous place for a party—all these orange trees for a backdrop." I'm imagining myself the duchess strolling through these magnificent rooms, presiding over banquets and festive gatherings.

In the depths, we crawl into the prison and deeper, into the dungeons. "I can't believe anyone could survive living here." I call to John from the rear of a long, tight, low-ceilinged room. The walls are thick with only a tiny slit for light. I don't want to imagine life here. "I'm sure glad I didn't live then...and piss off the duke."

Descending a long, wide, spiral stair into the courtyard at the end of our tour, we see three medieval-costumed people and stop for a picture with them. The young man channels Johnny Depp with shoulder-length, dark wavy hair, a trimmed goatee, an impish smile, and sparkling eyes. Did I mention I think he's really adorable?

We have lunch at a café across from the cathedral, then follow the crowd hoping we're on our way to the racetrack. *Boom, baba boom, baba boom!* Beating drums are coming up the street, a procession of blue-and-white costumed drummers and coronet players, followed by couples, children, and singles—all in medieval dress. They're heading into the castle, so we slip in at the end of the procession and follow them back over the drawbridge. Inside, the courtyard is now crowded with costumed residents. Hundreds of townsfolk in splendid dresses, magnificent capes, brocades, leather, and fur. It's like a grand movie set—or perhaps 1504. We wander through the crowd taking photos and eavesdropping on conversations. Returning to the street, we follow everyone once more toward the stadium.

Hundreds are already at the track. We slip into a spot at the center of the far turn. Behind us, folks are selling heraldry scarfs, and John buys one for me. It's blue and yellow with checkerboards and griffons on it. Wrapping it around my neck, I notice similar ones on the people all around us. Each Ferrara neighborhood represents an ancient dukedom with its own heraldry. All around the stadium, colorful flags and scarves define people's loyalties—like sports jerseys or caps. Friendly competition for claiming rights to this year's championships has everyone's adrenaline up, and the people around us are jabbering with excitement.

"We've landed in the San Giorgio section," John says after talking with another reveler.

Loud drumming comes from the street and eventually the procession enters the stadium. At least eight local groups, plus one from L'Aquilla, home of the recent earthquake, parade through the big oval. Each begins with their heraldry banner followed by drummers and trumpeters. Next comes the parade of citizens in their finery, archers and armored knights. Colorful flag throwers come next. Following a precise routine, the flags are twirled and tossed in unison. Lots better than batons. When the San Giorgio group parades by, the costumed couples turn and bow to us. Like all the other folks, we wave and shout our approval to "our" neighbors. After the last group passes, all the flag carriers run out and ring the entire track. Right in front of us is that dreamboat from my photo, and he's the leader of the entire show. Together, nearly 100 flags glide through the air in a choreographed routine, their colors tumbling over and over like swarming birds. It's a great show.

Now the races can begin. Captains of each group line up across the track and announce the first participants—the boys race. Off they go twice round the track, not practiced runners, just fast kids.

"*Vai, vai,*" we cheer with our fellow San Giorgians when our runner goes by. Go, go.

As the winner finishes, the San Michele group to our left pours over the barricade and onto the track. They all run to the finish line, hoist their hero onto their shoulders, singing and shouting. He receives a gold cup for his effort and is carried all around the track as the crowd stands and cheers. Next, the girls' race. The same thing happens. This time, the cheering squad waves a room-size flag that they carry onto the track and swirl around with their hero. The third race is with donkeys—big ones that the boys ride bareback, or as John puts it, bare-assed. It's a hoot.

The last event, what we've all been waiting for, is the horse race. Ten beautiful steeds stride onto the turf. Once again the riders are bareback. Flat-out racing on big, fast horses, bareback riding is *brave*.

"Look, there's a gray Arabian, my favorite," I say pointing to the sideways prancing mount. "I know who I'll be rooting for."

The starting gate is simply a thick rope stretched tight across the track on the turn just ahead of us. Behind it, another rope, stretched not quite so far, forms a corral. After much prancing and sidestepping, the horses start in. Number one walks nicely into place. Number two follows. Next is "my" Arabian. Like most Arabs he's a little skittish, but soon enters the corral. Lining him up isn't quite so easy though, and his rider struggles to get him in position. In the meantime, the number four is acting like there's a burr under his nonexistent saddle. Balking, rearing, and heading backwards, he does *not* want to go in. I watch his jockey's thighs grip the rearing steed. "Wow, that kid can ride!" No chance *he'll* be tossed to the ground.

After many failed tries, another rider comes up on his left and gently guides them through the opening. But now the gray horse is out of place, and number four is where number three should be. While they jostle trying to correct the situation, a few more enter the gate, each one being directed by name over the loudspeaker: "*San Paulo, San Pietro...San Giovanni, dentro*, in front of, *San Pietro. No, San Giacamo, dopo*, after, *San Michele...*" It's like watching a Jack Black comedy, and we have the best view in the stadium.

Finally they're all lined up in order—except the gray horse is facing the wrong way! Okay, start again. "*San Paulo, San Pietro, San Giovanni...*" Almost there, and...BANG...they're off...oops, a false start. They trot around the track and start getting into position again. After about 20 minutes, the fun of watching them from our vantage point ends. The rope falls, the gun sounds, and off they run.

Thundering around the track they pass us three times—the gray horse always in the back of the pack. On the last lap, right in front of us, the lead rider gets squeezed. His horse stumbles and almost goes down. Our crowd gasps. The rider saves his seat but loses his position and someone else wins. San Giorgio comes in fifth. Like our compatriots, we're disappointed and join in the wait-'til-next-year laments, *la prossima volta*. The cheering celebration starts again, but we turn back toward the Center. I'm happy to be moving again. My old crushed vertebrae from that long ago fall reminds me I've been standing nearly three hours. The crowd moves out onto the streets, and dozens of bicyclers glide past us heading for the Center.

At our lunch café sipping Campari and soda, we're surprised to be in the middle of things again. Above us, on a high parapet, the "Duke" is proclaiming the day's winners. Their crests are mounted below each of the four windows fronting the building, and their flags wave from the windows. In the square, the teams are singing and cheering. A standard is run up the flagpole followed by more singing. Eventually, everyone drifts away. Time for us to head out too. It's been an excellent day.

We think we could make friends in Ferrara. Something in human nature makes people seek connections. That's certainly been true of our time in Italy. We long to belong somewhere, to feel included, not like intruders. Today we started as visitors, but the racetrack experience pulled us into the San Giorgio community. We were part of their team, their neighborhood. How little it takes to make that happen. Today, it was simply a colorful scarf.

Maybe Ferrara is the place for us to spend the rest of our Italian year. We could get a couple bikes for transportation. Over the next few weeks, we search the internet for apartments. We call several Ferrara realtors but have no luck. For now, our ideal place remains elusive.

Trouble in River City

Sometimes you do something, and you get screwed. Sometimes it's the things you don't do, and you get screwed.

Chuck Palahniuk

Like the guys sing on the Rock Island Line in The Music Man: You got to know the territory. It's as true for Gary, Indiana, as it is for Bologna, Italy.

Specifically, you got to know the local laws. Otherwise, you are asking for trouble, trouble with a capital T, that rhymes with P which, in this case, stands for *polizia*, police.

Surprise. The laws in Italy are different from ours. For example, when you ride the train, it's not sufficient that you have a valid ticket. You also have to have your ticket re-validated with a time-stamp before entering the train—or else the conductor will hit you with a fine. We are well aware of this rule. So we always make sure to have our tickets stamped—except for the time that we did not.

It happened on the train from Florence to Bologna. We had just spent a lovely afternoon with Andy and Judy, American friends from Boca Raton, Florida. Because of their schedule, it was easier for us to take the train to meet them in Florence than for them to come to Bologna. The trip is only about an hour. Besides, how many times in our lives would we be able to say that we are going to Florence for lunch with friends? How cool is that?

We caught up over lunch in a nice little place that Andy recommended. The meal was superb, in part because Andy picked the wines. A collector and connoisseur, Andy knows how to select wines, even Italian wines. There was only one problem: we lingered a bit too long. After saying our goodbyes, we rushed back to the train station. When we arrived, our train was about to pull out. Nancy had the presence of mind to slip our tickets into the yellow box that stamps the time, and we climbed onto the train. We found two seats, made ourselves comfortable, and thoroughly congratulated ourselves on having mastered the Italian train system to the point where we could go from one city to another just to have lunch. That's when the conductor showed up crying "*Biglietti.*" Tickets. We're ready. Nancy hands him ours.

"They are not validated," he says. "Tickets need to be time-stamped."

"Yes, we know," I say. "We stamped them in Florence."

"There's no stamp," he says. "We require a stamp so that a ticket cannot be reused. There are yellow boxes at the station. There's no stamp."

I remove my glasses, holding the tickets close to my myopic eyes. There's no stamp. "But we stamped them. The machine made a noise. I heard it." Nancy confirms what I say.

"*Signore*, the ticket is not validated. The fine for not validating your ticket is 50 euros, each."

"A hundred euros! That's one hundred and forty dollars. That's crazy. We did use the yellow box. Maybe it malfunctioned."

"Did you align the arrows labeled *convalida*?"

Damn. I don't know if we lined up the arrows precisely the way he says. We were in a hurry. *Cripes, we stuck the stinkin' tickets in the stupid yellow box.* No, I didn't say that to him, but that's what I was thinking. But we did use the stupid machine. It made a noise. We hopped on the train. What the hell do I know? I want to tell him to buzz off but I know that will only make things worse. Besides, this poor jerk is just trying to do his job.

Nancy takes the tickets from my hand. She then goes through the "convalidation" motion. "The yellow box was at *Binario* 3, Track 3, where we boarded the train. I placed each ticket in like so. The machine made the customary noise. Because we were in a hurry, we did not examine the tickets carefully."

"Next time, Madam, make sure you check the tickets. Machines can malfunction. Enjoy the rest of your trip." Nancy's charm saved the day. But we were to face a day when nothing helped.

While driving on the road to Mantua, we learned the hard way that if you get caught speeding, you can protest, you can request a trial, but unless you want to spend several nights in jail awaiting your day in court, you have to pay the *multa*, the fine, to the *polizia* in cash, right there, right then. In our case, the fine was 155 euros, more than $220.

My defense: my wife has an appointment in 20 minutes—with an oncologist at the hospital in Mantua. *No, it is not an emergency, but do you know how hard it is to get an appointment with Dr. Franco? Yes, you schmuck, that Dr. Franco. The Dr. Franco, the noted practitioner. And, anyway, you red-faced, beady-eyed SOB, I was only doing 65 in a stupid 50 zone. Moreover, that uniform makes you look like a bleepin' storm-trooper. You jack-booted, over-stuffed pig...*

No, of course, I didn't say any of those things. But it didn't matter. Colonel Klink or whatever his name is was intractable. No way around it. We had to come up with 155 euros, cash on the barrelhead. No checks. No credit cards. Cash only. Exact change. What is it with Italian bureaucracy that they can't make change? Who has exactly 155 euros on hand?

Fortunately, my brother Robert was with us. Among the three of us, we managed to pull together the funds. The last 25 euros came mainly from a baggie we keep under the front seat. Loaded with all the small coins we never seemed to find useful, that day the baggie's contents were a godsend. By the time we counted out the last few cents, the baggie contained just three odd coins, one Chinese.

As we were departing, receipt in hand and already ten minutes late, the brown-shirt rat had the guts to express good wishes for my wife's health. *Speriamo tutto va bene con dottore Franco.* We hope all goes well with Dr. Franco.

What's with the "we?" Are you some sort of self-proclaimed royalty? You dirty, rotten piece of crap. As for us, that is we, that is I, me, this me, io, io spero, I hope you fall off your stupid, jerry-built motorcycle and break your stupid, fat ass.

No, I didn't say any of that.

But if the fines and the way they collect them seem oppressive, consider this: in the EU, sales tax is 20 percent. Oh, they call it by the fancy name of Value Added Tax (VAT.) In Italy it's called an IVA—*Imposta sul Valore Aggiunto*. But whatever you call it, it's a sales tax. And you have to pay it at the point of purchase. Even New Jersey only has a seven percent sales tax. For the record, sales taxes are indeed higher in Italy, but New Jersey's total taxes—real estate, income, business, etc.—make the Garden State one of the most highly taxed places in all of Christendom.

In Italy, the law states that payment of the IVA to the government is the responsibility of both the merchant and the customer. That's right, if the government is cheated out of its IVA, both the buyer and seller need to worry about being hit with a fat *multa* or even jail-time. That's why when you buy something, anything, even a loaf of bread, you had better keep your *scontrino*, receipt, until you get your merchandise home. For tax purposes, it's illegal for the merchant not to give you one and for you, the customer, not to insist on one. The Italian tax police, the *Guarda di Finanzia*, earn their keep by catching violators of both stripes.

You gotta know the territory. Gemma, our erstwhile landlady in Bologna, certainly does. She is an *avvocato*, an attorney.

We met her before we signed the lease. And we believed everything she told us. But the apartment wasn't what it was cracked up to be. The promised quiet location turned out to be Via Saragossa, the busiest, noisiest street in town— more like a highway, a highway where motorcycles zoom all night long. Even with the windows and shutters closed tight, the noise is loud. What will it be like during the summer? There is no air-conditioning. How will we be able to sleep with open windows? And our bed must have been designed by the same guy who, during the Inquisition, came up with the rack and the ball-crusher.

With closed windows and new mattress pads we bought at the local IKEA, we manage to survive April. But after a series of emails, it becomes clear that Gemma is not going to do anything to improve our living conditions. She had originally told us that we could install a portable air-conditioner. Although we were willing to buy a small window unit, it couldn't be installed in the windows, and any other kind of AC would require a compressor on the roof, which the building management will not allow.

On May 1st, Gemma's mother Elvira comes to the apartment to collect the rent. Like the motorcycle policeman, she insists on cash. Unlike our Colonel Klink, Elvira does not give us a receipt. Neither had Gemma. That's right! No *scontrino*.

By June 1st, the temperature in Bologna is over 90 degrees F. At night, the apartment is hot and noisy. Opening windows only makes things worse. Nancy is miserable. I am angry. Elvira comes to collect the rent. Same thing. Cash. No air-conditioning. No new furnishings. No new mattresses. No *scontrino*.

Did I mention I am angry? *Basta!* Enough!

By July 1st, we are in a quiet, beautifully furnished, air-conditioned apartment a few blocks from the center of Parma. If our Bologna experience was a nightmare, Parma will to be the answer to our dreams. We broke our lease? Yes! Here's how it went down.

In an email, I explained to Gemma that I had learned from the *Guardia di Finanzia* that a renter is legally required to demand an official receipt, *a scontrino*, from a landlord. Failing to do so is a crime. I went on to explain that Nancy and I would no longer be party to a deal that did not explicitly show payment of the IVA to the Italian government. *If you don't cooperate, Gemma, I'm going to report you to the Guardia di Finanzia.*

No, I never said anything like that. Nonetheless, Gemma, our beautiful, smart lawyer-landlord, now knew that we also knew something about the laws of Italy. Gemma got the message. Not only did she agree to let us out of our lease, she also agreed to return a portion of our deposit monies to us by July 10th. By then, we were already living in our Parma apartment.

I'm not exactly sure when we decided to leave Bologna but it was not a quick decision. For two months, we tried to make it work. But then we said to ourselves, this is crazy. Why do this? Let's make a change.

While we were taking Italian classes at Madrelingua, one of my classmates was a professor of biochemistry from New Hampshire. One weekend, he had gone to Parma to investigate the chemistry of cheesemaking. He knew Nancy and I were looking to move from Bologna. We had told him about Ferarra and Modena. He told us about Parma. "John, you'll love it. Beautiful city. Wonderful cathedral. Nice shops. And, listen to this. No graffiti. Can you believe it?"

Two days later we were there. Before going, I had called a realtor to look at three rental apartments. We arrived by train and grabbed a taxi at the station. The driver, an attractive, middle-aged woman named Luccia made a wonderful first impression. When I asked, "Do you have much graffiti here in Parma?" she smiled and explained that the people of Parma were too proud of their city to tolerate such nonsense.

"We catch violators and prosecute them. We even have hidden cameras to help. Violators are sentenced to cleanup details. They are also heavily fined. Repeat violators are jailed."

When we explained our mission, Luccia could not have been more helpful. In the ten minutes it took to get to our first appointment, she told us about some of Parma's best restaurants, the university, the hospitals, and even some of the history. About half the size of Bologna, Parma has many of the things we want. According to Luccia, Parma's opera company is second only to La Scala in Milan. The food is second to none. There are lots of green spaces and, something we did not expect, bikes. Everywhere we looked, there were people negotiating through town on bikes. It gave the place a sort of fairy-tale quality. We liked it.

"Oh yes. This is definitely a bike-friendly town. We even have places where you can rent a bike on one side of town and drop it off at another."

Luccia was a font of knowledge. By the time we reached our first destination, we negotiated a price for her to chauffeur us for the rest of the day. We looked at three apartments. All were air-conditioned with two bedrooms and two baths. The third was in the best location, a tree-lined street, Vialle Campanini, a short walk to Garibaldi Square, the town Center. It was a bit more expensive than the other two but still 25 percent less than we were paying Gemma. The owner Simona, a stunning woman with auburn hair and a beautiful smile, explained in Italian that she and her husband, two teenaged boys, and a dog all lived here until recently; their new larger apartment is two blocks away.

We told her that we liked the apartment, liked the city, but we wanted to sleep on it before making a decision. On the way back to the train, Luccia told us that Viale Campanini was considered to be one of the finest streets in Parma—very desirable. By the time we returned to Bologna, our minds were made up. Simona's apartment was the one.

The next day we called the realtor to say yes. Three days later we went back to Parma to seal the deal. This time we met Simona's husband Andrea, a tall, dashing fellow who speaks fine English. We signed a lease and gave them two months rent—for which they gave us an official *scontrino.*

Two weeks later, we rented a small truck, packed our bags, and left our apartment in Bologna for our new digs in Parma. When we arrived, Simona and Andrea were waiting for us.

We had already agreed on the furnishings to remain in the apartment. Simona and Andrea had decided to leave us a few extras, however, if we wanted them. An extra armchair? Yes, please. A sideboard? Yes. Another coffee table? Yes again. Then Andrea said, "We have two bicycles in the basement. Would you like us to leave them for you?"

"*Si,*" we said in unison. I thought to myself, we're going to like it here. And, you know what? I was right.

La Famiglia

The family is the country of the heart.

Giuseppe Mazzini

In only a few hours we've made the train trip from Parma past Venice and on to Trieste where John's cousin lives. Claudia Petralia is the daughter of John's uncle Anthony who remained in Italy and married a woman from that northeastern city. John last saw her 30 years ago. Her boys were teens then. Now the oldest is in his fifties. When John called a few weeks earlier, Claudia was eager to have us visit.

After settling into our downtown hotel, we hike the long hill that leads to her home. I know this will be an afternoon full of Italian conversation, and I'm feeling apprehensive about being able to understand everyone. When the street side gate opens, it isn't the old lady I'm expecting but a vibrant, youthful-looking woman who appears to be in her mid-70s. She has a square face, chestnut hair, and eyes that sparkle behind her glasses. She throws her arms around John and gives me a huge hug and *baci*, all the while chattering in rapid Italian.

"When did you get here? How is your hotel? It's been such a long time, John. You don't look any older." She steps back to take another look at him, "Well maybe just a bit. When was it? The last time you were here?"

"Maybe 1976?"

"And Nancy," she says turning to me, "it's so good to meet you. Did you walk from the city? Did you stop at any of the coffee bars? The city is filled with them you know...." She's pleased by my stumbling responses and reassures me that I'm speaking just fine.

"Come meet everyone," she says, leading the way briskly up a long flight of stairs, past fig and laurel trees, to the patio. She explains that the four-story house was built by her father. Her apartment is on one side of the first and second floors. Her son Stefano's family has the third floor, and Alessandro and his family are on the top floor. Lorenzo, her third son who lives in Padua, rents his unit which is opposite hers. It's so different from the way we live in America, where our families often spread all across the country.

Before long, all of us are gathered on the rooftop deck for champagne. Claudia's sons are tall and lanky with long, thin faces and dark hair. Alessandro's wife Valentina, a round-faced brunette, and Stefano's wife Susan, a blond pixie, join us for a toast as we watch the sun set over the harbor and the city. Even the kids join in. Then it's down to Alessandro's apartment for a dinner of traditional Trieste foods: boiled ham to start, asparagus risotto, then a rolled stuffed beef recipe that would normally have been made with horsemeat. Thank you for not serving Seabiscuit!

Over many bottles of wine, homemade bread, and a traditional Trieste cake that Claudia made, we laugh and share stories about the family and our interests. John recalls his visits years ago when Claudia's husband Stellio was alive. He was head of the Library of Venice and an internationally known James Joyce scholar. "Be sure to find Joyce's statue when you're touring the town tomorrow," Stefano tells us. "Dad would like that."

I'm able to understand most of the conversation and everyone but Claudia either speaks or understands some English, so when I get stuck they're ready to help. Despite the years, kinship and shared history pulls us into this close-knit group. My worry forgotten, I'm comfortable in their company. I ask Susan and Alessandro about how they prepare some of the dishes and exchange SKYPE addresses with Valentina. John teases Claudia about how she's too young to have these grownup children.

"I'm 86," she says with pride and I can hardly believe it. Must be all these hills and stairs that keep her so youthful. That and her warm and lively tribe.

After a day of touring the city, a visit to Miramar, a tiny castle built by Maximillian in 1860, and a photo with the James Joyce statue, we return in the evening for another meal together. Just like in the movies, we all gather at a long table on the patio for our *al fresco* dinner. Susan contributes a mushroom appetizer. Alessandro has made sardines with onion confit and fresh laurel leaves from the nearby tree. There are two pasta dishes, fresh vegetable salads, homemade bread, and hot, breaded sardines. John and I have brought wine and desserts.

The air cools after sundown but the warm conversation keeps the chill away as we laugh through the evening. Before we leave, there are photos and big hugs from everyone, especially between Claudia and me. We promise to see her in Padua when we go to meet Lorenzo's family. After just two days with them, I feel like I've known these folks my whole life.

In July Alessandro calls. "Valentina and I are taking the kids to London for a week in August. The apartment will be empty. Would you like to come and stay here while we're gone? I know Mom would love to have more time with both of you."

"That would be delightful," John tells him. "We'd love to spend more time with Claudia. She and Nancy really took to each other. And it'll be nice to get to know Stefano and Susan better too."

"It's set then. You're coming."

On the evening we arrive, we accompany Claudia, Stefano, and Susan to Castello di San Giusto for a special event. Stellio Crise, Claudia's husband, was a major figure in Trieste and his family is still honored there. Tonight the President of Serbia has come to open an exhibit celebrating the Serbian people and their Trieste community here. The Crise family is invited and it's a special treat for us to be with them.

Trieste is a port city with a Bavarian feel. Along the shoreline runs a wide boulevard lined with pastel-colored buildings and Art Nouveau lampposts. North of the city public beaches hug the coast. The next day we all go there for a swim. Just beyond Miramar, we park along the road high above the water and walk through a garden to the bathing entry. For three euros we're able to stay all morning. We change into our suits and take an elevator 30 meters down to the water's edge—where the "beach" is a wide paved area. Large pines along the hillside stretch their shady arms over half the pavement and tiny, green private changing houses are tucked in among the foliage.

"Are you ready for a swim?" Claudia asks me as she pulls off her robe.

"Sure. I'm ready to cool off and get a little exercise."

I follow her down the concrete stairs into the clear water and glide out for a few laps along the shoreline. Floating, my mind drifts back to LBI and all the times I swam with my friend Rhoda. I still can't believe she's gone. An absolute fish, she would have loved swimming here. Summers back home won't be the same without her.

After a couple of hours we've all had enough sun. Back in Alessandro's apartment there's time for a nap before dinner and a jazz concert.

We plan to spend some of the next day on our own, but first Susan has organized a visit to a famous home that's now the Civico Museo Sartorio. A teacher, she often takes her classes there. She's now writing a book about the museum. Having a personal docent is a treat. She leads our tour in Italian, but I grasp most of her commentary.

Later, when John and I are on our own, we wander into Piazza di Unita, the city's major gathering space where workers are setting up for tonight's big concert. It starts to rain so we duck into the Grand Hotel Duchi D'Aosta and take a table under the awning of Harry's Bar. "I remember this place from when I was traveling in the 80s," John says. "It was *the* place to stay. Too bad we can't stay here now."

"It's too pricey. But I'm glad we can look around inside. Eating lunch here, we can be part of the elite crowd for a while."

We share a plate of sardines with the soft, sweet onions that are a Trieste staple and fast becoming one of my favorite dishes, then take a cab back to Claudia's. There's a special dinner planned tonight, and I want to contribute so we feel a real part of it. Alessandro does the cooking in his house, and I feel right at home in his well-equipped kitchen. My polenta with mushroom *ragu* in hand, we go downstairs to Stefano's at eight. Claudia and three friends arrive a short while later and everyone has brought something for the dinner. Claudia's eggplant parmesan is my favorite—so light it dissolves in my mouth almost without chewing.

Claudia loves to laugh, especially at herself, and has ample opportunity as she's teased by her son, her friends, and John. I have a hard time following the jokes but John explains when I ask, and I can catch the gist of most of the other conversation. Meeting Claudia's friends, hearing about their travels together, we feel like part of *la famiglia*.

Being with these people is so easy. As an only child, the daughter of two onlys, I've joked all my life that my family reunion could be held around a card table. Maybe that's why I feel so good in this big, boisterous group. There's an ease about life here—a good way of being.

Susan has a plan for our next day: visiting the Gigantic Grotto in the hills behind the city. By volume it's the largest grotto in the world that's open to tourists. At the entrance, signs warn that there are 500 steps to the base of the cave, and another 500 back up to exit. "Think it'll be okay?" I ask John before we buy our tickets. "That's a lot of stairs."

"We'll be fine."

Trekking the damp stairs, we're getting colder as we descend. Our guide tells us the grotto was discovered in the mid-1800s and opened to tourists in 1908. Oil lamps and torches that lit the gargantuan space back then left black soot on some of the stalactites. Since 1957 the space has been electrified, but that's had another ecological impact. Plants now grow in the grotto, hundreds of feet below the earth's surface. Spores on tourists' clothing provided the "seeds," and heat and light from the big lamps enabled photosynthesis. Man's unintended consequences again.

From its base the grotto seems as big as St. Peter's Cathedral. When I look back toward the stairs, the people climbing down are tiny ants whose voices echo in the voluminous space. All around us huge stalagmite "plates" are growing from the floor. Stacked like tottering dishes, they form when water from the extremely high ceiling drops with such velocity that it spreads out on impact.

Now it's time to climb out. At first the stairs don't bother us much, but after 300 or so John and I are both puffing hard. Susan, Stefano, and little Francesco are well ahead of us by now. "Let's take a rest," I say leaning on a railing. John grips it hard, his chest heaving. A few minutes later we push on, pausing at each landing, frustrated by our failing stamina. I'm starting to worry about him when we round a bend to see the skeleton of a prehistoric bear that was found in the cave—and the exit. "It's good to be back outside again," I say rubbing my goosebumps and fears away.

We find Claudia sitting in the shade. "You made a good decision not going in," John tells her. "You're probably in better shape than we are but it's a *long* slog back up those stairs."

Later, back in the apartment, the couch feels especially good. John puts on some music and stretches out for a nap. I pick an English-language book from the shelf. Stefano calls at 8:00. "Time to leave for another jazz concert. Tonight it's Brazilian."

The sultry music in the main square lasts two hours. When it ends, we stop for gelato and a slow *passagiatta* before returning home. Trieste, like many other cities, morphs at night. Her streets crowd with diners, music lovers, and strollers. Wish we had the stamina to stay up longer!

We depart in the morning with hugs and kisses. Little Francesco's eyes light up when John gives him his LBI baseball cap. These delightful people have again made us feel like both honored guests and part of *la famiglia*.

Padua remains on our to-do list for many months. When we finally arrange to go, we email Lorenzo. His reply is prompt. He will meet us in town the evening we arrive, and Claudia will come from Trieste to see us too.

Arriving early in the day we have reservations to visit the Scrovengi Chapel where the famous Giotto frescoes are. "Remember the ones he painted in Assisi?" I ask John. "Some of them were pretty faded."

"You liked them well enough. You spent at least an hour in the upper church alone."

Here the frescos are well protected from the elements. That means we'll have only 15 minutes in the tiny chapel. We enter through an airlock to a small theater where a short film tells about Giotto and the paintings. When it ends, the doors at the opposite side of the room slide open, and we walk along a climate-controlled hallway to the chapel. I've done my reading in advance and have my trusty art guide in hand. Moving quickly and pointing out each panel, I hurry John around the room three times to "read" the cycles of frescos.

Although they're from 1305, the colors are as vibrant as if done yesterday—brilliant royal blue sky, bold oranges and reds, and gilt haloes and angel wings. The intimacy between Judas and Christ just before the traitor's kiss is planted is arresting. Jesus, perfectly calm, stares into the eyes of an almost simian-faced Judas whose lips are pursed. Behind and around them is a chaos of angry men, tilting spears and exposed daggers. Giotto knew how to capture the drama of a moment. Unfortunately we can't linger. Our 15 minutes are up.

I'd read about a monument to 9/11 that's across the street from the chapel. This is the second we've seen in Italy. The other was in Rome, a beam from one of the Twin Towers, an unexpected part of an antiquities museum. Trieste's substantial outdoor installation is entitled *Memory and Light*. On a grassy plain approached by a long marble walkway, two 50-foot walls of frosted glass meet at 90-degree angles. The inside of one is faced with granite that surrounds a rusted and bent steel beam—the gift of our State Department to the Veneto region. Like all Italian memorials, it has a large wreath.

"It's a beautiful tribute," I say to John as we linger near the sleek walls. "Even though it's in the middle of the city there's a peacefulness about it. It's always surprising to see a memorial to 9/11 outside the States. I'll bet most Americans would never guess that another country has such respect for us and our loss."

"Of course there were Italians in the Towers," John adds. "In a way, 9/11 was the world's loss."

We linger a few more minutes and return to our hotel to meet Lorenzo. Claudia's son and his wife Santina arrive around seven. Like his mother and brothers, he is delightful and exuberant, embracing John like the long lost cousin he is. Even thinner than his brothers, his receding brown hair is curly and he wears red-framed glasses. Santina is quieter. Her soft auburn hair curls off her face, and when she smiles her eyes almost disappear. She's congenial and her comprehension of a little English makes it easier for me to fall in with her as we walk around the city. As she narrates the sights for us in Italian, I'm pleased to understand most of what she's saying.

"You should come back here tomorrow," she says as we enter Palazzo della Ragione. "It's where the daily market is held. They sell everything from food to clothing to household goods. Take a look at the clock tower behind us." Santina points back across the piazza. "It shows all 24 hours, the phases of the moon, and the astrological months."

A few blocks away we hear music—an orchestra is playing in a courtyard. In the middle of a piece entitled "Train," the timpani is simulating a steaming engine—chooga-chooga, chooga-chooga. As the train is speeding down the track, the piano player's keyboard suddenly collapses onto the street. Unfazed, the pianist simply squats down and finishes the number with bent knees. A standing ovation.

Like the Trieste part of John's family, Lorenzo and Santina are easy to be with; our conversation flows with smiles and laughter. Before we part, Lorenzo arranges to pick us up the next evening for dinner in their home. "*Ciao, ciao. Ci vediamo a domani sera.*" We'll see you tomorrow evening.

On our own the next day, we return to the Palazzo della Ragione to tour the interior and visit the market that surrounds the building. Built in 1218 as the court of justice the upper floor is one giant hall. Its wooden ceiling arches perhaps six stories high. The walls are lined with frescos depicting religious, astrological, and seasonal subjects. An enormous wooden horse from 1466 at one end of the hall dominates the furnishings. On the opposite end sits the Stone of Shame. Here debtors would be stripped to only shirt and pants and made to climb the stone in front of a hundred townsfolk. They then had to proclaim their remorse three times before being banished from the city. It was a huge improvement over the preceding sentence—hanging.

The Prato, a classically designed oval park over what was once a Roman theater, is a green oasis in this medieval city. Encircled by a watery canal and statues of 78 famous men, locals and tourists relax here before heading to the Basilica of St. Anthony. Construction of the cathedral started right after the saint's death in 1231. It was completed nearly a century later. Inside, the walls and arched ceilings are covered in more stripes, stars, braiding, frescos, and gilt than a *Carnevale* best-costume winner.

In the piazza outside the basilica is Donatello's bronze, equestrian monument to Gattamelta, and I recognize the same huge horse we saw in the great hall. Now it's ridden by the mercenary soldier who led the Venetian conquest of Milan. Today is Friday, graduation day in Italian universities. On our way back to the hotel we see dozens of laurel-wreathed baccalaureates being feted by friends and relatives. Pelted with flour and mocked in cartoons posted to trees, the graduates are happily bearing the abuse.

Lorenzo arrives for us at seven and we head to the train station to pick up his mother. When she steps onto the platform, it's with arms outstretched to both of us.

"*Ciao Claudia, come stai?*" How are you, I ask with a two-cheeked kiss.

"*Bene, bene. E` mi piace molto di vedervi.*" Great. I'm so happy to see you.

Arm in arm we walk to Lorenzo's car for the drive to his home in the countryside. The house, a converted barn that they bought twenty years ago, could be on a postcard. Red brick with dark green shutters, it's surrounded by old fields that Lorenzo has tamed into lovely gardens. He laid the ground floor tiles himself, ones he recovered from a 15th-century *palazzo*. Santina shows us the furnishings that came from her grandmother; the high-relief carvings on the buffet like some I've seen in museums.

Upstairs in the large kitchen, the table is set and the aroma of my favorite—guinea hen—fills our nostrils. Our time together is as comfortable as a meal with my parents. Claudia is of course laughing all the time, the rest of us teasing her and learning more about each other. Son Ludovico and his girlfriend come in later and share our dessert. After dinner Lorenzo and I compete to see who can have more trouble trying to take a time-release photo.

I know it's late but I'm reluctant to leave. Claudia's family has added us like thyme and basil into the *ragu* that is their daily life. In Italy, *la famiglia* is all-important. People stay close, in proximity and relationship. We see multi-generations together on the streets, together in restaurants, together at events. Their lives are entangled and they seem to relish their shared time more than anything. It's one of the things I envy most about them. Feeling it myself is a gift I'll always treasure.

SOUTHERN EXPOSURE

The fact that year after year hundreds of thousands of people left the countries of Europe to come to this country was persuasive evidence that they were coming to improve their lot, not to worsen it.

MILTON FRIEDMAN

GROWING UP IN SOUTH PHILADELPHIA, I ROUTINELY HEARD MY PARENTS speaking in the Sicilian dialect. For example, instead of the correct Italian for "he'll leave at seven" *esce alle sette,* they would say *nesce alle sette.* Why the extra "n" in Sicilian? I have no clue. It's just the way it is. My friend Greg Vitale's parents spoke the Calabrese dialect. To them, *esce* was something like "nyessce." Joey Avalino's parents were from Naples where they like to make Italian sound like Russian by adding "sh" wherever possible; their *esce* sounds like "nesshsshay." Somehow, as long as we were speaking one of Italy's Southern dialects, we "Italians" understood each other.

Nonetheless, all of us Italo-Americans mispronounced Italian words. To us, *prosciutto,* air-dried ham, was pronounced "bra-schut." *Soppressata,* a type of dried salami came out as "super-sod." *Capicola* was "gabbi-gole."

The Italian word for eggplant is *melanzane;* for us it was "moo-len-yan". *Manicotti,* a crepelike filled pasta, came out sounding something like "mane-gutts." And because Americans want to pluralize even already plural Italian

99

words by adding an "s," it was not unusual to use words such as "spaghettis," "cannolis," and "raviolis."

We also made English words sound like Italian. A refrigerator was an "ice-a-box-a." But "ice-a-creama" was something you kept in the "frigeriffo," the freezer part of the ice-a-box-a. A bathroom was a "backa-housa," which was derived from the fact that an outhouse was typically located in the back of the house. To go up, you said "ungopa," as in "you go uppa." To go down, it was *unbash* as in *a basso*—to the base or basement. For Italo-Americans, the cinema was the "mo-pitch." Why? Easy! Because that's where you went to see the <u>mo</u>ving <u>pitch</u>ures. Get it? I'm embarrassed to admit that I was well into my teens before I realized that *mo-pitch* was not an Italian word. Similarly, to South Philadelphia Italians, the RCA Victor Company located across the Delaware River in Camden, New Jersey, did not make phonographs. They made "talkamachines."

If you've watched HBO's *The Sopranos*, you probably already know expressions such as "agida, bimbo, capo, cugine, goomba" and "goomah." But—to use a homey Americanism—here's the thing: in Italian, none of these slang words mean what Americans think they mean nor do their phonetic spellings bear any resemblance to Italian or any Italian dialect. For example, in the States, a "goomba" is usually taken to mean a gangster or a tough guy. In Italy, the word, correctly spelled "compare," pronounced com-pah-ray, simply means a friend from your hometown.

To be sure, Italians, even those in Sicily or Naples, have lots of words for Mafiosi or gangsters but none include the word *compare*—or as we'd say—goomba. In Italy, a bimbo is a male baby and not a dumb, blond pole dancer. "Goomah," correctly written as *comare*, is a female friend from back home, not a derogatory name for the capo's bimbo mistress, who may or may not also be his "cugine," which in Italian is the plural of *cugina*, female cousin.

One of the more interesting and controversial transmutations of Italian into a form of Italian-American dialect is the overused slang word "agida," variously written as "agito" or "acito." You'll usually hear it in the context of a warning: "Don't give me *agida*." So what does it mean?

Because you won't find any of the various spellings for "agida" in an Italian dictionary or for that matter in use in any Italian dialect other than in America, there is no official or correct answer. Nonetheless, my sources—actually, my brothers Joe and Robert—tell me my etymology is the correct one.

Unlike "goombah" and the other examples of American mispronunciations of Italian words, "agida" is a uniquely Italo-American *insalata misto*, mixed salad, comprised of various mispronunciations and misuses of three completely different Italian words. First, there's *agitare*—a verb meaning to stir up, to agitate. To be *agitato* in Italy is to be very excited; thus, a musical score marked *agitato* is intended to be played at a frenzied pace. The second word is *aceto*, a noun meaning acid as in *balsamic aceto* from Modena. Third, there is *agito*, meaning literally "I act." The conflation of these two Italian verb forms, *agitare and agito*, with the noun *aceto* has the extraordinary effect of making the meaning of the slang word "agida" greater than the sum of its parts. Because of its various origins, the exact meaning varies with the situation. For example, when Carmella says to Tony: "Don't give me *agida*," what Carmella is saying in Italian-American short-hand is: "Tony, you are annoying me so much that my stomach acids are boiling up to the point where you are about to experience projectile vomiting directly onto your stinkin' fat face. So, shut up. Now." On the other hand, if Tony says: I have *agida*," he's maybe telling you that he has an upset stomach or that he is in a sour mood.

Borrowing and bastardizing words cuts both ways. In Italy, a hairdryer is called a *phone*. A sweater is a *golf*. Weekend is *il weekend*. A computer is *il computer*.

As a wise man once said, context creates meaning. Anyway you slice it, the American view of Italy, Italians, and Italian customs comes at us through a prism lit mostly from the South. Not to put too fine a point on it: rich Northern Italians did not come to America.

Take my old neighborhood. Within three blocks of our house at the corner of McClellan and South 18th Streets, you could find all the basic products you needed, that is, if you were southern Italian. Even Mr. Schwartz who ran the hardware store on our corner carried espresso coffee pots in various sizes and shapes, colanders, pasta makers, and other assorted Italian specialty items. Holding court in his corner of the neighborhood, he spoke Neapolitan Italian so well that it wasn't until I was seven or eight years old that I realized that "Mista Shortza" was actually an immigrant Jew from Germany. Similarly, at Renz's German Bakery, the little German and Italian ladies behind the counter, could manage, some might say mangle, English, Sicilian, and Calabrese with an equal lack of proficiency.

My favorite was Ilky who always threw in some extra sweets for *der bimbi*. Also a German immigrant, Ilky was the widow of Richard Bruno Hauptmann, the convicted Lindbergh baby kidnapper/killer. After Hauptmann was found guilty and executed, the Renz family took Ilky in. She lived with them over the store. Every adult in the neighborhood knew her sad story. To us kids, she was just the "nicea old lady" who might give you an extra "cuppa cake" with your Boston Cream pie. Renz's did not sell cannoli.

All the other local stores, Rocky's Produce, Joey's Deli, Cheap John's, Fantini's Meats, Mattarazo's Chicken Store, Lanci's bakery, and a half a dozen others were owned and operated by immigrants from places like Napoli, Calabria, and Catania. To shop these Italian stores, my mother would "ziga-zaga" from one to another to observe selections of fresh vegetables, bread, fruits, Italian pastries like cannoli and ricotta cakes, luncheon meats, cheeses like *parmigiano*, never parmesan, and provolone. Her most common remark: *troppo caro*, too much. To be sure, we did more looking, haggling, and shrugging than actual buying—beyond the basics. For us, cannoli were reserved for Easter, Christmas, and maybe an anniversary. To paraphrase Clemenza in *The Godfather*: take the bread, leave the cannoli.

Thanks to my mother's extraordinary Sicilian culinary skills, we always ate well. Most nights we had pasta, lots of greens, fruits, and homemade desserts. Meat balls, sausage, and *bracciolo* were served on Sunday; Thursday was usually chicken, cooked dry the way I like it. And, of course, being Catholic, we had fish every Friday. During warmer months, the fish came to our streets via "the fish-a-man" and his pushcart. A colorful figure dressed in large, rubber fishing boots, he'd walk the streets singing *"pesce."* I particularly remember the way he'd chop off a fish head, mix it up with a handful of bloody guts and toss it there in the gutter for happy neighborhood cats to devour—all the while serenading the ladies with Neapolitan love songs. During colder weather, there was no fish-a-man but we still had fish on Friday. It was salt cod, *baccala*, made into the most wonderful delicacies you can imagine. Baked baccala. Baccala salad. Baccala fish cakes. To this day, I prefer reconstituted baccala to fresh cod. Just add olive oil and garlic.

That was then. This is now. Nancy and I are living in Parma. Known as the food capital of Italy, Parma is home to the Agency for Food Quality Assurance. Here we have access to the very best Italian foods you could ever want—and then some. Prices? Today, the dollar plummeted to $1.55 against the euro. So, restaurants are expensive. Think New York City. So we cook home a lot. At our various little *alimentari* or even at the Uns supermarket at the Barilla Center, 90 percent of what we buy comes from within a 20 kilometer radius of Parma. Frozen foods and imported foods are practically nonexistent. There is no such thing as frozen corn in Parma!

In addition to fresh produce, we are able to buy real Parma prosciutto and parmigiano for about half of what we'd pay in New Jersey. We drink acceptable Lambruscos, San Geoveses, Malvesias, and other Emilian wines for a fraction of what they are at our Buy-Rite in New Jersey. Heaven? Well...almost. The missing ingredient? Italian bread. What, you say? No Italian bread in Parma? How can that be? Well, it's like this.

For me, Italian bread is what some of you might call hoagie bread. You know: bread like we get in South Philly, bread made by immigrant Italians from Naples, Calabria, or Sicily, bread you can get to this day at Faragalli's, Nino's, Cacia's, or Sarcone's; bread with a hard, dark crust and yummy innards that can sponge up more red sauce or olive oil than a blue ShamWow. That's real Italian bread.

Take it from me, northern Italian bread—Parma bread—is a sort of a pale, lightly crusted concoction, easily split by hand, with a white, cakey inside that resembles—how else to describe it—American bread.

Fortunately, last week, three blocks from our apartment on Viale Campanini, just before the arch on Emilia Est, we discovered a new *paneteria*, bakery: *Antichi*

Sapore di Altre Terre, Antique Flavors of Other Lands. Their sign, a map of Sicily with a star marking Palermo, left no doubt about its origins. We investigated. The young owners were attractive, efficient, and chatty. Their ruggedly cute blue-eyed, red-haired nine-year-old, Paolo reminded me a lot of a kid from South 18th Street we called Rhino Nose. More important, his parents are bakers. Sicilian bakers! Their store is not much bigger than a Fiat 500 but what comes out of it makes my mouth water.

We've been there every day since it opened—sometimes twice. Paolo has even become a Phillies fan. Today he's sporting the 2008 World Champions T-shirt we gave him. We have dinner guests coming tonight so we're choosing some Sicilian goodies—cannoli for dessert and biscotti. The word *biscotti* literally means cooked twice. That's why biscotti are really hard and that's why they're perfect for dunking in either wine or coffee. But, most important, we buy two loaves of the most magnificent, wood-fired, brick-oven-baked, hard-crusted, totally wonderful, just like I remember, South-Philly-style Italian bread. Real Italian bread that you can eat with sublime Parma "brachutt" without risking a bout of "agida."

THE DOMINO EFFECT

The shortest distance between two points is not a very interesting journey.

RUBE GOLDBERG

PARMA'S TOURIST INFORMATION CENTER (TIC) IS STAFFED BY FRIENDLY young women who speak English, German, and Spanish. Unlike in Bologna, the Parma TIC has loads of information about what's going on in the city. Their staff makes up a weekly list of all the events: lectures, music, festivals, and *mostra*, special events. They're listed on the TIC website and also on printed pages available in their office. Located not far from the main shopping street and the *duomo*, John and I go there almost every week.

"I'm sorry," the curly-haired, young woman says, "but we don't have these printed sheets in English, only Italian."

"That's okay," I reply. "We can read enough to get the idea, and I use the English version of your website or Google Translate for the rest."

My experience in Bologna had been quite different. Its TIC is prominently located in Piazza Maggiore, the major square where most of the city's big events take place. One day we stepped inside to inquire about the current happening. Huge bandstands were being erected just outside the tourist center's windows, and we wondered what it was all about.

"*Parle inglese?*" I asked the woman at the desk.

'No, *solemente italiano*," came the reply. Just Italian. So with my limited vocabulary, I inquired about the activity in the piazza.

"We don't know," she quipped and returned her gaze to her computer.

"But it's just outside the window." If she bothered to glance through the room's glass front it was hard to miss.

"It's a political program. That has nothing to do with us."

When I asked about other city activities, she waved me with a dismissive look toward a rack of xeroxed flyers—all in Italian. Wait, if I'm a tourist who wants to know what's going on in the city, wouldn't it be a good idea if these folks would *tell* me!

Here in Parma on the other hand, we ask about transportation to events outside the city and are given bus schedules for the surrounding towns—and to the Parma fairgrounds. Crowded on the TIC's small display shelves are brochures, flyers, and postcards advertising all kinds of upcoming events. We find many of them on their published lists—but not all. Usually it's because the events are taking place in distant towns.

Each week I pick up the latest promotions and check out all the posters. We find postcards about summer jazz concerts at Piazza San Francesco, free concerts at the Auditorium Paganini (just minutes from our apartment), festivals of all kinds, and the semiannual *Mercanteinfiera*, the big antiques fair, as well as local performances, films, and outdoor and health-related events. That's how we learn about Culatello & Jazz. The poster on the center's window advertises an evening of magnificent food with music by Fabrizio Bosso, a trumpeter that we'd heard on CDs at John's cousin's home in Trieste. Because it takes place in a town in the north of the province, it's not listed on the TIC website.

To really know what's happening we have to look beyond the TIC. We study the daily newspaper *Gazetta di Parma* over cappuccino in a bar. Its weekly events list doesn't match the one in the Tourist Center. Mysteriously some things aren't listed anywhere. They're just put on posters that are stuck in shop windows and restaurants.

While walking one day, I notice a small flyer in a store window. Something about a chorus, it mentions the names of three singers from Parma's opera company. But the store is closed. There's an address shown for purchasing tickets, and it's not too far away—so we walk there. Arriving at a small *cartoleria*, stationery store, we head to the rear of the store and speak with the owner. A huge smile breaks across his face when we ask for tickets.

"Oh, yes," he says, "I've got them. Ten euros. I'm part of the chorus for the opera company and we'll have several of the singers in the performance." Wow. We can hear the opera company singers for only ten euros!

A few nights later we go to their terrific show. Toward the end, measured chords signal the start of Verdi's "Va Pensiero." Starting softly, the chorus builds to full volume. At the conclusion, the whole audience stands shouting *bravo*.

Getting informed takes persistence—and being observant. We miss out on hearing Christmas carols because we don't see the announcement. Instead of being sung during the holiday season, carols are sung in various churches—in *January*. We aren't looking for Christmas songs then.

Can you imagine Americans going from storefront to storefront, checking out posters and billboards to learn about concerts and festivals? Imagine us trekking to the local Chamber of Commerce office to pick up flyers for every program in the city. Back on our New Jersey island, flyers are posted around but no event planner would fail to list all the details in the *Sandpaper*—our local weekly. Everyone reads it to know what's going on. Americans use robust websites and powerful search engines to locate what we want to know. The Italians, it seems, are still wedded to the printing press.

Printing flyers, billboards, brochures, and postcards would be a great business to have here. Thousands of them are scattered around every city and town. Many thousands go unused or are tossed aside. Our American marketing method is more efficient and cost effective, right? Bombarded by thousands of commercial messages every day on TV, online, and in the papers, we filter our email, sign up for online notices, search and tweet our way through a morass of information to get to just what we want to know. Lost, though, is serendipity. How often do we discover something we aren't looking for? In Parma a flyer or postcard leads us to events that turn out to be surprisingly wonderful.

"Look at this," I say, eyeing the Culatello & Jazz poster. "Your cousin Alessandro had some of Bosso's recordings in his apartment. Remember? You liked him a lot. And Stefano told us he's the hottest trumpeter in Italy."

"I remember. He sounds like Clifford Brown."

"It's not in Parma though, and it starts at 8:30 so we'll have to use a car to get there. I can sign us up at the car share."

And so, on a beautiful evening in September we arrive at Roccobianco's castle where about 250 people have gathered. People are in jeans, beads, and sequins, a few Missoni dresses, and some backless ones—sans the ubiquitous, unmatched bra straps. The courtyard walls, lined with ivy, are flooded with blue and white light. Under a portico, glasses of wine, huge rounds of Parmigiano Reggiano, and butlered hors d'oeuvres are served. Fried zucchini is the hit of the cocktail hour; trays heaped with these crunchy sticks vanish immediately. Just before we head to the dinner tables, the waiters distribute brown paper cones full of even more of them. The sponsor, a spirits merchant, even has a cigar station—where John samples Davidoff smokes. Pulling the last draw on our way to the table, he gives my waist a playful squeeze. Being part of this sophisticated evening makes us feel very special.

At the dinner table, we do our typical American thing and go around to introduce ourselves to everyone. Our table mates are surprised and pleased by this uncommon attention. About 30 minutes into the meal, I exhaust my conversation skills with the retired couple on my left—who speak no English. John is having a friendly dialog with another couple from Parma, Andrea and Emmanuele. Andrea, a chemical distributor, speaks fairly good English, however, his wife Emmanuele, a nurse, knows only Italian. John chats back and forth in both languages, and we learn they are not only jazz fans but also opera buffs. When Andrea hears that we are too, he leans toward us with a conspiratorial grin.

"There's a special performance of Tosca at the castle in Sorogna next month," he says. "The tickets are free but very hard to get. I'll see if I can get some for you to join us. Give me your number, and I'll call you later in the week and let you know."

Dinner is a gourmet's fantasy. *Culatello* is a cured pork specialty of this area. The production is so small that it rarely leaves the region and is never exported. Tonight it first comes sliced very thin, served with little rounds of butter—the purest taste of the meat. Next, *tagliolini* is served with a creamy sauce of butter and chopped *culatello*, which I savor on my tongue. A pork fillet follows topped by crispy *culatello* and the brandy of the Castle Roccobianco, its delicate flavor the essence of Emilia Romano cuisine. Dessert is *limoncello* gelato and an almond cookie.

Now it's time for the jazz. We turn toward the stage as Bosso and his trio fill the air with wild music. Staccato notes swirl around the courtyard. How can he spew so many notes so fast? He's astonishing and the diners love him. Bosso and the trio play a long set and two encores to wild applause. We finally leave at about 1:00—our stomachs full, our heads pulsating—and with two new friends who have an inside track on special events.

Andrea comes through on his promise, and we're invited to a performance of Tosca in the Sorogna castle. Sitting in the upstairs hall, I think this is like being a friend of a prince in the 1700s, invited to his home for a concert. The long, narrow room we're in is decorated with frescos. About 200 chairs are set out. Just before the performance starts, the honored guests, Valery Giscard d'Estang, former President of France, and the Consul General of Japan make their way down the aisle. Prince Diofebo Meli Lupi takes a microphone and welcomes everyone to his home. I *am* the guest of the prince! Rather than limiting the performance, the small stage at the front of the room makes Tosca's heroic tale more intimate, its tragedy more palpable. It's John and my favorite opera. The voices are wonderful, the night an exceptional treat. With two-cheek *baci*, we part from our new friends with promises of getting together soon.

"Would you like to join us for Thanksgiving? " Andrea asks in November when we're gathered for cocktails. Thanksgiving? In Italy? "We have an American friend who always celebrates and she'd be happy to include you," Emmanuele adds.

"Why, of course! It would be wonderful to come."

A few days before the holiday, we travel to Rome to spend some time with Suzanne, an American friend on her way to spend Thanksgiving in Abu Dabi. She tells us she's carrying a few American delicacies in her suitcase—three bags of fresh cranberries and two pounds of dried corn. "We don't need all the cranberries," she says to me. "Would you like to have a bag?"

"Oh boy, would I," I answer, an idea already in mind.

The day before the holiday, I pick up oranges and make fresh cranberry-orange relish—an American Thanksgiving staple. Andrea and Emmanuele arrive to pick us up at 7:45, and we're off to Traversatolo, a little village southeast of Parma. We pull into a driveway where three men are smoking in front of a doorway.

"*Sono Silvano,*" says a broad-shouldered man reaching out a hand, "*il padrone.*" Silvano, the home's owner is in his fifties, balding, with gentle eyes. He ushers us into the house and up the stairs to a huge room that consumes nearly the entire top floor. Decorated in a rustic style, with Silvano's hunting trophies on the wall, it's already full of laughing guests and the aroma of the Thanksgiving bird. He introduces us to his wife, Claudia, our American hostess. With her short grey hair and dressed in an apron, she looks very Italian. Her soft voice, like *limoncello,* is sweet and soothing.

"My mother was American, but her family was very, very poor," she tells us as we slip off our coats. "Her parents kept their sons in the States but sent my mother to live in Italy with her uncle. It was an awfully hard life for her—on a farm far from the cities. The uncle didn't believe in educating girls beyond the basics. Life was about work. After she married, she came back to New Jersey where I was born. I came to Italy years later, met Silvano, and we've been married for 30 years. My two brothers live in upstate New York."

"What a wonderful thing to do, having Thanksgiving dinner," I say.

"I do it every year. I love bringing a little of the American culture here, and it's such a great holiday for family and friends. Like in the Pilgrim story, we're a mix of people here. Some of these folks are American ex-pats. A few of the women are my English-language students, and the doctors I work for are here too. I'll introduce you around."

"I brought a little something for the dinner," I say, offering my container. "It's cranberry-orange relish."

"Cranberries! Fresh cranberries! We haven't had cranberries in, oh, maybe eight years. What a treat! Look everyone...*cranberries!*" John and I are an instant hit.

Over wine, we meet the other guests. Later, we settle at the long table with Andrea, Emmanuele, their daughter Guiliana, and Paulo and Adriana. Paulo's a pilot for the Barilla family; Andrea is his American wife. Claudia joins us when everything is served.

Silvano is holding forth at the opposite end of the table. He speaks no English, but the warmth of his toasts and sincere smile need no translation. Others toast in Italian and John stumbles our Italian thanks for being included. Glasses click. *Salute!*

Dinner is Italy's version of the traditional Thanksgiving fare. Everyone contributes. Of course, there is turkey, but in no way does it resemble a Butterball. Long and flat, it looks to me like a bird the original Pilgrims might have eaten. And it's the *most* delicious turkey I've ever tasted, moist, and filled with Italian sausage stuffing. Gravy, peas and prosciutto, and potato salad are served. There's Pelligrino, the carbonated water named "pilgrim" that's a staple on every table in the country—and more wine. Five or six kinds of desserts are brought to the table, including pumpkin pie. By the time we're savoring its familiar spicy taste, we feel like part of the family.

We learn that Emanuele and Claudia both work for the doctors, that Paulo has flown the Barillas all over the world, and that Adriana, like Claudia, has traded her American life for one here in Parma Province. Claudia and Silvano's younger son Stefano sits with us for a while. He tells us about his engineering studies at Parma's university and that he and his older brother both have dual citizenship.

"I wanted them to have that advantage," Claudia tells me. "They can do with it what they want, and maybe nothing, but it could be important one day. Just recently, the two of them and my almost daughter-in-law started a little business together. Just a sideline right now, but they hope to grow it...literally. They're raising *apaci.*"

"Apaci?"

"You know, those beautiful creatures from South America with the huge eyes. Their fur is used in expensive yarns."

"Oh, alpaca."

"Yes, alpaca. My English is not as good these days," she laughs.

"Where are they?"

"The boys built a shelter for them on the hill at the top of our property. You have to come back and see them."

"We'll take you up on that." I want to get to know this family better.

Just then older son, Marco, his girlfriend Manuella, and their new baby Matilde arrive from their home in the building next door. The first grandchild, just 20 days old, she's the most beautiful baby I've ever seen. Napping in her mother's arms, she reminds me of the Anne Geddes photographs of sleeping babies as fairies, butterflies, and flowers. Claudia is beaming and smitten. Everyone coos and admires the infant.

"Matilde. That's not an Italian name," I say to Claudia.

"Oh, it's *very* Italian. The baby is named for Matilde di Canossa."

A little research told me more. A famous countess from the 11th century, Matilde is known to every Italian. At age 9, after the murder of her father and death of her older siblings, she came to rule thousands of acres across the northern part of the peninsula, from Mantua to Lucca to Florence and stretching toward Rome. She was courageous, cosmopolitan, and enlightened. Trained in military arts, she spoke German and French in addition to Italian. Matilde could also read Latin. A formidable ruler throughout her life, she is most famous for brokering Emperor Henry IV's forgiveness from Pope Gregory VII. A true defender of the faith, she protected the pope in his disputes with the young German emperor. In January 1077, she convinced young Henry to appear at her castle barefoot and bow before the Pope. Today the phrase *andare a Canossa*, to go to Canossa, means to beg forgiveness and eat humble pie.

Matilde built dozens of castles and cathedrals in her territory, supported charitable organizations, and was influential in the establishment of the first university in Bologna. In the 17th century, her body was moved to St. Peter's where Bernini had designed a sarcophagus for her. She was quite a gal and gorgeous too—hers a fitting name for Claudia's tiny granddaughter.

Dishes cleared, Claudia pulls out song sheets and we all sing a few Christmas carols—another of her traditions. We Three Kings. Away in the Manger. Deck the Halls. And Silent Night. The English voices are strong, the Italian a bit quieter, many just humming. I love singing Christmas carols, and sharing these familiar songs shrinks the world in this happy room.

Next, Silvano pushes back the chairs and puts on a polka. He and Claudia twirl around the room, laughing, while the rest of us clap with the music. They're good. A couple of women join in. Others then take a turn around the furniture. Maybe they're not so graceful, but their hopping and hooting adds to the fun.

Late into the night, it's time to leave. We're touched by this welcoming family and deeply appreciate this unexpected holiday celebration. We have much to be thankful for: our good health, our opportunity to be here in Italy, friends old and new, shared meals and warm conversation. These *pelligrini* from New Jersey couldn't be happier!

MURDER IN PERUGIA

One who deceives will always find those who allow themselves to be deceived.

NICCOLO MACHIAVELLI

MAYBE IT'S BECAUSE VIOLENT CRIMES ARE A RARITY IN ITALY—AT LEAST compared to the United States. (Last year, there were more murders in Philadelphia, the City of Brotherly Love, than in all of Italy, the country of *amore.*) Or maybe, it's because the news media are bored with the politicians. Whatever the reasons, amid the antiquity, the Michelangelos, Giattos, Cellinis, and Leonardos, along the narrow cobblestoned streets walked by Caesar, Pompey, and Cicero, inside ancient edifices where Dante and Petrarch once dined, in creaky classrooms where Galileo, Volta, and Galvanni explained the marvels of optics and electricity, in outdoor bars surrounding picturesque piazzas, and between acts at the opera houses, there are murmurs of murder.

The tabloids show us the victims and the perpetrators. A young woman was killed by her lover who turned out to be her sister's husband. A beautiful girl with a broken neck was raped and killed by her doting uncle. And then there are the women in Naples who married wealthy, older men to kill them for the insurance money. Meet someone at a *bar* and after you've talked a little Berlusconi, a bit of Obama, a touch of Palin, the conversation will likely move to the latest big story of murder.

During our time in Italy, no murder story is bigger than the Amanda Knox case. The tabloids called her Angel Face and Foxy Knoxy. Good looking but strange is the way I read her.

When we arrived in Italy, her first trial was going on in Perugia. The victim, Meredith Kercher, from Surrey, England, was only 21. At the time of the murder, Knox, an American from Seattle, was 20. Like so many fortunate, young American students we meet in our travels, Knox was in Italy taking a semester abroad—in this case specifically, in Perugia. She and Kercher had been housemates.

Kercher was found dead in her bedroom the morning of Nov. 2, 2007, with multiple knife wounds to her neck. Knox and two other students, 25-year-old Italian Raffaele Sollecito and 22-year-old Rudy Guede from the Ivory Coast, were accused of the murder.

The tabloids painted Knox as some sort of weird sex fiend. She kept a pink penis-shaped vibrator in a locked clear-plastic display box in the bathroom she shared with Kercher. Other housemates testified that the display had upset Kercher.

During Knox's first trial, she seemed to smile at inappropriate times. She wore a T-shirt that said "All we need is love." I don't know about you but if I'm being tried for murder, I'd want to present myself as someone who is serious and responsible. I certainly would not be throwing kisses to my codefendant and winking at spectators. Before the trial began, outside the police barracks, while waiting to be interrogated, Amanda was seen doing cartwheels. More germane to the case, her story kept changing.

Nancy and I follow the proceedings on TV and in the local papers. After all, this is a fellow American—a pretty young student accused of a horrendous crime—in Italy. Despite all the twists and turns of the case, compared to most other stories in the Italian news, this is one we can follow.

All three of the accused have denied being responsible for Kercher's death. Only Guede consistently stated that he was at the apartment on the night of the murder. According to Guede's account, he and Kercher had been making out. While he was using the bathroom, he claims to have heard Knox come in and argue with Kercher over money. Then he heard the two struggle. He figured it was an argument between the housemates and he turned on his iPod—until he heard a scream. When he ran into Kercher's room, he claimed he confronted a white, male figure "who tried to strike me." He backed down the hallway in the dark, fell, and heard the man say, "Let's go. There's a black man in the house." When he went to the window, he saw "the silhouette of Amanda Knox leaving." He said that an injured Kercher tried talking to him and reached for his hand. Instead of helping her, he fled, leaving traces of his DNA in the unflushed toilet.

In contrast to Guede, Knox changed her statement many times. In the first interrogation she claimed that she was at the flat when she heard Patrick Lumumba kill Kercher. Lumumba, a Congolese owner of a nearby pub, was arrested based on Knox's statement. He was later released—when a Swiss businessman came forward to testify that he was talking to Lumumba in his pub at the time of the murder.

Knox gave several versions of her story until settling on the one she used at trial: she was with Sollecito at his apartment and they spent the night smoking marijuana, watching a movie, and making love. She said she had gone home the next morning and found some spots of blood on the bathroom floor, but took a shower anyway before finding Kercher's body.

Sollecito initially said he was downloading cartoons and a movie at the time of the murder and that Knox was not with him. When the police discovered that his computer showed no activity during the time in question, he changed his story, saying that Knox was with him during the time in question but that his memory was hazy from the marijuana.

Guede was tried separately. He was found guilty and sentenced to 30 years in prison. He later appealed, and his sentenced was reduced to 16 years.

Knox and Sollecito were tried together before a jury consisting of two judges and six laymen. Although the trial was not carried on live TV, the story was all over the newspapers and newspapers are all over tables in coffee bars. Order a cappuccino, sit at a table, read one of the many newspapers. Amanda Knox, young, pretty, and bewildering, is on the front-page. I find her annoying.

I wonder how I would have behaved in her situation? I'm in a foreign country, a medieval town, where I am not fluent in the language. I'm 20 years old and accused of murder. Before I'm tried, I've already spent nearly a year in prison. No bail. At trial, I sit before two stone-faced judges who are peering down at me. Behind them hangs a three-foot high crucifix. In front of them on the evidence table sits my pink, penis-shaped vibrator. I've changed my testimony several times. The tabloids call me sex-crazed. The judges are righteous. If I'm Amanda Knox, I'm worried.

But Knox's comportment suggests something else. It doesn't ring true. Why does she smile so much? Is she having fun? Is she crazy? Why the gee-whiz Valley-girl what's-goin'-on attitude? Even OJ took notes incessantly and appeared to show interest in his proceedings. In the TV footage, Knox looks disconnected. One tabloid says she has the look of an angel. Or is it the look of a martyr? I'm not sure. But I do know that I want to reach out and shake her. "Get serious kid. This is not a school play. A young woman has been brutally murdered and the police say you did it. Even if they're right, and I think they are, quit acting like you don't give a damn."

During the trial, prosecutors argue that Knox, high on drugs and alcohol and irritated with Kercher for being "prissy," coerced Sollecito and Guede into a rough sex-game that ended with Knox slitting her housemate's throat. From my reading of the trial transcripts, it is not clear how the prosecution came up with their scenario because none of the defendants testified. Nonetheless, their characterization, using drawings, storyboards and actual photos from the dead girl's autopsy, feed into the media sensation. Foxy Knoxy has become a she-devil.

As Nancy and I get deeper into the case, we are convinced that Knox is guilty. If she is not guilty, why did she make up a story implicating Lumumba? And why Lumumba specifically? Did it have anything to do with the fact that he and Guede are both Africans? Remember, the murder took place in Perugia where Africans are not exactly a majority. To me, it was like saying, I was there with an African; Guede and I committed this murder. But instead of fingering my actual co-perpetrator, I'll give you someone who looks like him.

The prosecution also claims the murder weapon was a kitchen knife found in Sollecito's kitchen. Evidence shows that the knife had Knox's DNA on the handle and Kercher's on the tip. If Knox's lies and weird behavior were enough to put me on the fence about her guilt, the DNA evidence pushed me over. The jury agrees: guilty on all major charges. Knox is sentenced to 26 years in prison and Sollecito to 25. Although the prosecution had been seeking a life sentence, reading newspapers replete with man-in-the-street reactions, most Italians think the sentence is, if anything, too lenient.

In the Knox-Sollecito appeal trial, court-appointed experts—in consultation with American DNA experts hired by the Knox family—say that the DNA had been collected in a way that *could* have allowed for contamination and that the genetic information on the two main pieces of evidence could not be matched to the defendants with certainty. As both a flawed scientist and an even more flawed human being, I can tell you that there is a 100 percent chance that some "error" will occur in the sampling and testing of anything. Moreover, as the OJ case proved, one can always find an expert who will find errors in DNA evidence. Anyway, the new experts do their job well; the jury overturns the original conviction. After spending four years in jail, Knox and Sollecito are released.

So—were Knox and Sollecito guilty, or were they victims of a flawed legal system? The answer seemingly depends on where you sit. Italians generally think that Knox and Sollecito got away with murder. Americans seem to think that Knox was railroaded. They see Perugia as some sort of medieval backwater incapable of solving a crime of this color and complexity.

Ironically, Americans who were quick to criticize Italian justice had little to say about the million-dollar book offers Knox received within days of her release. I understand that the Knox family has legal bills to pay. Maybe a lucrative book deal will give them enough money to compensate Patrick Lamumba for losing his bar. Maybe Knox and Sollecito will go on to do great things with their lives. Knox already has a book deal. There's also talk of a movie. Making lemonade out of lemons? Yankee ingenuity? Opportunistic? Maybe. But, as I watch Knox parading before TV cameras, I can't help wondering how a grieving mother in Surry must be feeling about Italian justice.

Art Education

Art enables us to find ourselves and lose ourselves at the same time.

Thomas Merton

An artist is never ahead of his time, but most people are far behind theirs.

Edgard Varese

I never much liked Madonnas. Raised a Methodist, the only time I ever encountered one was on Christmas Eve when as a teen I would go with all my friends to midnight mass after our own church's eleven o'clock carol sing. On those cold nights, the saintly statues and youthful Madonnas placed around St. Phillip's were as mystifying to me as the odd chanting of the priests.

Then in 1986 I went to Italy with my best friend Bonda. The perfect traveling companion, she loves history and art and enjoys researching a trip almost as much as the adventure. I never had to worry about seeing all the right art and architcture. Bonda made sure we did. We visited Rome, Florence, Venice (the big three) as well as Spoleto and the Umbrian countryside. For three weeks, we visited great museums and churches—lots of churches. Everywhere madonnas in blue cloaks and gilded halos cradled adult-looking toddlers with beatific smiles. I didn't like them much. I preferred the pastel Impressionists we'd seen the year before in Paris. *Those* women had some life. I couldn't understand why these flat, staring Marys, with almond eyes and hollow looks, are they so venerated.

It's not that I don't enjoy different artistic styles. I started art lessons when I was in grade school and once considered becoming a graphic designer. Much of my youth was spent at the Carnegie Museum in Pittsburgh, where classic statues and a scale model of the Parthenon fed my interest in ancient Greece and Rome. My memory of the thick, swirling gobs of paint and passionate brush strokes of Van Gogh is as vivid as his colors. In college I wanted to take some art courses, but required classes and the practicality of a speedy graduation left me no time.

Like most Americans, I'm a self-taught art lover. I've enjoyed exhibitions touring Philadelphia, New York, and Washington. And I listen to docents and browse local museums and galleries wherever I travel. Over the years, I've learned to appreciate sculpture and have gladly gone to contemporary exhibitions. But I always pass up the galleries of 13th-century Christian icons.

One day our friends Giuliano and Teresa call to invite us to go with them to Ravenna—to see San Vitale. I recall our conversation with an artist in Bologna who recommended this church, and I'm eager to go. Giuliano, an encyclopedia of Italian culture, tells us that it's one of the most important churches in Italy. "This church was built on the place where Saint Vitalis was martyred," he explains. "It was started by the Goths and finished by the Byzantines—all in the 6th century. The mosaics here are possibly the finest Byzantine mosaics."

We park and walk the short distance to an octagonal, brick building with simple, arched windows all around that reminds me of a two-tiered wedding cake. Not especially impressive, but inside...it's *round*. Half-domes supported by two floors of graceful columns frame the circular center where the domed cupola soars five stories over intricate, marble floor mosaics. From beyond the arches, the windows fill the room with natural light. Angels float from the dome's center—high above the arches. Seemingly detached from the surface, they appear to reach down to us—far below.

"How did they do that?" I ask no one in particular. They're floating, so alive, so real. And the colors—ivory, maroon, and pink— are as elegant and beautiful as a Victorian valentine. I love this place!

Teresa comes to stand with me gazing up at the ceiling. *"Bellissima."* Gorgeous. Touching my elbow, she points to the apse where golden mosaics catch the light. Together we walk over to stare, and I feel my mouth draw open. Every inch of wall, ceiling, and arch is adorned with intricate designs and detailed paintings made of tiny stones. A youthful Christ with huge brown eyes stands between Saint Vitalis and Bishop Ecclesius who founded the church. Moses, Jeremiah, Abraham, the apostles, and a host of others fill the walls and line the arches. Behind them all, the background is gold. Theresa tells me it's to represent the glow of heaven. The figures have so much depth, I think I could stick my fingers in the folds of their robes. Teresa wanders on but I have to take in every detail, ponder every symbol, marvel at the elegance of the designs. John comes searching for me some time later.

"I've never seen anything so fabulous," I say as we walk into the garden. "I guess I have to rethink my ideas about Byzantine art. And those angels. Nobody even mentions them. Weren't they amazing floating off the walls?"

"Yeah, they reach right out to you."

"I think this is the most beautiful church in all of Italy," I add when we reach our friends. Giuliano and Teresa murmur their agreement, clearly pleased that *we* are pleased. How fortunate we are to have met these amiable people. Their excitement to share their knowledge gives us a rare insight on the Italian experience—and lots of laughs as we stumble with the language.

Giuliano is on the move again, *"Andiamo.* There's much more to see," he says, leading the way to another building. "These mosaics are even older..."

A few weeks later, we are finally able to see the *duomo* in Parma. All the other times we've come it's been closed. But today, both it and the city's iconic baptistry are open. In medieval times, only baptized Christians were allowed inside the cathedral, so separate buildings were built for this ritual. On the day of the baptism, celebratory crowds would accompany the aspiring Christian—first to the baptistry and after the ceremony, in triumph, to the entrance of the *duomo.* So like Christians of old, we start with the former.

Built between 1196 and the early 1300s and constructed of tier upon tier of pink-and-white Verona marble, the baptistry's octagonal shape supports five rows of decorative columns above its arched entrances. A foot-wide parade of real and imaginary animals is carved round the perimeter walls. After we pay, we step through a tiny door into its single room.

On the ceiling, marble spokes divide the dome into 16 parts. Each is painted with a saint, an apostle, and a scene from the Bible. The gleaming gilt of heaven surrounds them. The five-story walls are covered in frescos—each painting made to tell a sacred story to the uneducated populous.

"John, look at these walls. They were painted in the 14th century, 800 years after the San Vitale mosaics, but they seem much cruder. Flatter and less detailed. No wonder San Vitale is so famous. Then again, it was the Dark Ages and I guess a lot of artistic knowledge got lost."

"Do you see this?" John says, walking around the enormous eight-sided emersion basin. "Stairs, outside wall, and interior wall, all carved from a single piece of marble. And after 750 years, only one small crack."

"I guess they didn't lose their stonework knowledge." I flip through the slim brochure. "This says those statues above the altar represent the zodiac signs. Look, there's my Aries ram. And above them, the statues show what people do during each season. See, there's planting, harvesting, and taking things to market."

It seems odd to have signs of the zodiac in a building designed for Christian rituals. But the Church had to build on what the people knew. They often co-opted pagan rituals, so why not zodiacal signs. I tuck the brochure into my bag. "Let's go now. I want to see the church."

Just across the square, the *duomo's* 1106 facade echoes the baptistry with three tiers of columns near the top. On the right, the bell tower with its huge clock rises twice as high as the cathedral. Slipping through the door on the left, we walk slowly toward the nave.

"Oh my God! It's unbelievable. Every *inch* is frescoed—like the Sistine Chapel, but three times as big." I don't know where to look first.

The entire ceiling is covered with geometric designs, faux statues, and portraits inside laurel medallions. Huge figures cover every wall. They're so life-like you think you might test their muscles. They're realistic yet their soft beauty transcends the terrestrial. Flanking each other at the top of every pillar down the nave are two huge figures seated on clouds. "Those people above the pillars lean right off the wall," I say to John, pointing to a man bending to write on a tablet, the sole of his foot extending directly out toward us.

After a moment he says, "Spiderman. They remind me of Spiderman comics."

"*Spiderman?*"

"Spidey was always jumping off the page at you, stepping out of the frame, just like these guys."

"*Punto.*" You've got a point. "The scale is certainly superhero. I love how enormous they are. Biblical superheroes. Above them, see, those sections are stories from Jesus' life—the annunciation, the birth, in the temple with the elders..." I continue down the nave loosing John somewhere along the way. As I near the front of the *duomo*, I look into the half-dome of the apse. There, floating just below the ceiling, is the most beautiful angel I've ever seen. Wrapped in gauzy white fabric that's wafting in the breeze, the curly-haired youth is blowing a trumpet. She must be a foot below the ceiling! But she's a painting. How can that be?

Because the central stairs to the choir level are roped off, I go up along the side. I twist my head back and gape at the painting in the humongous dome. What *is* that? In the center someone is falling from the sky, clothes blown upward by the descent. All around the edges of the dome, swirling upward towards the heavens are clouds—and hundreds of legs, feet, and naked bodies viewed from underneath—not a cathedral-like sight. A crowd is shown at the base of the dome, looking up. It's extraordinary and baffling. Maybe it's the *Final Judgement*. I'll have to find out. I stand with my neck craned up until I can't endure the pain any longer, then head back toward the front of the cathedral.

The entire entry wall is frescoed with Christ's ascension depicted from inside this building. At the mezzanine level, astonished figures gesture skyward while angels descend headfirst from the clouds as Jesus rises to the roofline. At floor level, even the huge statues that stand guard at the door have turned their gazes upward in surprise. Massive. Emotional. Unconventional. This church is spectacular. And it's here, where I *live*, so I can come back. I've got to learn more about it and the artists who created these effects.

Back at the apartment, I pull out the book I've bought about Parma's art and learn that the dome of the cathedral was done by the city's most famous artist Antonio Allegri called Correggio after his hometown.

"His statue is the one in Piazza Garibaldi," I tell John, "tucked into that niche near the Town Hall."

"He must be famous. He's the only one there except the great Garibaldi."

"Well," I say as I read, "I sure got it wrong about *that* painting. I've got to go back and look again."

The dome's theme is the *Assumption of the Virgin into Heaven!* The floor under the dome is meant to be her tomb, so the viewer is looking up from her grave. At ground level, the apostles watch in wonder while above them a host of angels carries Mary upward on clouds. She's reaching her arms out to her Son, who is descending to take her heavenward. So it's *Jesus* flying through the air. Around them, like a swirling vortex, are all the luminaries of the Bible—Adam and Eve, Judith, Isaac, Jacob, David—and hundreds of angels playing musical instruments and singing, their limbs shown in dramatic foreshortening.

Correggio had painted the dome of nearby San Giovanni the Evangelista in 1521. That painting shows Jesus descending towards the elderly, dying St. John, who's surrounded by the other disciples. This dramatic portrayal of Christ's descent from a golden heaven to the eleven below was so loved by the bishop that he commissioned Correggio to fresco the much larger dome of the cathedral in 1526. This fresco was so imaginative, so strange, so unorthodox, however, that many of the priests hated it and wanted it removed. As the story goes, some years later Titian was passing through Parma. The priests took him to the *duomo* and asked what he thought of the "puddle of frogs" in the dome. Titian looked up into the enormous rotunda and replied, "If you had enough gold to fill this dome, it would not be enough for the value of this painting." And so it stayed. Although the story is apocryphal, it is based in reality. Correggio's masterpiece, with its illusionist perspective and dramatic composition, was a style not attempted again for a hundred years—until the Rococo period of the 18th century.

I'm hooked. I want to know more about Correggio—and also his contemporary Francesco Mazzola—called Parmigianino because Parma was his home. Parmigianino painted that dazzling angel in the *duomo*. A statue of him is in the piazza beside Santa Maria della Steccata—where some of his best frescos decorate the large arch at the entrance of the sanctuary.

And so, like many an Italian, the art of my "hometown" inspires my exploration of Renaissance art and history. We go back to the cathedral whenever we're in the neighborhood and I study every detail. We visit the National Gallery in the Palazzo della Pilotta, which has a special section dedicated to Correggio and Parmigianino. There, I'm able to see at eye level the original central fragment of Correggio's fresco *Coronation of the Virgin*. It was salvaged from San Giovanni Evangelista's rear wall, when the choir section of the church was enlarged. The new construction copy was painted by Cesare Aretusi in 1585. Up close, the softness of Correggio's figures, not at all feminine but gracefully angelic, is much easier to appreciate. To me, his style foreshadows the fuzzy, softly rendered figures of the Impressionists. (Aretusi's *Coronation* by comparison is stiff and flat.) I marvel over and over at Correggio's huge painting *The Martyrdom of the Four Saints*. For me, it's an almost perfect painting—composition and emotion rendered with grace.

Correggio died mysteriously in 1534. He was only 45. Yet his influence on future artistic styles has been profound. The illusion he created in the *duomo*— of imaginary space replacing natural reality—foreshadowed the Baroque style of the next century. When we go to the Uffizi in Florence, the final room we visit, number 33, is named for him—though it holds only three of his paintings. In the Vatican Museums we see two more. Soon he becomes the measure against which I judge others. I'm thrilled one day when I recognize his style from across a room in a private museum in Rome.

Gradually I've come to enjoy peering into Virgin faces. I've learned to "read" the symbols that tell the paintings' stories. Mary is always wearing a blue cloak, so she's easy to find. Other saints have their identifiers. St. John appears with a black eagle and a book. St. Cecilia is surrounded by musical instruments. St. Stephen, perhaps the most painted saint, is always nearly naked—his body pierced with arrows. A priest we know thinks St. Stephen was painted so often because it was the only way the Church was comfortable showing a naked, male body. Maybe so.

Poring over *Art for Travellers, Italy*, I read about the evolution of the Renaissance. This rebirth of enthusiasm for the classical arts and philosophy of Rome began in Italy. It began with Giotto, who decorated most of Assisi's San Francesco Cathedral in the 14th century. Fra Angelico, born in Florence, was commissioned to paint the walls of his monastery there. Fra Lippi, Mantegna, and famous Florentines Botticelli, da Vinci, Michelangelo, and Raphael followed. The Renaissance ended with 16th-century Venetians Titian and Tintoretto. Afterward, Caravaggio and the immortal sculptor Bernini continued to define Italian art into the 17th century.

"When we go to Florence next week, we have to visit the Museo di San Marco and the cloisters that Fra Angelico painted," I say to John. He's happy to have me as tour guide. He's fond of saying, "Nancy does all the work." So I schedule us to see Florence's Duomo Museum, the Uffizi, and the Fra Angelicos in San Marco.

It's January, and all the sights in Florence are tourist-free. We meander around the *duomo*, able to appreciate its details without the crowds. In the Uffizi, we spend nearly an hour in a large room of Botticellis—with only a handful of other visitors. His pensive blond Madonnas are extraordinarily lovely. Trailing along with a small student group, we learn that his magi have the faces of his Medici patrons.

The next day, inside San Marco's courtyard, we head along the loggia to see Fra Angelico's 1441 *Crucifixion with Attendant Saints*, billed as one of the greatest frescos of all time. "It's pretty faded," John says. "Probably being exposed to the moisture doesn't help. What do you think?"

I contemplate the forms on the crosses—and the witnesses gathered on the ground—trying to fit the style into my newfound artistic sensibility. "The figures look rounder, more three-dimensional—I think more advanced than earlier works we've seen. There seems to be a suggestion of perspective in it."

We stop to look at three more frescos, then visit a gallery just off the loggia that's lined with much smaller, brilliantly gilded works. These paintings have exquisite detail but we decide they aren't as advanced as the frescos. As we're leaving the room, we notice a man in street clothes who seems to be standing guard. Always eager to practice his Italian, John stops to chat with him.

"The paintings here don't seem nearly as advanced as the frescos in the loggia."

"Oh, no," the man replies, "it's exactly the opposite."

Wrong again, *stupido*. Time to listen and learn. For the next 20 minutes the man leads us around the room, pointing out ravishing details and the *perspective* in these paintings. "Church paintings like these were for the education of the people, and Fra Angelico put all his best efforts into them—to convey the stories. Perspective was a new thing, and he used it to emphasize people and objects in the painting. See, the sitting Madonna has a lap that looks dimensional, not just a flat garment."

We learn his name is Alessandro, and his voice is full of passion as he shares his knowledge. "The paintings done for the monks—the ones around the cloister—didn't need this attention to detail. The monks knew the stories, so Fra Angelico didn't bother with the perspective and special details for them."

We spend a long time peering through the glass at *The Last Judgement*. Dozens and dozens of people are divided by Christ in the heavens. On the left are the faithful, their faces full of happiness. On the right, the damned, including kings and even a pope, are suffering in Hell. Each face, no bigger than a quarter, is meticulously rendered. I wonder who inspired each of them? Did Fra Angelico, like Botticelli, paint people he knew? This painting is one of the most beautiful I've ever seen. For a moment I wish I could find a poster of it. But no poster could come close to the brilliant colors and depth of detail I see before me. My mental photograph is all I'll have.

Pointing to the intricate gold trim on the garments, Alessandro says, "Often the painter would write a hidden message here, or somewhere else in the painting. It might be an anagram of his name, a date, or a comment." He leads us to another painting, his voice excited. "Here's the one I want to show you. See this writing in the nobleman's robe? Can you read the date?" We squint to see through the glass reflection. MCDLXII. 1452.

Bidding goodbye to our art teacher, we head upstairs to the monks' quarters. White walls and wood ceilings define this serene space. Both color palate and stillness sooth the mind. Each monk had his own room, cell, with a heavy, wood door and perhaps a tiny, leaded window. In all of the fifty-odd cells, Fra Angelico frescoed a scene from the life of Christ. One, entitled *The Mocking of Christ*, is extraordinary. A blindfolded Jesus, holding a ball and staff, sits on a fake throne. Around him, floating in space, the disembodied hands of his torturers deliver blows to his head. On the left floats the head of a man doffing his cap as he appears to blow air at Christ.

"Can this be a painting from 1440?" I ask John. "It looks more like a Dali. All it needs is a melty clock."

"What do you think inspired him to do that?"

"I can't imagine," I say, fascinated. "Who would have thought that surrealism was born in a Florentine monastery!"

I like linking 600-year-old paintings to more modern ones. I'm not sure any art historian would agree with me but if art truly is in the eye of the beholder then it works for me. Seeing connections makes my experience more meaningful, and that's really the point of looking at art. The more I notice and try to compare, the more I enjoy it. Perusing colorful brochures and newly purchased art books, the Renaissance world seeps into my pores. Through the artists, their subjects, and the stories, I'm becoming comfortable in the "old world" that surrounds me here. And a growing sense of mastery tugs at me to keep learning.

We visit the Sistine Chapel on a holiday to Rome, and I remember being here with Bonda all those years ago. The ceiling was just starting to be cleaned then, and we could see just a single panel in the "new" vibrant colors. Now that all of the chapel is brilliantly colored, I find myself a bit disappointed.

"I'm sure it's heresy, but I think Correggio could have done a better job," I whisper to John, turning round and round, my head craned hard against my shoulders. "Michelangelo was an incredible sculptor, but his paintings look too much like statues. They're kind of blocky and thick. The central figures of God and Adam, now they're glorious, but the others...when he does that exaggerated perspective, some of those people just end up with tiny heads and big feet."

"And there's no Spidey effect."

We're on thin, artistic ice now. "Correggio would have had them flying off the ceiling," I say, leaning in close so other visitors can't hear. "But I guess we're prejudiced."

"We sound like every Italian," he laughs. "*My* church is the most beautiful. *Its* painter the most talented. I think we're becoming natives."

Back in Parma, we take most of our visitors to the city's National Gallery. I've become attached to the early paintings there. The guards are watchful, but I've managed to snap a few photos of my favorites. Even the Leonardo. One of my standard stops is Michelangelo Anselmi's *The Sacred Family with St. Barbara and an angel*. The first time I looked at the Virgin's face I was smitten. Rendered in Correggio's soft style with light illuminating her half-turned face, she is more lovely than Mona Lisa. Her demure posture is reminiscent of a Botticelli Mary. On every visit I spend at least five minutes with her.

One day we return to Bologna—to visit friends and to go to the *Pinacoteca*, Bolgona's National Gallery. Correggio's contemporary and Parma's native son Parmigianino (Girolamo Mazzola) has a painting there, *Madonna and Child with Saints*, that reminds me of the great Art Deco artists. The solidness of the figures, St. Margaret's blond curls, and St. Jerome's muscular arm foreshadow Deco's strong forms.

I'm drawn now to inspect every blue-clad Mary. I love to peer into their faces, to compare the attitudes of the figures and complexities of the stories each one tells. After many months of viewing, I've even become fond of the flat, gilded altarpieces from the early part of the millennium. In the *Pinacoteca* galleries, I examine each one closely. Their soulful eyes gaze across the centuries and touch my heart.

I've fallen in love with Madonnas.

STRANIERI

I'm not interested in preserving the status quo; I want to overthrow it.

NICCOLO MACHIAVELLI

THE DICTIONARY DEFINITION IS STRANGERS. BUT, DEPENDING ON THE context, *straneri* has different connotations. As tourists in Italy, we are here to spend our money, to contribute to Italy's GNP. We are not here to use the Italian welfare system. And because we are Americans, not members of the European Union, even museum visits cost us full price. There is no senior citizen discount for non-EU visitors. Like the busloads of Japanese tourists who regularly invade Venice, Florence, and Rome, we are the most desirable type of *stranieri*.

We are the sort of law-abiding, trinket-buying, gondola-riding *straneri* who locals greet with smiles on their faces and euro signs in their eyes. Is there any other type? Well, yes. The *clandestinos*—the clandestine ones—the illegal immigrants. There are an estimated five million of them—10 percent of the country's population. They come from Africa, eastern Europe, and the Far East. They come for the free healthcare, the free schools, and jobs.

Around the major tourist attractions, the illegal immigrants are everywhere. On St.Mark's Square, tall, young black African men sell knockoff handbags, Yankees hats, and cheap jewelry while gypsy women of all ages beg by the church steps. We have no way of knowing if these people are illegal, but—I know this is going to get me in trouble—they seem that way to us.

On the train from Anzio to Rome, legal Russian immigrant women in their thirties and forties complain to us in perfect Italian about how the influx of illegal immigrants—some from Russia—has made it tougher for them to find work as housekeepers. In Pisa, happy to find street parking near the leaning tower, we find it necessary to pay off two African "security" guards to watch over our car—after one informs us that unwatched cars are prone to getting flat tires. The cost: two euros, about three dollars. Hey, I'm from Philly. Three bucks to park on the street seems like a bargain.

Immigrants, legal and illegal, are changing the face of Italy. And I know I'm going to get in even deeper trouble for saying this, but we feel fortunate to be here before these changes make the country and the culture unrecognizable. We want to experience old-world Italy, not some new polyglot version.

Today is December 8th. We are in Venice. Despite the exorbitant prices—a martini at Harry's Bar costs $26—and too many *straneri*, legal and illegal, we love Venice. We love martinis but Harry's is not on our radar. Instead, we meet our friend Patrizia at a local wine shop where we select two reds, a San Geovese and a Cabernet. Instead of a high-priced lunch at a local restaurant, at Patrizia's loft apartment off the Grand Canal we share a variety of appetizers and the *vini*. An American living in Venice, Patrizia will always be a *straneri* to the Venetians. But to us she is a font of valuable information. Where to eat. Where to shop. The best times to go to the museums. "Want a cheap gondola ride?" she asks us. "Take the *traghetto* across the Grand Canal. You'll have to stand up the whole way along with ten other people but it only costs two euros." A great deal.

We ask her the best place to buy a mask for *Carnevale*? This is pushing Patrizia's knowledge. She does not have a specific recommendation. Instead she directs us to a certain section of the city where some of the best artisans are to be found. "But," she says, "beware of the knock-offs. Cheap reproductions of traditional designs. Made in China. Not good."

After lunch, armed with specific directions from Patrizia, it's time to launch our search. We are off to find Via Santo Croce, located two *vaporetto* stops east and then a short walk. We have our maps, a small one and our large street map. The street we want is near St. Paolo Square. Patrizia says there are several authentic mask-makers in that area.

The rain is now more than a drizzle, and it's getting colder. Welcome to Venice in early December. Luckily we wore our rain gear. I'm wearing a dark green Orvis parka with beige Eddie Bauer rain pants over my jeans. I have on my Phillies cap, and I'm carrying a black golf umbrella that says Firenze in large red letters. Nancy is wearing overly large black rain pants and her long, white Lands End squall coat with big, dark streaks across the front, vestiges of the fall she took yesterday in the rain. Her ankle is not swollen but it hurts, and she is walking with a slight limp.

We've found St. Paolo's church and are now looking for the correct alleyway to Via Santo Croce. I'm positioned on the church steps trying to read the big street map under the arch of the entrance. I'd go inside to escape the rain but the doors are locked. Meanwhile Nancy is walking across the square to determine what the street sign directly in front of us says. I'm hidden from a woman who is walking directly towards Nancy. She is well dressed, middle-aged, tentative. I'm on the alert. I hear her say *"Mi scuzi. Sta cercando lavoro?"* Excuse me, are you looking for work?

Nancy looks perplexed. I know she understands the woman's words but she looks confused. "It's your blond hair," I say in English. "She thinks you're a Russian." Startled, the woman smiles, does an oops, excuses herself, and hurries off before we can ask her where to find Via Santo Croce.

"It's my dirty coat, isn't it?"

"No, it's your hair. And your knit cap. They make you look like a Cossack—a cute little Cossack woman. Looking for work, baby? I have a job for you."

We're laughing so hard we almost miss the sign. It's hard to read. Faded letters. S. Croce. From a distance, it looks like "SCROCE."

The street carries us around a bend where we begin to see them. Masks. Carnival masks of various shapes and colors are pouring out onto the streets. The first store we see has masks that, to our eye, are not much different from what we've seen on the carts in St. Mark's Square. We move on. The merchandise improves. Three minutes later, we're standing in front of a store window that calls to us. This must be the real thing. No two masks are exactly alike. The designs are intricate, creative. The colors are brilliant. This is what we are looking for. In the window alone, there must be a couple of hundred papier-mâché *Carnevale* masks. Deep in the store's recesses, we could see the mask-maker hard at work. We step in. He gives us a welcoming smile but continues with his work. We ask in Italian if we can look around. *"Perche no; accomodate."* Why not; help yourselves.

As we look, we speak English to each other. "English or Americans?" the mask-maker asks. Americans, we say. "We're coming back for Carnival in February, and we'd like to wear authentic masks for the occasion," I say.

"I am so pleased to hear you say that. Too many people are satisfied with cheap copies made in China." His English is perfect.

"Oh, please speak Italian," I say. "We need the practice."

In Italian, he goes on to tell us about the need to preserve the ancient craft of mask-masking. "Here," he says, "we make masks the way they have been made for a thousand years. It's a dying art. You know, there are only a half-dozen of us left in all of Venice. There used to be hundreds. Today, the Chinese come in and buy up old established businesses for three times their value. They sell mass-produced junk. And it's not just the masks. Those Murano glass beads you see them selling on carts in the Square—completely fake—not from Murano at all. They're all made in China."

He's now up from his bench. A tall, handsome man in his mid-thirties, he introduces himself as Pradi, master mask-maker. He's giving us an animated primer on the finer points of his craft. As he is speaking, an attractive, middle-aged woman in a mink coat comes in. He introduces us to Signora Martine, the shop owner. After she leaves, Pradi tells us that her husband Antonio Martine is the grandmaster mask-maker. "I studied with him for ten years. He is a wonderful teacher," Pradi says as he shows us some of his teacher's work.

"Madame Martine had an unusual accent," I say. "What part of Italy is she from?"

"Oh, she's not Italian. She's from Puerto Rico."

"And Antonio?" I ask.

"From Argentina. But he's been here many years."

Nancy has selected a mask made by Pradi. It's a white-faced beauty with gold, green, and black hair shooting high above the forehead. Gorgeous on Nancy. We've seen similar styles selling in St. Mark's Square for ten euros but now we know they were cheap Chinese knock-offs. This one made by Pradi costs over a hundred. Feeling less adventurous (translate that as cheap), I select an unpainted mask that looks like something the Lone Ranger would wear, but white, not black. Also made by Pradi, it costs eight euros.

We ask him to sign the backs. He does. We look closely at the signature. It looks like PRADEE. "Is it Pradee?" I ask.

"Yes, PRADEE."

"That's an unusual Italian name."

"Oh, I'm not Italian. I am from Croatia. I still have a home there. I go back whenever I can. One day I hope to return permanently. But, for now, I need to make a living. There's very little demand for mask-makers in Croatia."

Hmmmm, I think. Didn't my father, an immigrant from Sicily, have to ply his craft as a stonemason in the States? Wasn't it mainly Italian immigrants, *straneri*, like my dad who built most of the great buildings in Washington, D.C.? My dad helped build the Federal Reserve building. He also did repairs on the Capitol Building and the White House. In the 70s, he practically single-handedly rebuilt Philadelphia's Custom House on Chestnut Street. So, why is it not entirely fitting and proper that today in Venice we sons and daughters of immigrants can buy original art crafted by *straneri* from other lands, legal or otherwise?

ALL IN A DAY'S WORK

Nothing is really work unless you would rather be doing something else.

JAMES M. BARRIE

I'VE SAVED OUR VISIT TO THE PARMIGIANO FACTORY FARM FOR WHEN BONDA and Ted come to visit. It's the kind of thing she and I always like doing together. We have to be at the farm by 9:00 am, so we are up early. Only a few kilometers from Parma, it doesn't take long to find. As Ted pulls into the driveway, a young man emerges from a nearby building. Dressed in a long, white apron and knee-high, white rubber boots, he could play center for the Parma Panthers.

"We're here for the tour."

"I'll get my mother," he replies with a shy smile, then ducks back inside the building.

Anna emerges a few minutes later. About five feet tall and stocky, she too is wearing a white apron and boots—as well as a huge smile.

"*Benvenuto*, welcome, welcome. You've come to learn how we make Parmigiano."

We've been looking forward to this for a long time and are excited to know more about Parmigiano-Reggiano, the Undisputed King of Cheeses as Mario Batali calls it. Following her inside, we see the young man and an older one moving from one huge caldron to another.

"It's a family business," says Anna. "My husband used to be a belt designer for Louis Vuitton, but it was very hard on his eyes and he wanted to find something else. I was a nurse at the time. We've been married 42 years." Forty-two years! That means she's over 60 and still working hard. Her eyes are warm and her face animated. Waving her hands for emphasis, she charges on. "We decided to learn to make cheese. My husband apprenticed for five years, then we bought this place. That was 30 years ago. I had two children, a daughter, and my son, who works with us now. The factory supports all of us," she adds, her face beaming.

Over the next hour and a half, Anna explains the process for making the King of Cheeses. "We're up at four every morning. No vacations, not even Christmas. We work 365 days a year." I can't believe someone who works so much can be so upbeat, but her enthusiasm is effervescent.

"First we scoop off the heavy cream from milk that's been resting overnight in the trays up here." She leads us up a metal staircase to a loft area above the production floor where we can watch the men below. Everything is spotless, if a bit wet.

"We clean very thoroughly. If the inspectors find any loose paint or rusting metal, they can close us down. *Everything* is strictly controlled. The cows, the feed, the process."

"The cows?" says Bonda.

"Yes, all the cows are local and eat a diet of local grasses. A farmer can purchase a cow from somewhere else, even someplace like Germany, but it has to feed here for a year on the designated program before its milk can be used for our cheese."

"Amazing," I mutter to my friend. "What happens next?"

"The milk is put into a centrifuge to remove the second cream. Each of the creams is used to make butter, first quality and also second."

Looking at the floor below, we watch the two men sink their arms over their elbows into the swirling, pale liquid and bring up what looks like tiny, white pebbles. They roll the pebbles in their fingers, then drop them back into the warm liquid. The air is humid from the cooking, and Anna tells us that they carefully control the temperature in the room. She's enthusiastically shouting now over the noise of the machinery.

"The milk goes into those huge, copper kettles. They're sunk into the floor and taper at the bottom to about two feet in diameter." We walk over to peer into an empty one. It's nearly eight feet deep and bright copper inside. "We add a special enzyme, a natural product, that catalyzes the cheese."

John, always the chemist, asks, "What kind of enzyme?"

"It comes from the stomach of young calves. It used to be pretty messy and difficult to be exacting, but now it comes in a powder." She shows us a can about the size of a pint with gray-white powder inside. "That big metal arm stirs the milk while it's heating—until it forms tiny grains." She hurries down the stairs, dips her arm into the milk mixture, and brings up a handful of the white granules.

"How do you know when it's finished?" Bonda asks.

"By feel. When it reaches precisely the right temperature, 41.5 degrees Centigrade, the cooking is finished."

We learn that's when the real work begins. As we watch, father and son dip a huge piece of cheesecloth into the milk mixture in one of the caldrons. Both men have broad, strong shoulders and muscular arms. Working together they swirl the cloth through the liquid, gathering granules with each pass. After about five minutes, they have an immense ball of soft cheese in the cloth.

After tying it up, they hang it from a pole that's suspended over the caldron and then empty the remaining watery contents through a drain in the bottom. The cheese will hang here to drain for a few hours, Anna explains. Ted wants to know how much it weighs.

"Each wheel of finished cheese is 80 pounds, but wet, it's over a hundred. When it's drained, we put it into those plastic molds you see on the table over there. They're imprinted on the inside with the distinctive Parmigiano-Reggiano design, the number of our farm, and the month and year of production. As the cheese ages and the rind forms, the design turns brown so you can see it. After it sets up, the wheel is removed from the mold and put into one of these saltwater baths. We have to turn it every two hours."

This sounds like far too much work for me. I'm just glad I can *buy* such a marvelous product. We inspect the vats in which yesterday's production is floating in the salty liquid. It will stay there, turning and turning, for about 20 days. After the saltwater bath, the wheels are put into clear water—for more time and turning. Then they're moved into an aging room. We follow Anna into a room with rows of wood shelves reaching all the way to its 20-foot ceiling. Hundreds and hundreds of cheese wheels line the shelves. The smell is a bit musty—and very delicious.

"Every two weeks, we take each wheel down from the shelf." Anna gestures to a mechanical lift that reaches to the top row. "When we started, and for many years, we did it all by hand, carrying the cheeses down and up a ladder. They need to be cleaned to keep the mold off." A sort of gigantic shoe polisher does this.

I can't *imagine* this life. Working every day of the year, hauling 80-pound cheese wheels up and down a ladder, turning, turning, turning. What kind of people want to do this? Anna is excitedly explaining the next steps.

"They stay on the shelves for 24 months, then an inspector comes to check each one. He uses a small hammer to whomp it on the side." She strikes one. WHOMP! WHOMP! If it sounds right, it gets the seal of approval—literally. The inspector carries the official Parmigiano-Reggiano seal—which he burns into the rind.

"If it doesn't sound right, he'll test it using a long plunger like this one." She holds up a ten-inch-long needle. "There may be some air pockets in it which won't impact the taste. Then it's marked "second grade," and the inspector scores the rind with bands so that it can't be sold as first quality. If it doesn't *smell* right, though, we have to discard it."

"So how much do you produce here?" John asks.

"We make eight or nine wheels a day and finish up about eight o'clock at night."

Oh, my god, what a life! But she's still chattering on in excitement. Her pride is palpable, and so is the love that goes into this product.

"I must tell you a story," she says. "When my son was born, he had a stomach disorder and was unable to digest milk of any kind. Not even mother's milk.

The doctor told us that he would die in a few days. Of course, I didn't want to believe it. So I took the granules of cheese, from the beginning of the process, and fed them to him. He kept them down. And he thrived. The cheese saved his life. It's a miracle product." As she told this little story she became a bit more serious, but then she laughs, "You saw him. He's six feet tall and burly enough to sling those cheeses around with ease."

We laugh too. "That's for sure."

Returning to the production floor, we watch the men maneuver a huge ball into its mold. They pose together for a photo, arms over bulging shoulders, each smiling broadly. They don't say much. But then Anna has words enough for all of them. And we're enchanted.

"We sell all our cheese through a cooperative," she explains. "All the producers do the same. Everyone gets the same price for their product. And we're really pleased that both the quality of the cheese and the price we get has improved in recent years. No one else can claim Parmigiano-Reggiano, you know. Now, would you like to taste some?"

Would we! Our mouths have been watering for an hour. We follow her into a small showroom where a neat table is laid with a white tablecloth. On it are honey, balsamic vinegar from Modena, some fruit, white wine, and, of course, a wheel of cheese. Anna digs huge chunks from the wheel with a small triangular blade and serves them on paper plates. "Try it with the honey," she says.

Like the cheese, the honey is local and all natural. I dip my hunk of cheese into a pool on my plate. Salty, aged Parmigiano bites into the smooth sweetness of the honey. *Oh, so good.* Next, we taste a little aged balsamic—20 years—the best. Just a drop or two on the cheese is enough to explode its sweetness in my mouth. *This must be what they serve in Heaven.* The four of us shuttle back and forth around the table, savoring the cheese with some fruit and wine, more honey, and more balsamic. What a breakfast!

Of course we each buy a huge chunk—and a ceramic dish for serving the shaved granules. The dish looks like a tiny wheel of the cheese. I note the number that indicates their farm—333 on the side of a piece. Here in Parma, we buy this heavenly product for about $7.00 a pound. Quite a bargain considering the $17.00 or more we pay back home, but *this* cheese is *so* worth the price. Where can you buy so much love for so little money? Maybe someday, I'll find a piece back home with the farm's 333 on the side. Now *that* would be a miracle.

Parma has more shops to repair bicycles than for autos. Almost everyone rides a bike. That is, if they aren't on a Vespa or another brand of motor scooter. We see businessmen in suits and soccer shoes and women in short skirts and five-inch heels riding bikes to work. Moms with their *bambini* in upfront child seats pedal to schools, markets, and parks. Old men and women ride their *bici* to the shopping center, the supermarket and the *ferramente*, hardware store. People routinely walk their dogs while bicycling—and chatting on their cellphone. In winter, women in magnificent fur coats peddle around town. People here even ride bikes in the snow.

Our *bici*, complements of our landlords Andrea and Simona, are typical city bikes. They're specially designed for city travel and can carry up to 50 pounds of extra weight in the front and rear. We buy a basket for mine, and a couple of bungie cords for the rear racks. Outfitted, we join the biking masses.

Threading the sidewalks past strolling pedestrians, other cyclists, and the ever-present baby carriages is exhilarating. Most streets have dedicated bike lanes, but traveling down Via Repubblica into town, bicycles weave around cars and buses—sometimes three abreast. A little scary.

I haven't spent much time on a bike since I turned 16 and got a driver's license. Back on our narrow New Jersey island, there's only one main road, 18 miles long. Few stores are open except in summer, so biking is an exercise endeavor. But who wants to ride up and down a long, boring road? Not me. In Parma, however, my bike is freedom. Instead of a 20-minute walk into the Center, we arrive in seven or eight minutes. Picnicking in the park across town is a breezy 15-minute adventure.

On my bike, I feel young again. Walking it from the storage room, out the driveway, and through the gate, I can't wait to hop on. Swinging my leg through, I settle onto my seat and pump gently along the shaded sidewalk on the designated path. No complicated gears to shift. City bikes have just one speed, like the trusty one of my youth. Cool air blows my hair, and I pull my sunglasses down to keep my eyes from watering. Where to explore today? We love pedaling the wide avenues that ring the city where the old walls once stood. Their four lanes of traffic are bordered by the equivalent of four more of sidewalk. Huge trees offer shade from the summer sun, and here and there we see people chatting on benches. We cycle miles and miles without a thought.

"I think my front wheel is bent," I tell John one day. My bike had always felt a little unsteady. Now I've fallen twice. First, on the way to the big supermarket I hit a bump on the sidewalk and toppled sideways into the sign outside a gas station. No damage. Then, on the way home, my basket overloaded with groceries, I'd figured I had room enough to ride across a big intersection rather than stop and walk. Bad decision. I'd barely turned into the crosswalk when the bike suddenly heeled to the left, and I careened into a woman walking with hers. Groceries scattered over the street as I struggled to avoid knocking her over too. Traffic stopped in both directions as I tried to gather myself and my produce. A kind man helped pick up my things and then led me to the other side. Now I have two bruises on my leg and a bigger one on my ego. But I've figured out the problem. The wheel had been bent, and the added weight shifted as I turned. *Kaboom.*

That's how we meet Rizzi. He owns the repair shop not far from our apartment. When we enter he looks up from the adjustment he's making. "*Che cosa vogliono?*" What do you want, he asks, eyes darting around the room.

"We have a bike that needs a new wheel," John replies.

His eyes widen like an inflating tire. "A bike!" You'd think he's never heard of such a thing.

We give each other a wary glance, then walk outside with him. Lean and wiry, with unkempt hair and restless glances, he mumbles to himself as he brushes the wheel. Spinning it first one way then back, he mutters some more. It's like watching someone strum a guitar, singing a private song. Back and forth, first the front wheel, then the rear. "Yes, a new wheel," he says at last. "I can fix it. Come back on Wednesday."

We return the next week and wait while he finishes with another customer. The shop's front room is the size of a small bedroom and so thick with bikes you can barely move. They're suspended all across the ceiling and stand eight or ten deep against the walls, in a tight embrace of metal handlebars. A narrow path leads from the front door to a back room where a tangle of tires and frames climbs nearly eight feet high in his workshop. Just outside the workshop door hangs a faded poster-sized photograph of a bike racer. "Is that you?" John asks, removing his glasses to squint at the photo.

"Oh, yes," Rizzi's slightly nervous reply. His eyes don't connect with you for long, but flit back and forth. He straightens up a little. "I rode the Tour de France and Giro di Italia when I was young. Twenty-six years ago. That's me with Greg LaMond."

"We watched the Giro come down our street when we lived in Bologna," I tell him. "It was amazing. They went by *so* fast. We tried to pick out Lance Armstrong but it was impossible." He nods but makes no comment, and we pay our bill. My *bici* repaired, I'm carefree again.

We visit him several times in the ensuing months—for a new tire, a brake adjustment, and then, when John's bike is stolen, for one to replace it. Picking through his tangled inventory, he mumbles to himself. "Not this one...maybe... no...here. Oh, this would be better." Finally choosing an aging, gray one, he spins the wheels back and forth before declaring it just right.

Sometimes we just stop to say hello when we're passing by. He's open nearly every day and works until after seven. John loves chatting with Rizzi, and I enjoy watching his comical behavior. On one of our visits he introduces us to his son who is sitting behind the cramped counter looking bored. Another day, John draws him into the racing conversation again.

"*Guarda*," he says reaching into a drawer below the counter, look. The cover of the magazine he produces, *Il Giro a Parma*, has a black-and-white photo of him on his racing bike. With pride he flips to several other photos of him including one from the Tour de France. "That was 23 years ago," he says wistfully.

I ask him to pose next to the poster for a photo with the magazine, and he puts on a shy half-smile. Then he asks a customer to take a photo of the three of us. Arms around the two of us, he finally breaks into a full grin. Then, with a nervous laugh, he returns to his muse with the two spinning wheels.

Takeout is different in Italy. Our favorite is the chicken store, a *polleria*, where we go every week for at least one meal. Three blocks from our apartment, the seductive aroma of roasting poultry fills the street—enticing everyone headed for the post office. It's hard to resist. Steam covers the front window on which a collection of Winnie the Pooh animals is painted beneath the *Polleria* sign. The store opens mid-morning when the first batch of rotisserie birds is ready and closes when they're sold out—usually around 2:30.

The mother and daughter who work here must have been born with their smiles fixed in place. Octogenarian Mama, her thinning, gray hair tucked into a poofy white cap, wears a heavy apron over her clothes. She works behind the refrigerated counter, which is filled with fresh poultry, eggs, and butter. Her 50-ish daughter, Rose, wearing a blue smock, works the roaster. Occasionally a somewhat slow, young man, perhaps Rose's son, handles the cash register. The women, especially tolerant of my halting Italian, make it one of my favorite places to visit.

"*Buongiorno, signore,*" I say, entering the tiny place. For the moment I'm the only customer, but that is sure to change. Only four or five can fit inside the spotless store. When it's busy others wait patiently outside.

"*Ciao. Come stai oggi?*" asks Rose.

"I'm very well, thank you. Especially when I come here for the best chicken in the world." I nod to Mama whose smile broadens. "I'll take one. Cut up, please."

Rose selects a golden bird from the ones resting beneath the circulating rotisserie. Placing it on a large metal tray and holding it in her bare hands, she uses shears to cut it into pieces. I've watched her do this many times. Fresh from the rotisserie, the meat is scalding hot. Her face, beneath red-dyed hair, is moist from the heat but she's lively and seemingly tireless.

"How can you hold that steaming bird?" I want to know.

She works rapidly, dissecting the chicken into eight or ten pieces in less than a minute. "I've been doing this for many, many years. My hands are used to it," she says with a shrug.

This little store supports them all. I imagine Mama restocking the cooler case each morning while Rose loads dozens of farm-fresh fowl into the rotisserie. With strong arms, she hefts skewers of eight chickens around using big tongs, moving them lower as they cook. Six days of hard work each week. I don't envy her.

I watch as the hot juices pool around the fresh-cut meat before she adroitly wraps it into a double foil package. Mama slips it into a plastic bag that I tuck in my carryall bag.

"*Sei euro*," Mama says.

I hand her six euros and turn to leave. "Oh, I almost forgot. On Thursday, I'd like to have a...." I can't remember the word, so after a moment I start flapping my arms and quacking.

"*Anatra!*" laughs Rose. In other circumstances I might not have done this, but I never feel silly with these women. Their hearts, like the chicken, seem warm and comforting. "*Venerdi. A che ora?*"

"Three o'clock."

"*Bene. Ciao, ciao, signora. A venerdi.*" Rose waves her greasy hands.

Back home, John and I prepare some salad and unwrap a loaf from the "Italian Store." Whatever the women do to this chicken is a miracle. Tender, sweet, juicy, it's like nothing we've ever experienced. We lick the juices from our fingers and pick every scrap from the bones. It's our weekly foray into heaven.

Not far from Perugia is the town of Deruta, famous for centuries for its painted pottery. For years I've coveted their bowls, jars, place settings, and platters—with their hand-painted, brilliant-colored designs. Like pasta, pottery designs vary from city to city, many dating back before the Renaissance. The most classic design, with flowers, curlicues, and bearded griffons in gold, blue, and green, is from Florence.

When we arrive in Deruta, the variety of designs and shapes in the stores is mind-numbing. We pass up the megastores along the entry road and drive to the hilltop to walk among the artisan shops. John follows patiently from store to store as I rhapsodize over the workmanship and different patterns. In one tiny shop, we speak with an artist whose giant round plaques, some featuring portraits of medieval men and women, sell for thousands of euros.

"In this part of the country," he tells us, "every child learns to paint on clay. It's just part of their general education. Some do well, others not so much. You can find all levels of quality." His craftsmanship is far beyond our pocketbook, so we keep looking.

We find a young woman seated inside the window of her shop adding delicate yellow feathering to a blue design—like the "eyes" of a peacock's tail—on a dinner plate. Her work is beautiful, and I like the depth of her colors.

"How long does it take to finish a plate?" I ask her.

"In total about a day, but it's done in stages. I work on several pieces at the same time."

"Do you make the pottery too?"

"Oh no. We buy the shapes we like and paint the decoration."

As I'm salivating over her wares, I notice a newspaper article tacked inside a cabinet. Its byline is from the New York Times.

"Is this about you?" I ask her.

"Yes," she says with a shy smile. "Several years ago, the paper did an article about Deruta. Several of us were featured."

That settles it. I'm buying something here. I find a large oval dish with a green and yellow design on a cobalt blue background.

"It'll look great paired with Mom's flow blue dishes," I say to John. My weakness for dishes is worse than for shoes but it's genetic. I already have several cabinets full of my mother's antique collection, my own Wedgwood and Spode, Grandma's Noritake, and at least a dozen other patterns. The last thing I need is another plate but John knows how much I've been wanting some genuine Italian ones.

Rolling his eyes he pulls out his wallet. "I like that one too," he says. "How are you going to get it home?"

That's not going to be a problem. "I'll hand-carry it."

Before we leave town, we find another shop where two brothers turn out lovely patterns and buy two large platters. My carry-on is going to be heavy.

When we first arrived in Bologna and walked along the portico on our way into town, we'd pass a few *parrucchieri*, hairdresser shops. Curiously, they never seemed to have more than one customer, and sometimes there were two people working on that one patron.

"How can they make a living?" I'd said to John. "I wouldn't want to go to someone who couldn't attract customers."

When it came time for me to get a haircut, I searched out a large shop not far from Piazza Maggiore that was bustling with customers who all looked great when they left. The Chinese man who cut my hair spoke a little English and was unfazed when I handed him a photo of a tousle-cut Sharon Stone. After 30 minutes, I had the same style.

In Parma I asked our real estate agent, Giuliana, who looks like a movie star, for a recommendation. "I'll get you an appointment with my hairdresser, Oriana," she said, picking up the phone immediately. The next day she insisted on driving me there so I wouldn't get lost on the bus.

Oriana's shop, which she shares with Simona and a shampoo person, is in a residential neighborhood. Though I've been there many times, I've never seen another patron unless it's Simona's. When I arrive I'm whisked to a sink where the cute shampoo guy gives me a five-minute head massage while he bathes my locks. No one in the shop speaks any English. But that first day, I'd shown Oriana the photo of Sharon Stone.

We stumble through a few pleasantries while she carefully cuts, but I'm quickly out of words. I can't chatter as I do with my hairdresser in New Jersey.

Behind me, Oriana and Simona chitchat back and forth. I'm intrigued watching Oriana work. Moving slowly and deliberately, she cuts tiny strands. Every few minutes, she takes a measure holding hair on both sides of my head to see if they're equal. The process takes at least 45 minutes. Then, it's back to the sink again to wash the loose hair from my scalp.

Clipped and rinsed again, I watch as she blowdries then twists and pulls teeny strands this way and that—until I look ready for a camera closeup. There's nothing studied about it. It looks completely natural and uncoiffed. The best haircut ever. Ninety minutes after arriving, I hand her 30 euros.

I understand now why these shops are never crowded. Like Anna and the chicken ladies, Oriana takes great pride in her product and in making something perfect. Like Rizzi, she treats her work with reverence. Like the Deruta artist, she takes her time and creates a work of art. Oriana, like many ordinary Italians, is an artisan.

VOLUNTEERING

The art of living is more like wrestling than dancing.

MARCUS AURELIUS

CHRISTINA IS PUTTING US THROUGH OUR PACES. "MOVE WITH THE MUSIC.
Your hand is a mirror. As you dance, watch your reaction in the mirror. How
does it make you feel? Now, hold the mirror towards your partner. What's the
reaction? Are you both having fun? Keep dancing. Follow the rhythm of the
beat. Move with the music."

Along with ten other volunteers, we're in a dance therapy training session at
the Parma Senior Center, moving to Vivaldi's *Spring* from *The Four Seasons*. It's the
second training session we've had this month. I'm not having fun.

Our career as volunteers in Parma started a few weeks back, when I answered
an ad in the Parma Gazette that sought volunteers to work at a food festival
sponsored by Kuminda, an organization that raises funds to feed the hungry in
Africa and elsewhere. I called the telephone number and spoke to Marina. She
slotted us in for duties on a Friday night. The food festival was being held at
a park several miles from our apartment. We'd been there before on our bikes,
but because we'd be working late, we decided to go by bus. Using the local map,
Nancy worked out our route. We needed to take two buses. Forty minutes later,
we were at the entry looking for Liza, the local Kuminda director. A young

149

woman behind the greeting desk directed us to a tall, pretty brunette dressed in black jeans, black riding boots, and a black T-shirt. Striking.

After a quick exchange, she knew what we were to do. We'd help Alegria, the young woman we met on our way in. Not to worry, Alegria would fill us in on the details. That's when we learned that we were to be greeters. It seemed a strange assignment for two Americans—until we learned that Alegria was from Peru. She spoke several languages including Italian and English. But she did not know much more about Kuminda than we. Fortunately, some of the literature in front of us was in English. The three of us quickly became experts.

Then it happened. A bus carrying half of Tokyo unloaded directly in front of us. Japanese tourists. Some spoke English, no Italian. They had lots of questions. Nancy, Alegria, and I became indispensable. "Yes, madam, Parma ham and cheese are the best in the world. You'll find selections at booth 56." "No, sir, we are not Italians; no, not Germans; we're Americans." "Yes, sir, Kuminda is an African word; it means harvest." "Yes, yes, certainly, you can make a donation. We do accept personal checks. Thank you. Thank you. *Grazie. Grazie.* Please leave us your email address as well."

Soon we were holding court in English and broken Italian. In addition to all the Japanese tourists, we met some German hikers wearing lederhosen—I don't know why—several Africans, all wearing Yankees caps, two Aussies, an American businessman, and more than a few Italians who wanted to practice their English and give us exotic foods to taste. *This* was fun.

Volunteering suited us. By evening's end, Marina sought us out. A 24-year-old pixie with red hair and freckles, she explained how she coordinates more than 35 volunteer programs for the city of Parma. Kuminda was just one such program. "Liza was very pleased with your work. Unfortunately, the Kuminda events are over for this year, but if you are interested, we have many opportunities for volunteering. I'd like you to consider working with some of our other organizations. What other sorts of things do you like to do?"

Nancy and I looked at each other, clueless. We explained that we'd be in Parma only three more months. We were not candidates for a long-term assignment.

Marina went through her list. Visiting prisoners? Working at the hospital? Helping drug addicts?

"No, maybe, and no."

"Wait. Do you have a car? If so, we have many elderly that could use help shopping?"

"Sorry, we don't have a car. "

Then she says, "What about dance therapy? The senior center needs dance therapists. Do you like to dance?"

Do we like to dance? Why, we're practically pros. We have a space off our living room that we use for dancing. Nancy loves it when I whirl her out of the kitchen to dance with me to Jo Stafford or Tony Bennett. Helping old folks with dance therapy. We can do *that*. Nancy is all smiles. We nod in agreement. We're going to be dance therapists. Perfect. "Sign us up."

Two days later we received an email from Christina, a Ph.D psychologist, dance therapist, and more. I don't understand all the initials after her name or even all that she has written, but I do get the part that welcomes us to her group and the time and place to meet. We're to come to the senior center on the other side of town on Friday night. Before replying, I checked with Nancy. "Bill and Peg will be here that night," she says.

Friends from New Jersey, they'll be staying with us. The dance therapy session is on the second of their three-night visit. Rather than cancel out on the dance therapy, we decide to give Peg and Bill the option to either come with us to dance with old people—or they can go out on the town where we can meet them later.

I email Christina explaining that there might be four of us coming to dance with old people. Let me know if that is a problem. Her response was in English: "No problem."

When we give Bill and Peg the news, they are eager to come with us to the senior center. Extra bonus: Bill has a rented car.

Parking is a pain. We get to the senior center about five minutes late. Hey, this is Italy. We enter a large ballroom. Chairs and wheelchairs are pulled to one side. Save for an old gentleman behind a coffee bar, the place is empty. I walk over to the bar and ask the *barista* about dance. He looks back at me quizzically, scowls and says, "There is no dance tonight. The next dance is in three weeks." I tell him there must be a mistake, verify that we are at the correct senior center, and ask for Christina. "Who is she? Never heard of her. I am in charge here. I run the dances. There is no dance tonight."

Just then, a half a dozen women come through the door. The leader—tall, slightly built, aquiline features, bleached blond hair, in her late thirties—comes over to us and says, "I'm Christina. You must be Mr. Petralia. Happy to meet you." She then has a quick *sotto voce* with the barista. I cannot hear, but it is clear Mr. Know-it-all is more than a little unhappy that he was not informed about tonight's proceedings. I give him one of those looks as if to say, I was right and you were wrong. He scowls back.

After a few quick introductions and explanations, Christina says, "Glad to have you all join us. Ready to dance?"

She guides us to a room off the main ballroom where four other women are huddled. She introduces us as visiting Americans, fellow trainees. Then she gathers us into a large circle. Including Christina, there are 13 of us. Save for one woman who had to be over 80, the other women range in age from 20 to 50.

Christina sits on the floor in the Lotus position. She motions to us. Join in. Most do. Nancy and Peg have no problem. Bill and I sort of kneel. The elderly woman can't get down that far. Christina gets her a chair, then returns to her spot on the floor. She is holding a ball of twine and talking very fast. I ask her to go *piu lentamente,* slower, because I'm the translator.

Holding an end of the twine, she rolls the ball across the floor to the woman sitting next to me. The young woman knows immediately what to do. She holds the twine, rolls the ball to Peg. A quick study, Peg grabs the twine and rolls the ball to another woman. Soon we all have at least one section of the twine. I must have six or seven.

Christina explains that we're all part of a system. How we got here is irrelevant. We are a team, bound together by a common objective. Instead of rolling the twine back up, she takes out scissors. (Where did they come from?) She cuts a piece and wraps it around her wrist. She asks Bill to tie a bow in it. We repeat the process until each of us has a piece of the twine tied to one of our wrists. We are a team.

Now standing, we join hands. Christina puts on some African music. "Hold hands, move to the music. Move to the music."

When it turns out that this volunteering session is really a two-hour training session—no dancing with old people tonight—we all take it in stride. Christina plays CDs with excerpts from Mongo Santamaria's *Watermelon Man*, a Bach fugue, a little Vivaldi, and possibly in our honor—Sinatra's *New York, New York*. According to Christina, each piece has a relevancy to our training. Between fighting to hear over the music and my lack of fluency, I do not always understand. Nonetheless, I am translating and laughing. There is no senior dance tonight, but we *are* seniors and we're having a ball.

We all have fun, especially Peg and Bill. Nancy and I get to meet the other volunteers, practice our Italian, and contemplate the day when our team will be helping needy elderly folks move to the music.

A week later is our second training session. It's more of the same. Wait a minute. When do we get to use what we've learned? Where are the old people? Do I need to become Fred Astaire to dance with a 90-year old *nonna*?

At a break, I pull Christina aside. "How much more training do we have to endure before we dance with seniors?"

She looks at me, "Signor Petralia, we explained in the mailing about the certification. My program is funded by the state. The grant is very explicit."

"What mailing? We got no mailing. We're here because Marina told us that you needed help getting old people to be more active. How many more of these training sessions are required?"

"My grant requires that I conduct five training sessions, each lasting two hours. In these sessions, you'll learn dance and interpersonal skills—to be granted your certification."

"What certification?"

"Your Dance Therapy certification. When you are certified, you will be qualified to do dance therapy anywhere in the European Union."

"You mean we can't dance with seniors until we are certified?"

"That's right, Mr. Petralia. You must be certified. It's required."

The next day, I called Marina to ask if any certifications are required to help prisoners.

TASTINGS

Eating is a cultural act in Italy. Civilization is formed at the table.

PAULO BARRATTA, DIRECTOR VENICE BIENNALE

Everything you see I owe to spaghetti.

SOPHIA LOREN

THE ITALIAN RELATIONSHIP TO FOOD HAS NO COROLLARY IN AMERICA. OUR daily obsession with the minutia of sports statistics and the lives of celebrities is as close as we come. Italy's variety of pastas, greens, meats, and fish rivals the inventory of a Sports Authority shoe display. Whereas an Italian celebrates the differences from town to town, region to region, American measure excellence through consistency. We expect to buy exactly the same hamburger or fried chicken in Peoria, Orlando, and San Diego. We look for commonalities; Italians search for nuances.

Vegetable stands and supermarkets here are full of produce that's unknown in America. Veggies look different too. There are four-inch zucchini rather than the foot-long ones we know and giant fennel heads, twice the size of the ones we find at home. Purple artichokes are the size of a tennis ball, not a grapefruit. I find curly radicchio, feathery radicchio, and radicchio that looks like purple romaine as well as different varieties of bitter greens and bibb-type lettuce with wine-colored spots and veins. The pears aren't big like ours but they have more flavor.

The modest Uns market where I do much of my shopping has a case of fresh, handmade pasta every day. Long curls of *tagliatelle, garganelli,* and *maccheroni,* sit beside green, brown, and white gnocchi. Ravioli is stuffed with ricotta, spinach, herbs, radicchio, or squash. Tiny tortellini are filled with mortadella and pork— for *tortellini in brodo.* Italians revel in the subtleties of pasta, its shape often unique to a town, designed to transport the local sauce perfectly onto the palate. Handmade fresh every day, Italian pasta is delicate and light, not chewy. It never overwhelms the other ingredients in a dish.

Restaurant meals are an exploration. We try to discern the ingredients hoping to develop a more discriminating appreciation for the taste, texture, and regional accents of Italian food. When living in Bologna, John and I frequented Osteria Traviata on Thursdays when their specialty was a trio of pastas. The charming hostess, whose husband is the cook, explained their distinctive tastes to us, and we tried to discern what we'd learned as we ate. My favorite was the lasagna. Made with just three delicate layers of spinach pasta and a modest amount of meat sauce, vegetables or perhaps béchamel spilling onto the plate, it tasted nothing like the lasagna I've always known.

Even meat products are local. In Bologna, where it originated, mortadella is king. At local festivals we've seen logs of this foot-wide, slightly savory sausage that are over four feet long. Always flecked with small chunks of lard and some-times with pistachios too, it's something I learned about when I met John. We enjoyed imported mortadella back in the States, but the "baloney" I grew up with in Pittsburgh derives its name—and nothing else—from Bologna.

Not long after our arrival in Bologna I decided to teach myself to make its trademark dish—*tagliatelle con ragu*—what Americans, but *never* Italians, call pasta Bolognese. My ultimate goal is to find an Italian cook who will teach me, but for now, I have to work untutored. I'd ordered *ragu* in several *ristoranti* and knew the meat is minced, not ground—its silky sauce is tossed on spinach pasta. Today, I would master the sauce, and use fresh pasta from the market.

On my computer are many of my favorite recipes but for this I turn to Google and my hero, chef Mario Batali. As the Food Network's *Molto Mario*, he's probably done as much to educate the American mind about Italy's unique regions and customs as he has our palate about the marvelous flavors they've produced. I loved hearing stories of local produce and regional meat preferences as he prepped his latest recipe. From him, I learned that the secret ingredient in *ragu* is milk. I find two recipes and decide to integrate them. Now, with shopping list in hand, I'm off to the market.

At the butcher, I spy chunks of meat labeled *manzo, maile, e tacchino*. Beef, pork, and...something else. I don't know the word, and I am too embarrassed to ask. It's light meat and already cut up, which will save time, so I buy the trio, pointing to the cubes, "*Un kilo de questo, per favore.*" The recipe calls for a quarter pound of pancetta so I have the butcher cut a nice thick slice.

Meats in hand, I head back to my kitchen and start to read again. Mince the meat. It's nearly two and a half pounds! Good thing I have a new cleaver. It takes over an hour and when I finish, my arm feels like Oscar de la Hoya used it for punching practice. I can barely pick up the cleaver. Worst was the pancetta—a salt-cured pinwheel of spiced pork and white fat—that's dicy to dice. But the next steps are easier. I make my *soffrito*, add the meats, and finish the recipe.

In the evening, my arm still aching, I proudly place the dish on our table. "*This,*" says John, his arm still poised after his first taste, "is a level six!"

"I started with Mario's recipe, but I modified it, so now it's mine. It'll be a long time before I do all that chopping again, though."

And it is delicious. The tiny chunks of meat give another level of texture to the sauce which clings to the fresh, green pasta like a Versace gown. The next night we have the leftover *ragu* on fresh pumpkin ravioli—and swoon.

A few weeks later while searching for sliced *coppa* ham. I happen upon...packages of *chopped* pancetta. There are two different kinds—regular and spicy. No more dicy slicey! Another *ragu* is in our future, and I am the happiest camper in Bologna.

So here's my recipe. Be sure you have a heavy sharp knife.

> *5 tablespoons extra virgin olive oil*
> *3 tablespoons unsalted butter*
> *1 medium onion, diced*
> *3-4 carrots, finely chopped*
> *3-4 celery stalks, finely chopped*
> *5 garlic cloves, peeled, crushed, and finely chopped*
> *1 package chopped pancetta*
> *3/4 pound beef chunks, diced small*
> *3/4 pound pork chunks, diced small*
> *3/4 pound turkey breast, diced small (That's the* tacchino.*)*
> *6 ounces tomato paste*
> *1 cup whole milk*
> *1 cup dry white wine*
> *Kosher salt*
> *Fresh ground pepper*
> *1 pound fresh spinach tagliatelle (or dry)*
> *Parmigiano-Reggiano for grating*

Heat the olive oil and butter in a 6-8 quart heavy-bottomed saucepan over medium heat. Make soffritto by combining the onions, celery, carrots and garlic and cook very slowly, stirring frequently until the vegetables are soft and translucent but not brown. This should take 15-20 minutes. Add the pancetta and, when it starts to brown, the remaining diced meats. Turn heat to high, stirring to keep the meat from sticking together as it browns thoroughly. Reduce the heat, and cook for about 20 minutes. Add the tomato paste, milk, and wine, and simmer for 1 1/2 to 2 hours. If the mixture becomes too dry, add a bit of water or wine. Season with salt and freshly ground pepper. Set aside to cool.

Prepare the pasta. Add about 2 cups of ragu to the pasta, and toss to coat evenly over high heat. The balance of the sauce can be frozen. Grate Parmigiano-Reggiano over the finished dish, and savor a taste of Bologna.

On a brisk October Sunday, we head to Parma's Barilla Center for a food-tasting. The past three weekends, we've been going to Academia Barilla, run by the pasta maker, to learn about the Emilia-Romagna specialties; tomatoes, Parmigano-Reggiano, mushrooms, and today *salumi* and *culatello*. Coveted by the residents, a small amount of *culatello* is produced north of Parma. I must admit, the subtlety of the taste is lost on me, on both of us. *Culatello* costs about four times what Proscuitto di Parma does, but to us they taste pretty much the same. Our Italian friends, however, rhapsodize over the differences.

"I think the Italian palate is so much more sophisticated than ours," I say to John while we wait in Academia Barilla's cooking theater for the program to start. "Maybe we'll learn a little about what makes *culatello* so special."

Our speaker is a producer from Zibello, where the finest *culatello* originates. "It all starts with the weather," he explains.

The Po valley, which Guiliano warned was full of fog, is the perfect micro-climate for curing what some have called myth not meat. In 1891, Gabriele d'Annunzio wrote that *culatello* "is aged only in the square of land surrounding Zibello, where the air of the Po is often humid and good for the mold that preserves this fatless cut of meat."

Only 30,000 of these hams are produced each year as opposed to nearly ten million Proscuitto di Parma, it's nearest cousin. Instead of curing the entire hind leg, *culatello* uses only the muscular portion from pigs bred, raised, and slaughtered in either Emilia-Romagna or Lombardy. After this heart of the thigh is removed, skinned, deboned, and salted, twine is wrapped around it to produce the signature pear shape. Over several days, the meat is massaged with salt and peppercorns and sometimes garlic and wine—the porcine version of a trip to the spa. Then it's encased in a pig's bladder and stitched snugly closed. Bound in twine with producer and date labels, it goes into the cellar for 14 to 48 months. The *salumaio* minds his *culatello* carefully, opening and closing the cellar's windows to the Po's breezy mist from which it acquires the *muffa nobile*, the noble mold, and moving the hams around the cellar every few months. This nuanced process needs patience and instinct. The result is deep burgundy, almost purple in color, with scalloped edges. I now understand why *culatello* is nearly $100 per pound—even here in Parma.

"*Culatello* production started in the 15th century," our speaker continues, "but was dying out in the early 1980s when a number of producers banded together to protect the process. We secured a DOP (Protected Designation of Origin) from the EU and enforce the old, authentic methods. In the past few years, some large producers have started curing meat in high-tech facilities for the minimum time. No Po river mist. It's not the same. Only the DOP ensures the real *culatello*."

"And I thought DOP was only for wine and champagne," I whisper to John.

"I hope we get a taste after the lecture," he says. And we do, a tiny taste.

The crowd in Barilla's test kitchen is tighter than a clump of Sangiovese grapes. We weave from table to workbench picking up thin slices of *coppa*, *salumi di Felino*, called the Prince of Salami, prosciutto, and *culatello* while sipping fizzy Lambrusco from the region. Closing my eyes, I try to distinguish *culatello's* nuanced flavors. "It's really delicious, maybe a little sweeter than prosciutto. But I'd need a lot more tastes to discern the differences. And a lot more time to keep tasting."

"We'll never get it back home," John says, licking the residue from his fingers. "Not enough produced to meet the demand here. So we better enjoy it now."

"Maybe we could just stay." He nods agreement, then heads back to the table for another taste.

I fantasize all the time of lingering in Italy. Another spring. Another winter. Seeing the things we missed this year. Going back to those we loved. Our other life exists on a distant planet. Strangely, I don't miss it. Italy's *dolce vita*, sweet life, bewitches me like dark, savory chocolate. My inner chocoholic craves more. But we only have a year and it's already October.

John's brother Robert is visiting a few days later so we have a car and Robert loves to drive. "Let's do the Prosciutto and Wine Road," John suggests, and we both agree. We've seen references to this gourmet trail at Parma's food fairs and had recently picked up a brochure.

Heading south toward Langhirano where most of the wineries are, we search for the brown-and-white signs for *Strada dei proscuitto e vini*. The brochure map, it turns out, is of little use. Up and down the verdant hills, we find and lose the trail over and over—without locating a single winery. Finally, on a road not far from Traversatolo, we see a sign, not about wine. It says *biologico*.

"Let's try this," says John. "Who knows what they have here."

In the driveway, a large German shepherd heralds us as a slight man in his 50s emerges from a large, industrial building. "*Sono Signor Cunial*," he says reaching out a hand.

"*Sono John Petralia. Mia moglia, Nancy e mio fratello Robert.*" He explains that we're looking for a winery.

"We have a small-production winery here," Signor Cunial says. "But all our wine is biological. I don't use any pesticides or chemical fertilizers. Would you like me to show you around?"

"*Certamente.*" Sure.

Following him toward the building, we first take a look at the huge grape crusher. "This machine is a lot bigger than I need," Cunial explains. " Now I have less than 100 hectares of vines, so I rent it to other producers in the area. I hope one day to keep it busy myself. But using biologic methods, it's hard to have large vineyards."

"I'm a chemist," John says, "so I know a little about the chemistry of wine. How did you get interested in working only organically?"

"The vineyard is a part-time thing for me right now. I'm a professor. My specialty is pesticides."

John laughs. "So of course your own wine is pesticide-free."

"Right. What I know about them is what makes me want to keep them off my own food and wine. But they have their place. If you want to feed the world, you have to use pesticides. Let's go inside, and I'll show you the aging tanks."

The three-story room is spotless—with huge stainless-steel tanks aligned like giant tin soldiers down one long wall. Oak barrels rest two-high along another wall. At the far end, bottles of red and white are arranged on a table. Cunial brings three glasses to an upturned barrel that serves as a tasting table and opens a bottle of asti. The flavor is unexpectedly full bodied. Cunial explains that the small bubbles are an indication of proper fermentation. He invites us to consider how they play on the palate rather than attack it. Next he taps one of the "soldiers" for a sip of the past year's vintage.

"It should be good," he says as we sniff our samples, "but who can tell at this point? We'll know better in March."

We purchase several bottles and leave with a promise to bring other friends. "Call me in advance," says Cunial, handing me a fresh watermelon and hubbard squash from his garden. "I'll put together a little something for you."

We return with friends Jane and Bill a month later. This time Dr. Cunial has prepared a tasting of whites. First we sample the "juice," then a whiff and taste from the oak barrel and finally the bottled result. John translates as Cunial explains the process of growing, crushing, filtering, aging, and bottling. Bill has lots of questions, and the back and forth leaves Jane and me free to consider our choices from the rack of bottles.

Heading down the twisting driveway after our visit, Bill says, "Your Italian is really good, John. I don't know how you followed all the technical stuff."

"It's getting easier," he replies. "And it helps to have a basic knowledge of the chemical process."

It's true. He did a great job. I'm always impressed with how well he converses here—and the doors it opens for us. My own conversation is improving, but my Italian skill is better in the kitchen.

This morning I'm experimenting again with one of our favorites—chicken livers. The recipe I'm concocting is in its third iteration. To the butter and oil I've browned them in, I'm adding a bit of Marsala. On other occasions, I've tried pinot grigio and Italian riesling. I want something just a bit sweeter today. I splash in a little of the dark liquid and finish with a pinch of "Teresa's salt,"

now a staple in my Italian kitchen. Several months ago my friend Teresa brought me a jar made by her Bologna butcher. It's sea salt from Cervia mixed with fresh herbs that give it more punch and flavor than regular salt. You can see green flecks among the coarse grains. And because it's so flavorful, I can use less. Better for John's heart. Thankfully, I found a butcher in Parma who has it. We still call it Teresa's salt. Like every other food here, salt is varied and celebrated. I can buy several varieties in the supermarket—including a delicate pink one—only three euros for two pounds.

On a visit with Teresa and Giuliano to their summer place in Cervia, they took us to the Salt Museum. Located in the old Salt Tower warehouse, the well-arrayed museum tells the history of salt collection and its role in Italian culture. The town has been famous for salt production since Roman times. Covering about three and a half square miles, Cervia's salt flats are now part of a nature preserve. But from June through September workers still rake deposits of the crystals into mounds, then spread them out to dry in the sun. Much less refined than Morton's, Cervia's salt contains traces of minerals not found in most. In 2004, the Slow Food organization recognized it for its extraordinary quality and flavor.

Called "white gold," salt has been used in amulets and rituals, for preservation, and for political power. Controlled by the government until about 30 years ago, salt was exclusively sold at *tabacchi* shops—where tobacco sales and tax collections also take place. Examples of colorful *Sali e Tabacchi* signs hang on the museum wall, and they're still seen today outside many stores. Our visit coincided with a festival. Stalls lined the canals offering salted anchovies and sardines arrayed in circular designs inside wooden casks, salty perfumes and lotions, bags and gift boxes of Sale di Cervia, and handmade salted chocolates.

I'm remembering our salty adventures as I serve the wine-tossed livers with an arugula salad and crusty bread. "What do you think?" I ask John.

He slides a piece of liver into his mouth and pauses, eyes rolled upward as he considers the taste. "I think I like this one."

"So what do you think is in it?"

"Chicken livers, maybe a little wine...and just the right amount of seasoning."

I take a bite and let the wine-soaked liver dissolve on my tongue. "I used Marsala and Teresa's salt. Can't cook without it."

"*Sagra di funghi* next week," a mushroom festival, I read to John when we stop to see the posters at the Tourist Information Center. "It's in Borgo Toro, the heart of the mushroom country. That's not too far, but we'll need a car."

"If it's anything like the prosciutto festival, it should be fabulous. We can get one of the car share vehicles, see some of the countryside, and make a day of it."

The day is perfect—sunny and not too hot. We drive southwest through the hills, following our Google map. A huge banner points the way to the mushroom festival. It's spread over a large pasture with several gigantic tents and a few low buildings. On our way to the first building, we stop to watch families enjoying the amusements. No roller coasters or Tilt-a-Whirl here. A woman with a racket is showing her son how the tetherball works. An old fellow plays tabletop shuffleboard with a younger one. Other tabletop activities are set on wooden sawhorses. I'm reminded of the simple diversions of my childhood, long before video games.

Inside the building, rows of long tables are covered with burlap. On top, a hundred or so plate-sized baskets hold mushrooms of all sorts. Mushrooms like we've never seen. They're gigantic and tiny, brown, yellow, speckled-orange, red, and white, ruffled, flat, and cone-shaped. Some look like petrified turds. It's a splendid display.

We prowl through the vendor tent and buy porcini pasta, three truffles, some local honey, a *salumi*, and a few pounds of dried porcini. Every mushroom vendor displays open boxes of varying sizes and qualities of highly treasured Borga Tora fungus which tempt the crowd. At a wine merchant's stand, a slender young woman points to the award and photo behind her and tells how Prince Albert of Monaco awarded it to her sauterne. As she wraps up a bottle John grins at me. "Time for lunch," he says. "You've bought enough."

The blue-and-white dining tent reminds us of firehouse dinners back in New Jersey. You pay upfront, find a table, and kids serve you the food. Clad in red shirts, youngsters dash around serving maybe 300 diners mushroom risotto, mushroom pasta, sautéed mushrooms, marinated mushrooms, and everyone's favorite—fried mushrooms. The outdoor kitchen can't keep up with the demand. Finally our wait is rewarded. Delicate, fried, fresh porcini have a texture softer than regular mushrooms and a velvety taste like warm butter.

"Fresh ones have such a different flavor," I say savoring a bite of risotto. "It's such a shame they're only available for a few days a year."

John's mopping the last of the buttery sauce from his plate with a piece of bread. "It makes you appreciate them more."

"It's so Italian. Holding big festivals so you can gorge on foods that only last a few days or weeks. Enjoying the *now* of life. I'd gladly give up year-round strawberries back home, if we could get sweet, tasty ones during their season."

"I agree." He pauses, then gives me that naughty-kid look. "Wanna get another order of those fried ones?"

Down a tiny street behind Santa Maria della Steccata is Rigoletto, our favorite Parma trattoria. We learned about it from a local friend who's a foodie. But for the longest time we couldn't figure out how to eat there. It wasn't hard to find with its three globe lights and vines crawling up the facade—but the iron gate was always locked, and there was no sign about the hours—or even a phone number. Finally one day we think to try the phone book. It opens at eight John learns—an hour later than other places. No wonder we've always found it locked up when we were walking past around seven.

Eight-fifteen the next night, we're ushered to our seats by Fabrizio, the affable owner. On the menu is a roasted leg of *faraona* which he recommends. What he places in front of me is some kind of chicken leg. At its end, the exposed bone is black. So simple, but incredibly delicious, it's tender and cooked to perfection. I order it nearly every time we return, which is often. Then one day I just have to say something to Fabrizio.

"*Questo e` meraviglioso.*" This is wonderful I say, almost swooning.

"*Grazia, signora. Mia moglia Antonella é una cuoca molto fine.*" My wife, Antonella, is a very fine cook.

"*Vorrei che avveva in America,*" I say sadly. I wish we had it in America.

He looks at me quizzically. "*Lo si puo trovare li`.*" You can find it there.

"*No, no. Non mai ho visto,*" I've never seen it.

"Guinea hen!" he exclaims in English. "Of *course* you have guinea hen in America."

Oh. Well, yes, I guess we do. But you certainly don't find it on the typical restaurant menu. Nor in the supermarket. Here these overly large chickens with the black legs and feet still attached are at the Uns and every other market I've shopped in. The attached feet make me a little queazy about buying them. I guess the Italians leave them on so you're sure you're getting a real *fararona*—and not just some big, old chicken.

But Antonella's melt-in-your-mouth *fararona* is the hands-down best, so we bring many of our American friends here when they come to visit. After listening to a strolling trio play in Garibaldi square, we lunch there with John's old business partner Gene and his friend Carolyn. We dine there with our Franciscan friend Father Tom and with my best friend Bonda and her husband Ted. And when our *amici* from LBI, Enrico and Lydia come for a few days, we make sure to take them there too. (Originally from Rome, Enrico came to America as a teen. He and Lydia are our Italian *famiglia* at the shore.) Rigoletto never disappoints. And I always recommend the black-legged bird.

Parma's Ristorante La Greppia is where we discover black rice. We decide on dinner there with Bill and Jane after a long day exploring Parma's Wednesday market and the museums. More formal than Rigoletto, La Greppia also has superb food. Our waiter suggests an appetizer of black rice risotto with shaved truffles. Unlike any rice I've tasted before, it has a nuttiness that complements the smoky truffle flavor.

The next time I'm in the market, I head to the grains and pasta shelves. There it is. Venere black rice—complete with a few recipes. This special rice is grown in Italy. It's a cross between an Italian variety and an ancient Chinese one that was favored by the nobility. I love its dramatic presentation. It pairs especially well with seafood, but you can toss it with a chicken curry and vegetables or with grape tomatoes and feta. Here's one of my favorite preparations.

1 cup Venere black rice

4 small seppia (cuttlefish) cleaned and chopped into rings, tentacles divided, if large

2/3 cup peas, fresh or frozen

2 cloves of garlic, chopped

1/3 cup chopped fresh parsley

2 tbsp olive oil, or more to taste

Bring 3 cups of water to a boil, and add the rice. Allow it to simmer for about 45 minutes to absorb the water.

In a medium skillet, heat the olive oil, then add the garlic and sauté until just softened. Add the seppia and continue to sauté for another minute. Add the peas and continue cooking until the seppia are cooked, one or two minutes more. Add the rice and parsley to the skillet and stir to mix. For a creamier dish, add a pat of butter and swirl to melt. Serves two. Heaven.

Butter. I always thought butter was the province of the French and Paula Deen, and that Italians cooked exclusively with olive oil. Much as I tried, my risotto was never as creamy as the ones I had in fine Italian restaurants. And here the pasta dishes have a smoothness that binds the flavors in a way I could never achieve.

One of Academia Barilla's Sunday afternoon open house events features the King of Cheese, Parmigiano Reggiano. Set on the long stainless steel table of their kitchen are four rounds of different ages ready for tasting—12 months, 18 months, 24 months, and 32 months. As the cheese ages it gets more salty and crumbly. My preference is the 24 for snacking and cooking, and the 32 for a special treat. When it's older than 36 months, they tell us, Parmigiano is really deteriorating.

On the opposite side of the room, a crowd is waiting for a sample. One of the chefs is whipping up risotto in a pot the size of a small barrel. Stirring the pot every few minutes, his tall chef's hat and round face remind me a bit of Mario Batali. Balanced on his shoulder as he works is his son, a boy about three who's enjoying the attention of the crowd.

The chef tastes the risotto when it's nearly finished then adds a huge bowl of shaved Parmigiano. I think he's finished when he reaches for another bowl and tosses in about three pounds of *butter*. After a few minutes he tastes again, then adds another two pounds. Now I get it. Butter. The secret ingredient of Italian cooking. Sure enough, my risotto is now as good as Barilla's, and my pasta dishes have that silky smoothness that melts on your tongue. Butter, I tell you. That's the secret.

Venice introduces us to another Italian specialty—white polenta. Polenta, ground cornmeal, is an Italian staple. You slowly add a handful to boiling water, stirring constantly with a whisk and simmer. In America we can buy polenta in a quick-cook form or even precooked, wrapped in plastic. I often use it as a side dish for roasts, as the base of an appetizer, or with any kind of meat or mushroom *ragu*.

Lunch at Venice's Hosteria all'Ombra, near Garibaldi's monument along the tree-lined street that bears his name, is where we first learn about white polenta. The menu pairs it with *frito misto di pesce*, fried seafood. When the stocky owner, who would be at home on *The Sopranos*, comes to take our order, we ask about it.

"White polenta comes from the Veneto area. It has a more delicate taste than the ordinary yellow kind and therefore is especially good served with seafood," he explains in Italian. "It doesn't compete with the fish."

Our dish arrives—rings of calamari and tiny whole shrimp in a crispy tempura style batter. The polenta, much lighter-tasting than the kind we know well, is delicious—the perfect complement to the fish.

Venice is also where we try *cannolicchi*, razor clams. Their long brown half-shells litter our Jersey beach in summer, but we never dreamed of eating them. I always considered them part of Atlantic flotsam. One evening a waiter tempts us to give them a try in a mixed seafood salad. About four inches long and white, they might be mistaken for a pasta, but their flavor is sweet and delicate. Like the newly discovered blossom you now want in every bouquet, soon we're looking for them each meal.

Fried zucchini flowers are another of my favorite Italian specialties. In the markets, I sometimes see four-inch zucchini with the blooms still attached to the stems. In season I can buy them wrapped in plastic in the veggie section of the supermarket here. But I leave preparing them to the experts. For one thing, I don't have a deep fryer. For another, while they taste wonderful, I can't yet bring myself to cook with lard. The best ones I've tasted are at a stunning restaurant overlooking Lake Como called Al Veluu.

Our neighbors, Johnny and Joyce have come for a visit. We travel together to their favorite town of Bellagio on Lake Como's eastern shore. We're staying at La Limonera, a place they discovered a couple years earlier. Tucked behind flowering hedges, the several apartments are comfortable and private, and there's a marvelous view of the lake from the terrace. Al Veluu is one of Joyce's favorites, so Johnny's made reservations for all of us.

The restaurant has arranged a taxi to take us up the twisting road from the ferry. We arrive about ten minutes later at the *ristorante*, which clings to the hillside. From the dining terrace there's a breathtaking view. Between courses, Luca, the young owner, shoulders his six-month-old daughter amid coos from the diners. On his menu is something new to me—stuffed zucchini flowers. Luca explains they have ricotta and a bit of anchovy inside. When they arrive, the three large blossoms have a crunchy brown crust and savory filling. Outrageous. Our lake fish is delicious too, but we savor most sharing this experience with our friends.

Mesmerized by the fading light, sparkling stars, distant moon and camaraderie, we realize quite late that we're the only diners remaining—and the last ferry is about to depart. Luca calls the taxi and we all pile in. Like a Gran Prix auto heading to the finish line, we rocket down the hillside, the three of us in the rear seat hurled side to side on every hairpin turn. I'm convinced we might not make the boat (because we've careened off the hill) but the driver deposits us at the ferry just in time—and we live to eat another meal.

Several memorable meals occur when the four of us visit Cinque Terre. On the drive around the bend from Portovenere, we discover La Grezia, a tiny version of its popular neighbor. It's not undiscovered. Several 100-plus-foot yachts are moored in the harbor. Along the waterfront road, Trattoria Locanda is serving lunch. John and I order a warm octopus salad and a mixed seafood dish to share. Joyce asks for the sautéed branzino. Then Johnny orders...spaghetti with meat sauce.

"Johnny," my husband cautions, "there's a marina across the street. You should order seafood here. You don't order meat on the waterfront." Johnny is unconvinced. When his meal arrives, he says it's good. Then he tastes our octopus salad.

"That's really spectacular. I wish I'd ordered some of that. Joyce," he says, leaning over toward her plate, "let me taste your fish." He cuts a portion of the white flesh. "This is wonderful too."

Joyce nibbles a bit more, then passes the fish to her husband who finishes it. "You're right *again*, Professor," he says to John with a grin and a toast. "When in Rome..."

I wonder how the American palate became so unexceptional. Our culture encompasses foods from around the world and, yes, we have fabulous restaurants. But to the average American, "good" is more, not better. We love mounds of greasy foods, sandwiches you can't get your mouth around, and heap cheese on almost anything. Our fast food nation is conditioned to microwaved and steam-table entrees and bland bagels the size of a lunch plate. I wish every American could taste what we eat here—fresh and simple food. Food as it should be.

Living in a Foreign Language

Life isn't a matter of milestones, but of moments.

Rose Kennedy

September already. This is our sixth month in Italy. The halfway point. Only six more months to reach my goal: become fluent in Italian. I'm determined. *Ma, non e facile.* But, it's not easy.

I speak at about a fourth-grade level. I can go shopping. Talk with a sales clerk. Ask for an exotic light bulb at the hardware store. When I am feeling really brave, I can initiate idle conversation with strangers on a train or in a bar. But challenges present themselves constantly.

Last Saturday, our TV was on the fritz. My usual tech service person, Nancy, was at the market. I called the satellite provider for help. Degree of difficulty: 10. Holding the phone in one hand, pulling wires with the other and listening intently while gasping "please repeat that," I finally threw in the towel. "Do you have an English-speaking agent?" Her response was equally exasperated. "Yes, call back Monday. Ask for Marco." Then she hung up.

Monday. No way. It was Saturday. The US Open Tennis matches were on this weekend. We can't wait until Monday. I decide to call back, but this time I enlisted Nancy, now back from shopping, as chief cable puller. I translate instructions to her in English. She does the heavy work. I call back, and get a different representative, Eugenia. Together, in Italian, we successfully determine the problem with the TV is—what else—the decoder box. Eugenia will mail us a new one. "Mail. No way. There's the tennis matches."

"Okay, if you hurry. Come to the company office with your old decoder box. We'll replace it. But, hurry. We close in an hour." It takes no little effort to get there—on bikes—before closing, but the outcome is worth it. We make the exchange. Degree of Difficulty: 10+.

Not only do we see the tennis matches, we are also able to watch our morning news programs. Here in Parma, I typically rise about two hours before my wife, have a cup of coffee, watch the news, and then prepare coffee for Nancy. By the time we're at our favorite café reading the Parma Gazette, I have a headstart on the news. I understand the brief coverage of national news, but most of the local news is hard to grasp. Nonetheless, I get a certain voyeuristic pleasure—sort of like reading someone's diary—out of knowing what's going on in Parma.

Among the stories I've been trying to follow is the saga of Parmalat—a large multinational dairy company based in Parma. As best I can figure, the company founder and CEO Calisto Tanzi has been accused of embezzling tons of money from the company. Nancy and I have a loose allegiance to the company because we have been using their milk since we arrived in Italy. We like the shape of their containers. At our local Uns market, Nancy buys the one-percent-fat variety that comes in a smart-looking dark, blue plastic bottle shaped like the old-fashioned milk bottles we knew as kids.

When the Gazette writers refer to "crack" Parmalat, first I am confused. But now I've determined that they are not talking about milk spiked with cocaine. I've since confirmed that "crack" is Italian newspaper lingo for broken or bankrupt. You might ask, why is it not written "bankrupted" or even "cracked" Parmalat? I don't have a good answer except to say that when Italians borrow English words, which they do frequently, they take the word but not the associated grammar. So, the Italian word for computer is *computer*, but several computers are still *computer*.

No matter how you write it, crack or bankrupt, Parmalat is definitely broke. Here, it's a front-page story with lots of subtleties that I know I am missing.

Still, I'm getting enough to know that Tanzi, a major contributor to the Catholic Church, owner of the beloved Parma soccer team, champion of the poor, and local rags-to-riches hero is in big trouble. The authorities estimate that he has embezzled about 400 million euros. But they can't find the money.

One morning at Feltrinelli's book store, I see a new book prominently displayed with the title: *Il Tesoro di Tanzi*, The Treasure of Tanzi. A three-foot-high poster above the books reads, "Startling revelations about the Parmalat affair." Hmmm. Might be interesting. Wonder if I could manage my way through it.

As I peruse the book, I'm thinking. I'm having enough trouble getting through my *gialla libri*, yellow books—American detective novels translated into Italian. They're written at about a sixth-grade level. Filled with dialogue, I find them an effective way for me to improve my language skills. My favorite is Mike Shayne, private eye; he solves cases by breaking heads.

But there's something drawing me to the Tanzi book. Nitty gritty, local news. Dirty laundry. Inside stuff. No one back home knows about Tanzi and crack Parmalat. In our honor, our book club is reading Grisham's *Playing for Pizza* because it's set in Parma. A fun read. But, this! This is real life, written in Italian. I should buy it.

It's 15 euros, $22. Pretty steep. Should I buy it? Just then Nancy tells me we need to get going; we have to get to the market before it closes. Relieved that I don't have to make a decision, I drop the book back in the pile. I can always buy it another time. Besides I've committed to reading *Il Gattopardo*, The Leopard, by next April for book club. Feltrinelli has ordered two copies for me, one in English and one in Italian. They'll be here next week.

After shopping, we meander over to Garibaldi Square, where we decide to treat ourselves to *pranza*, lunch, at Café Orientale. Halfway through our meal, Nancy squeals, "Oh my God! A greyhound." Before I can finish swallowing my bite of a glorious chicken Marsala, she is out the door and halfway across the piazza shouting at the startled woman and dog *"posso toccarla, posso toccarla?"* may I pet her, may I pet her?

In the time it takes me to explain to the waiter—we'll be back, don't clear the table, we're just over there talking to that woman with the dog—Nancy,

Yma, and Sugar are already fast friends. To my surprise, the women are speaking English. Unsurprising is Sugar's pose, the one that says, Yes madam, I am a greyhound, and you are not. Now, you may pet me, but try to control yourself.

Our beloved greyhound Cho Cho San died two years ago. During our time in Italy, this is only the second time we have seen one. The other time, we were on a train whizzing past the Castlefranco stop and Nancy was beside herself.

Like Cho Cho, Sugar was rescued from a dog track. In many parts of the world including the United States, greyhounds are considered livestock—like pigs, chickens, or goats. Their livestock status effectively puts them outside the usual humane laws. Sadly, killing them after their racing life is normal practice.

We learn from Yma, Sugar's raven-haired owner, that four-year-old Sugar was rescued from a track in Ireland. Together Yma and Sugar make a strikingly beautiful pair. For us, having a real live greyhound to pet is heaven. As luck would have it, Nancy happens to have something in her pocket for Sugar. Peanuts. Salted peanuts. Yup, they were Planter's, which are popular in Italy. Sugar is in heaven.

Yma, named after a folk singer from the 60s, we learn, is half British and half Italian. She speaks both languages brilliantly. After several minutes of chatting, petting (the dog), and squealing in two languages, we are making arrangements to meet again.

"Let's meet for a drink tomorrow evening. I'd like you to meet my significant other Livio." Sure we say. We'll meet tomorrow night here at Café Orientale for drinks. On our way home, Nancy stops at the Uns Market to buy a few things for dinner—plus several packs of salted Planter's peanuts.

When we see Livio, Yma, and Sugar the next night, they arrive as a matched set. A taller, slimmer version of George Clooney, Livio strides in wearing a black Armani suit, white shirt, dark tie, and the pointiest, shiniest black shoes I've ever seen. Yma, beautiful in a white trench coat, black top, black pants, and black shoes with five-inch heels, turns heads as she and her black-and-white princess follow Livio into the bar.

With Sugar happily munching salted peanuts, the four of us enjoy a variety of bar snacks, prosecco, and conversation—mainly in Italian. Livio understands some English but prefers to converse in Italian. That's fine for us. We need the practice.

We learn that he is a forensic accountant and Yma is the firm's office manager and marketing director. Livio's partners include his father, brother, and several other accountants. As we converse, I am quickly connecting dots. Partner in big accounting firm. Armani suit. Drives a Porcshe. Apartment in town. Boat in La Spezia. Beautiful girlfriend. Adopted greyhound. Sailor. Author.

Wait. Did you say author? "Yes," he says, "I've written a book about Tanzi. Do you know Parmalat? Do you know Tanzi? My book is called *The Treasure of Tanzi*. Would you like a copy?" He reaches into his brief case and hands me the book.

"I had this book in my hands just yesterday, at Feltrinelli. I almost bought it." As I'm talking, Livio is autographing it for me. Well, here I am holding an autographed copy of an important book while getting a briefing from the author himself—all in Italian. I can't believe it. He mentions derivatives. I say "Enron." He smiles and says *punto*—literally point. We're on the same wavelength.

"Like Ken Lay and Jack Skilling at Enron," Livio explains, "Tanzi used derivatives and special-purpose entities to skim an estimated four million euros from Parmalat into his own coffers. I first became suspicious of them when Yma and I were sailing in the Bahamas. That's where Enron had set up their special-purpose entities. So whom do I encounter there dressed in business suits? People I know from Parma. Executives from Paramlat. Accountants—a little embarrassed to see us." I haven't opened the book yet but I already know that Livio is going to break this case. Unlike Mike Shayne, he's going to do it with brains not brawn.

My only other opportunity to discuss an important book with its author was when our book club read *Prisoners of Hate* by Dr. Aaron T. Beck. That was a great experience. Beck, the father of cognitive behavioral therapy is a superb writer; his discussion with our book club was special because he gave us added insights to his theories. Would I have another opportunity to do something similar with Livio?

"John," Livio says, "read the book. When we meet again, we'll talk about it."

This prominent author has just given me an autographed copy of his book, and now he wants to discuss it with me. In Italian. I'm not kidding. In Italian. We're going to discuss derivatives, financial intrigue, the Parmalat case—that Parmalat, crack Parmalat—all in Italian. How great is this? If there is a better reason for me to have worked so hard on improving my Italian, I can't think of it.

WAITSTAFF

Pleasure in the job puts perfection in the work.

ARISTOTLE

COLD WIND STREAKS MY CHEEKS WITH TEARS, AND MY NOSE IS STARTING to run. "Let's try that little place just behind the *duomo*," I say as we cross the cathedral's square. "We've been wanting to go there."

It's Monday and many of Parma's restaurants are closed, but Angiolo d'Or's bright lights pour through its windows, making tiny shimmers on the wet cobblestone piazza. We step through the door into the warmth. A typical *trattoria*, its tables are set with double white cloths and each one holds a small vase of fresh flowers. The lone waiter hurries toward us with a welcoming face.

"*Buonasera*," he says. We choose a table by the windows and notice only one other is occupied.

"It's early. Not yet 7:00," John notes. Over glasses of local prosecco, we warm up and peruse the menu but before we can finish, our waiter approaches with a recommendation. He's tall, lean, and appears to be in his early thirties, impeccable in a starched white shirt and black pants. I like his Italian. It's precise and easy for me to understand.

"Have you tried *bagna cauda* before?"

Bagna cauda. Some kind of bath? We give him a puzzled look. "No, we haven't. What is it?"

"It's one of our specialties. A warm broth, heavy on garlic, that's served with fresh vegetables for dipping. Very good on a cold night. You should share as it's quite large."

"OK," I say, "and for *secondo* I'll have..."

"Oh, don't order anything else yet," he councils. "If you want more after the *bagna cauda*, you can always order it then."

"Fine," John replies handing over his menu. "We'll have the *bagna cauda*."

When it arrives in a six-inch pot over a sterno burner, the consistency is something like slightly thick chicken soup, the aroma like being wrapped in a warm, fuzzy blanket. On another plate is a careful arrangement of raw vegetables: large purple radicchio leaves, celery and carrot sticks, mushrooms, and thick slices of fennel. We each pick up a long leaf of radicchio and swirl it in the steaming brew. The broth forms tiny lakes between the ribs of the leaves. The taste, not especially garlicky, is smooth, delicious, and buttery.

"Mmmm, this really hits the spot tonight." I swirl a carrot and slide it into my mouth. Savoring the tasty warmth, we sip our wine and talk about the afternoon, slowly working through the collection of vegetables. Before long, the other couple leaves and we're alone in the dining room. Our veggies finished, we settle back, satiated.

"*E` buono?*" the waiter asks with a quizzical smile when he returns.

"*Si, eccellente!*"

"Americans, right?" he says in perfect English.

"Yes, we're living in Italy for a year," says John. "We love it here in Parma. *Come si chiama?*" What's your name?

"Marco. I lived in the States for a while."

"Really, what were you doing there?" I ask.

"I was working in a restaurant here, and a man from Chicago was a frequent patron. When he got ready to go back to America, he asked me to come work for him in his restaurant there. I didn't know much English at the time but I accepted."

I'm always impressed that people can move to another country with such ease—not knowing anyone or the language. "That must have been quite an undertaking," I say.

His mouth curls up and I notice his dark eyes. "It wasn't too hard. I started as a busboy. But I noticed that the waiters didn't know much. They didn't even know how to open a bottle of wine properly." He says this with sad distain. "So I showed them, and sometimes they might ask me to do it for the customers. I showed them several other things too. Within two weeks, I was made a waiter. Then three months later, they made me manager."

"Three months! How did the other waiters feel about that?"

"Some of them, the ones who were really incompetent and nasty, I fired. The others didn't mind. We got along fine. I stayed two years."

"So why did you come back here?"

He hesitates a moment. "In Italy, being a waiter is a *profession*. It's not like in the States where people just work for money. Here, I have a salary and a respected position. In the USA, everyone works for tips. They don't care about service, just money. They have no pride in what they do. I *love* what I do. I love good food and helping people enjoy it. The only thing missing in my life is a girlfriend."

"I have a young friend in Estonia..." I venture.

"Don't be matchmaking," chides John. "I'm sure Marco is quite capable of finding his own girls."

We linger over *caffè* and a shared dessert, then pull on our coats for the chilly walk home. "If your Estonian friend comes for a visit," calls Marco as we head to the door, "be sure to bring her here."

Like the memory of *bagna cauda*, Marco's comments stick with us. Walking through the deserted streets, we talk about our favorite pizza place, Don Alfonso's, where young Giuseppe always hurries to wait on us. He and all his fellow waiters are unfailingly pleasant and efficient despite the crowds that sometimes overwhelm the modest restaurant. We tease him that he looks like a youthful Dustin Hoffman, a name that means nothing to him. Forever grinning, he loves to practice his few words of English and is always grateful for our correction in pronunciation or a new word.

"Waiters here are so efficient," I say. "With none of the 'my name is Jason and I'll be your server tonight' we're used to back home. Only way we find out a waiter's name here is to ask him."

"They just focus on the job," John says. "I don't care what someone's name is as long as the service is good." We're turning the last corner toward the gate of our apartment house. "You got your key?"

"Sure. Right here in my little purse pocket." We unlock the gate and start up the stairs. "But that comment about it being a profession," I say as John unlocks the apartment door, "I guess he was talking about how he *feels* about his work. I think it's about pride."

Months later, in the back seat of Giuliano's Lancia, Teresa and I are catching up on the family news. We're off for a few days with them to tour Lago di Garda, Italy's largest lake. John and her husband are chatting in the front seat in animated Italian. Over the course of our friendship, Teresa and I have crafted a successful communication scheme from my halting Italian, interpretive hand gestures, rephrasing, and the occasional call to the front of the car.

"*E come stanno i nipoti?*" I ask. How are the grandkids?

"*Bene, bene,*" she laughs. All well. "Alberto is about to graduate from his studies as a radiology tech." That one took a front-seat call. "He's working as a barista every weekend at one of the elegant hotels in Cervia. His English is excellent, so they are happy to have him. But soon, he'll be looking for work in his field."

"And Alessandro?"

"He's about to start the next phase of his schooling. He'll be studying to be a waiter."

I know I look confused. Studying to be a waiter? "What kind of school is that?" I ask her as if it's the most normal thing in the world.

"It's several years," she says. "There are three courses of study: cooking, wait staff, and reception. You study them all. He wants to be a barista,"

"Like his big brother," I nod. Alessandro adores his brother. All the family are crazy for America, but Alberto has painted his room red, white, and blue, and a photo of New York's skyline covers one wall. Like his brother, Alessandro has taken to wearing T-shirts with Old Glory on the front.

"Right." She loses her smile for a moment. "But he needs to practice his English. Alberto loves to speak English. Alessandro, not so much."

"We'll give him some practice when we see them next."

I'm about to ask more, but get distracted by the passing scenery and turn to watch as Giuliano navigates the twisting hillside down toward the lake, past tidy homes and grape arbors. Most of the slope is covered with vineyards. Low stone walls define the roadway and the vines come right up to the berm. We round a corner and Giuliano swerves, barely missing an elderly man who's set up his ladder in our lane—to pick grapes from his arbor. The old man barely notices—safety concerns, we've realized, are an American thing.

The road slithers down to Torri di Benaco where we stop for a stroll. The tiny, ancient village is tucked between its modern cousin and the water. Fronting the lake is a modest castle with tulip-fluted battlements around its parapet. A wooden orangery snuggles its rear wall. Built to protect the fruit from cold weather, the trees inside it are heavy with citrus. Following the road around the castle, Giuliano poses the three of us for a photo by the tiny u-shaped harbor where day-sailers, a *carabinieri* boat, and rowboats in red, aqua, yellow, and green are moored.

"*Come si dice queste...,*" I point Teresa to the water, "*queste...*" I can't even remember the word for birds, but that's not what I want. I flap my hand up and down,

"*Cigni.*" Swans. She laughs as we watch them bob upended to feed near the rowboats. "*Sono divertenti?*" Aren't they funny?

Just beyond the harbor's mouth, a wide dock awaits the incoming ferry. On the opposite side, bistro tables fill the first-floor arches of Albergo Gardesana and onto the shaded piazza. The cobblestone narrows into a pedestrian street where shades of ocher define the buildings and we browse their shops and fruit stands. Walking back along the seawall, sheltered dining areas cantilever over the water. On the opposite shore we can see the tawny buildings of Maderno and Toscolano crawling up the steep slope.

"I think you were right," I tell Giuliano. "This is more beautiful than Lake Como. And it's flat. You know John and I like towns that are flat." We've already been speculating about what it would be like to spend a few months here.

"The other side, not so much," he says. "There all the towns are rolling down the hill."

John's gazing out at the water and I can guess what's on his mind. "Bet it's good for sailing," he says. Right again.

"My son had a sailboat here for several years," Giuliano says. "The winds are better on the northern end of the lake. And at the far end is the best windsurfing in Europe."

We head back to the car, visit several more calendar-worthy towns and gardens along the lake's eastern border, then stop for the night in Riva di Garda at the northern end. Our hotel overlooks the main piazza where tables of lively diners cluster near the small harbor.

Giuliano recommends we try the hotel's restaurant, on a balcony overlooking the action. Our waitress, a pretty girl of about 20 in neat black pants and jacket with a crisp white blouse offers some suggestions for our dinner. "I'm sure the food will be good," John says in Italian, "but do you have to be pretty to work here?" His standard line gets the expected blush.

"No. I'm in training here."

"In training? How so?" he asks.

"I'm studying to work in a restaurant. It's part of my school curriculum to work part-time while I go to school."

Sounds like Alessandro's program. "*Che studia?*" I ask her. So what do you study?

"It's a five-year program. The first two years are general education. Then I spend this year studying to be a waiter, another studying to be a cook, and the last one, studying reception. I'll have three degrees."

"That's a long time," I say.

"You work in each of the areas while you study, so you get practice and work experience. I work here several times a week." During our meal, she is attentive and handles her table duties without being intrusive. The next morning I watch her and another young woman as they tend the breakfast bar. Shuttling back and forth to the kitchen, they ensure the plates of meats, cheeses, breads, and fruit are never empty. They crumb the table each time they replenish something and arrange the plates carefully, adjusting the design. Constantly busy in the large dining room, they smile when summoned to a table. When one of them arrives with our cappuccino, there's a delicate swirl of brown espresso and a dusting of cocoa on top.

Sipping my steaming cappuccino, I say to John, "I think this training program is a good thing. It certainly makes for a well-run restaurant. Remember that waiter in Angiolo d'Or in Parma. This must be what he was talking about when he said being a waiter here is a profession."

"If he learned all the skills in school and through practice, I guess managing a restaurant wasn't such a huge undertaking for him."

"Right. But I think a lot of it still comes down to attitude. Studying something, mastering it gives you confidence no one can take away. You're getting that way about your Italian. What they understand here is that mastery is more than book-learning, more than a degree, and not limited to college grads. Italians put value on apprenticeship and passing down the proven way of doing things. We've seen it in lots of professions."

"It's certainly true of the artisans," John says. "Our mask-maker, the gondola builders, that woman who painted your new bowl."

"And the cheese-makers and salami producers. They talk about what they do as if they're talking about their children. Quality they say, always quality. It's the core of what they do. They create something that's desirable—coveted and enjoyed by others. And they're *proud* of it."

He glances over at the girls carefully resetting a table. "There's respect here for the work that goes into quality. It's part of the Italian sensibility, to choose only the best."

I scrape the last bit of frothed milk from my cup into my mouth. "I'm coming to understand that—the desire for quality, for an authentic experience. Part of our enjoyment is getting to know the Italians' nuanced tastes and appreciation for things well done. It's part of why I love living here. Maybe I'm becoming a little more *Italiana*."

Many months later, we're invited to the wedding of Yma and Livio, our young friends from Parma. We're gathered with about 40 others in Cattolica's town hall for the ceremony. Patricia, the bride's English mother, and Umberto, her Venetian father, live in Italy. Umberto, an engaging man who speaks several languages, welcomes the guests with special thanks to those who have traveled far for the occasion. He mentions the relatives from England and the friends from Australia. "And John and Nancy are here from America." We're flattered to be singled out in the small gathering. And he continues. "As many of you know, we lived in America for a while and appreciate all the friendships we developed during those years. Italy and America are closely tied. We have shared a lot. And Italy owes a great deal to the Americans. The bonds between us go back many years. America has always been a friend to Italy, even in its darkest days. That's why I'm especially pleased to welcome John and Nancy today." We never expected this. I'm touched and honored—and very proud to be American.

The bride is breathtaking, the groom elegant—movie-star gorgeous both. The service is brief and the reception, in an elegant hotel overlooking the Adriatic, chatty and informal. Champagne, oysters, and a huge wheel of Parmigiano to nibble while we all get to know each other. Later, at a table with the bride's English family, we share risotto brimming with fresh shrimp, tiny clams, and scallops; tender lettuces and radicchio sprinkled with aged balsamic; and grilled lamb, pork, and chicken. Yma and Livio move casually among their guests. Too busy talking, I miss the array of miniature desserts that surrounds the sea foam blue wedding cake decorated with white chocolate shells and starfish.

During the reception, Patricia and I find ourselves in an unexpected, personal conversation—sharing our life history. I ask her how she met her husband and she smiles the way a woman does remembering the early years of a well-loved marriage.

"Umberto was a waiter when we met. I had come to Italy for a visit with friends. We married not long after. He was very dedicated, worked hard, and got promoted through the years. Eventually, he managed several different hotels in London. We lived for a few years in Bermuda. Then we moved to the States for a while—where he managed the Plaza in New York."

The Plaza! The hotel I grew up reading about in my most favorite books about Eloise—the rowdy six-year-old who lived there. The place we visit whenever we're in its Central Park neighborhood—to suck up its elegant charm. Umberto managed the *Plaza*. All I can say is "Wow!"

I guess this Italian system produces more than confidence and pride. From waiter to managing New York's premier hotel...now *that's* a career track.

THE THEORY OF IMPERFECTION

What wisdom can you find that is greater than kindness?

JEAN JACQUES ROUSSEAU

Half of the American people have never read a newspaper. Half never voted for President. One hopes it is the same half.

GORE VIDAL

OUR CABIN MATES HELP SPEED UP THE TWO-HOUR TRAIN RIDE TO CERVIA. The two young Bolognese women pepper us with questions in broken English. Our responses, equally fractured, are in Italian. No, New Jersey is not the same as New York. Yes, we've been to Miami. Los Angeles, too. It turns out we're all getting off in Cervia. We're going there to stay with Italian friends who have promised to teach us to make homemade *tagliatelle.* The girls admit they can't cook. Not interested. They're going to Cervia for the beach—and, as they put it, to get away from too many *mommonies* in Bologna. *Mommonies?* Who knew there was a word for Italian men who continue to live at home—with their daddies and mommies—well into their thirties? Turns out, Bologna is a real *mommonie* town—at least that's the way Angela and Gia see it.

Over the loudspeaker, we hear *In arrivo per Cervia,* arriving in Cervia. As we say goodbye to our chatty cabinmates, we spot Giuliano and Teresa waiting for us on the platform. We're about to enjoy Cervia with great friends, capped by a pasta dinner at their home.

When Giuliano and Teresa make pasta, they start with flour, eggs, and water. Teresa places several cups of flour on a three-foot-square, one-inch-thick plywood board. She forms the powder into a one-foot-diameter circular dam that will hold the water and eggs. Using her hands, she molds the goo into a pasty ball, then kneads it over and over. Then Giuliano takes over.

Using a four-foot-long maple dowel, he deftly rolls, folds, and rolls again. The process transforms the ingredients into a firm but pliable quarter-inch-thick dough that covers all but the extreme corners of the board. None of this is new to me. I watched my mother and aunts make "homemades" a thousand times. What is new is the Giuliano's philosophy.

"You need to roll to a certain, consistent thickness. But you don't want it perfectly consistent. If I wanted perfection, I would put it through our pasta machine." He points to a gleaming, stainless steel device that sits prominently on the shelf behind him. I know about these devices as well. I gave my mom one for Mother's day in the early 70s. It was proudly displayed in the kitchen of the home where I grew up. Mom used it a few times but mostly she made pasta the old fashioned way: *a mano*, by hand.

Giuliano also does the cutting. "First you roll the dough into a log. Then you cut the log into pinwheels. Try to make the cuts even, but not too even. There's an attachment for the pasta machine that I could use to cut the *tagliatelle* into perfect strips. I prefer to cut using a knife."

Using a thin, nine-inch blade, he slices through the log to create piles of pinwheels more or less the same thickness. After they are cut, Teresa sprinkles them lightly with flour, gently shakes them out, and drops them loosely onto a plate.

The ribbons sit for about an hour while we tour the garden. Here we pick a few herbs, some of which—basil, parsley, and sage—will season the pasta we are about to enjoy.

The water in the pot is already boiling. Teresa carefully gathers enough of the ribbons for the four of us, about a third of what is sitting on the board. She hands them to Giuliano who slowly, gently—yes, reverently—places them into the water.

"You don't need to hurry this. There's no need for each ribbon to cook exactly the same. Indeed, you want to have a bit of variation in the cooking. It's these slight variations in thickness and cooking that excite the palate—in a way that makes you say Ah. That's why you use a wood board, not marble. The wood grain imparts texture to the dough. It's these little nooks and crannies that hold the sauce. When the pasta is perfectly smooth, the sauce slides off. Not good. Instead, you want a little variety. Not too much. Just the right amount. The same is true of its hardness. You want variety there as well. You want sections of each strip to be cooked slightly differently. Some parts a bit more *al dente*, more resistant. Variety. Diversity. Sort of like America. Imagine. A black man as president! I don't think that could happen in any other major country. John, you should be very proud "

"I am, Giuliano. Indeed, I am. Thank you."

Two weeks later, President Obama ia awarded the Nobel Peace Prize. And I write a letter to our hometown newspaper. Meanwhile, we enjoy a great meal featuring some of the most imperfectly perfect pasta we have ever eaten.

Letter to Editor of the Sandpaper, Long Beach Island, NJ

Re: Nobel Prize to President Obama

PARMA, ITALY October 12, 2009. Columbus Day

As Americans living in Italy, we think it's fair to say we were less surprised about our president getting the Nobel Peace Prize than most of our friends back home. You see, from our perspective, Europeans love Obama, not because he's president but because he's an American success story. And Europeans love the fact that we have so many such stories.

To prove our point, all we have to do is walk into any *enoteca* (that's a fancy name for a wine bar) in Parma; order a local red; start chatting with locals; they're quick to realize that we are foreigners. Are you Germans? English? No, we are Americans, we say, from the United States. That's when it happens. Big smiles. Nods. Oh, Americans; that's wonderful, they say; Great country, great people; we love America. We love visiting America. This is usually followed by a recitation of cities: New York, Las Vegas, Miami, and San Francisco are the most frequently mentioned. When we tell them we live in New Jersey…that's near New York, the smiles grow broader. I love New York, someone will invariably sing. So it goes.

So, why do you like Americans we ask? There's no one answer but we would sum it up this way. Europeans see us as their prodigal brothers. They stayed home to tend the farm while we went off to sow wild oats. In short, they're envious. Like so many Walter Mittys, Europeans would like to drive a big SUV instead of a Fiat. They'd like paying $2.50/gallon for gas instead of $10.00. They'd like to see themselves capable of electing a black man as president, not just because he's black but because it would be so rebellious. They like that our country was started by rebels; they like that we still have tea parties, that we seemingly protest everything, especially government proposals. They'd like the opportunity to be a bit less responsible, to experience the thrill of going off alone into the big, bad world. How else to explain all the James Dean images? He's everywhere. They like that, at age 23, Mark Zuckerberg, the inventor of Facebook, is already a billionaire. They like that nothing seemingly holds us down. From their perspective, we have created a system that favors the creative, the hard working, and the risk-takers. By contrast, here in Italy 70 percent of young men between the ages of 25 and 29 still live with their parents. When they finally do leave home, 90 percent remain within 50 kilometers of their original family home. While they might be adventurous motorists, Italians, like most modern Europeans, are not exactly known for striking out on their own. Unlike in soccer and rugby, in America, balls leave the park. Outta here! Who doesn't like that?

Anyway, without taking anything away from President Obama, our view from here is that the prize belongs as much to Army Specialist Joey Martinez fighting in the Gulf, to Ryan Howard of the Phillies, to Mark Zuckerberg of Facebook, to job-creating small businesspeople on LBI, to your immigrant neighbor down the street, and to all of us who call ourselves Americans.

Happy Columbus Day.

WINTER TRAVEL

The traveler sees what he sees, the tourist sees what he has come to see.

If it's tourist season, why can't we kill them?

UNKNOWN

WINTER. IT'S NOT AS COLD HERE AS IN NEW JERSEY WHERE THEY'RE HAVING a frigid season. Our apartment is cozy but getting out every day is what we like to do. Food shopping, errands, reading the newspaper in a café, or stopping into an unexplored church. "What'll we do today?" I ask John over our November-morning coffee.

"Let's ride over to the Tourist Center this afternoon, see what's going on for the Christmas season. We can pick up something for dinner at the Uns and maybe go out for a drink this evening."

Like most Parmagiani, we ride our bikes all year. Well, *we* don't ride in the snow, although the natives do. Today it's crisp and clear, so we peddle into town without much effort, gliding along the familiar streets. Later, our favorite martinis in hand, we warm ourselves by the fire at the bar of Grand Hotel di Ville.

"The *appertivi* here are the best," I say, biting into another tiny, beautiful crostini. There are always four or five elegant offerings on the bar, so it's one of our favorite hangouts.

"I think we should plan a little trip," John says tossing down his third *olivita* bite. "How about we go back to Florence for a few days?"

"I still can't believe it when I say I went to Florence for lunch!" Visions of the pink, green, and white cathedral and baptistry materialize in my mind—and the tiny shop where I bought colorful, handmade jewelry. "That was really cool, but there's so much more we need to see."

Our only Florence visit this year had been in sunny June when we met some friends there for a meal. Crowds mobbed the main piazza and we couldn't even see the famous bronze doors of the baptistry, so we skipped the *duomo* and happily explored the tiny side streets on the way to the restaurant. After *pranza*, lunch, we happened onto a store selling Florentine paper and watched the owner make swirling, multicolored designs the way they've been done for hundreds of years. Like oil on water, the ink colors float on the surface of a gel that fills a box. The paper-maker spatters the gel with brown, yellow, green, ocher, and tan, then uses a wire comb to make the traditional flowing patterns. He lays a sheet of paper on the gel then gently removes it. The delicate pattern remains on its surface. But he can make only one pull per design. "The real masters," he told us, "could repeat a pattern."

Before we left, we crossed onto the Ponte Vecchia for a photo reminiscent of one we took many years ago. John posed again with the bust of Benvenuto Cellini, sculptor and goldsmith, whose autobiography—considered the world's first—we have read.

"Early January would be good." I say, pulling back to the present. "We shouldn't have any problem getting a place to stay then. But I'll have to make sure the museums are open."

Browsing the web later that evening, I locate a B & B near San Croce. It's in a pretty good location and reasonable. Google Earth shows a lot of graffiti at the street level but we see that in all the major cities here. It's a shame.

We arrive in Florence in cold January rain, settle into our room, pull on our rain gear and set out again. I've got my iPod loaded with Rick Steves' walking tours and we start with the *duomo*. Partnered with a local guide, Steves does a good job describing the church and bell tower. He doesn't think much of the interior, though.

"I disagree," John says. "I think the simplicity is beautiful. And look at these floors!" Forming huge squares each in a unique design, the green, red, black, and gray marble contrasts with white Carrara. Today only small groups of people are scattered around the interior.

"If it were summer, we'd never be able to see the patterns for the crowds. Now, even with that life-size crèche in the middle, you can really appreciate the different designs. I like the one over there with the interlocking circles. It reminds me of the ceiling of the Pantheon in Rome."

"Well, the Pantheon was part of the building of this church. Remember that book, *Brunelleschi's Dome*?"

"You read it, not me. What was it again about the Pantheon?"

"The dome here is enormous. The church stood open for years because no one could figure out how to make a dome big enough to cover it. Brunelleschi decided to go back to the Pantheon which the Romans had built around the first century, to see how they supported the dome. It gets its strength from a double-wall construction, but like so much of Roman innovation, the formula was lost. Brunelleschi's double dome allowed braces to be hidden in between. Brilliant engineering."

I look up to admire the dome's execution. "Too bad the painter wasn't as brilliant. This *Final Judgement* fresco is pretty ordinary."

We dash across the puddled square from the cathedral to the Duomo Museum where the most important exterior pieces have been moved to protect them from the elements. Donatello's four statues from the bell tower are here, reproductions are outside. Up close, you can appreciate Donatello's genius.

"He's so much better than these other sculptors," I say when I've scrutinized all the statues. "His details and ability to capture lifelike attitude make his work much more lifelike." In another room I admire the Della Robbia friezes.

"I thought he was mostly known for ceramics, but these children are delightful." Stepping out in bas relief from pieces that once formed a choir loft, groups of cherubic children sing and play various instruments. I can't help but smile.

Dramatically lit in another room is Donatello's *Mary Magdelene*. Surprisingly carved of wood, the style so modern she could have been done in the 20th century, she's a haunting figure. We also find the cutaway model Brunelleschi made to show how his construction would work and admire a model of the cathedral and baptistry, which are hard to appreciate from street level.

Before we leave, we inspect the samples Brunelleschi and Ghiberti submitted in the competition for the bronze doors of the baptistry. It's easy to understand why Brunelleschi lost. A marvelous engineer, he was not such a fantastic bronze caster. His slightly cruder square is done in pieces that are bolted together, while Ghiberti's is one piece that has much finer detail.

Outside again we raise the umbrella and head to the Mercato Nuovo. Rick Steves suggests we find the X on the raised marble floor that marks the spot where, as punishment, robbers were dropped from three stories above. A good reason to be honest. After 20 minutes walking back and forth with no luck, we finally ask one of the merchants.

"You'll never find it," he replies in Italian. "It's over here." He pushes through a rack of leather jackets, shoves a large box aside, and there it is.

"*Grazie per il suo aiuto,*" I say, snapping a photo. Thanks for your help.

We get lost in the dark, rainy streets on our way to the Arno but discover a ceramic gallery where we get some relief from the constant drizzle, and I get to ogle some modern masters. I have enough ceramics experience to marvel at the size of the flat wall pieces and the execution of their vibrant details. Inspired and warm, we head across the Golden Bridge in search of the artist studios of the Oltrearno.

As usual, the directions from the article I read aren't quite right. We wander along the streets poking into doorways, but find nothing open. As we're about to give up and head back, we spy a huge, marble statue marking the entrance to some kind of studio. Inside, a lovely young woman with large, brown eyes and soft wavy hair introduces herself; Rubina Romanelli, the sixth generation of a

Florentine family of sculptors and artisans. One of the Romanellis sculpted the bust of Cellini that John likes so well. Under Rubina's tutelage, we spend an hour learning about some of the museum-quality pieces her family has created and collected. Our favorite is an oversized nude, dancing pair, Isadora Duncan and friend, done by Romera Romanelli. Unfortunately it's way beyond our price range. Because the best photos of John and me are always taken when we're dancing, I ask Rubina to snap one of us and Isadora.

Bidding *arrivederci* to Rubina, we set a path to our final destination—the Golden View Open Bar. Steves' tour book says we need reservations several days in advance but when we arrive at around 7:00, there are hardly any diners. We choose the modern bar area and are seated along the window—with a spectacular view of the lighted Ponte Vecchio reflecting on the river. In the light drizzle, it's eerily beautiful. Sipping my prosecco, I'm enchanted. Tonight Florence is our personal jewel box.

Across the candlelit table my guy looks especially handsome right now—like my own Medici prince. Once again I think how lucky I am to have married him and lean across the table, glass extended. "A pretty good day, wouldn't you say?"

John gently clicks my glass, reaches for one of the tasty treats that accompany our drinks, and places it in my mouth. "Only thing that would have made it better would be taking Isadora home to our personal dance floor," he says with a grin.

The next day we visit the Uffizi, one of Italy's greatest art museums. Arranged in chronological order, it's the easiest way to see the development of Renaissance art. Recalling the crowds when Bonda and I shlepped through here many years ago in sweltering August heat, I'm pleased when we arrive to find only a handful of people in any room. I'll be able to drown myself in my favorite paintings. In the Botticelli rooms, I linger half an hour examining the Madonna faces, admiring the almond-eyed children, comparing his Venus and his *Primavera*.

"What a difference it makes to just relax here and soak it all up," I say, returning to John who's found a bench for rest.

"You look as long as you want," he answers. "I'll just wait here." He's tired now, but I've got to linger a bit longer.

Exiting the museum much later, we stop to admire the statues that line the street side of the Uffizi's loggia. There are about 30 of them—artists, philosophers, explorers, writers, and scientists. All Florentines. Dante, Cellini, Vespucci, Petrarch, Giotto, Michelangelo, Leonardo, Donatello, Machiavelli, and Lorenzo the Magnificent are among them. No wonder this was the birthplace of the Renaissance. The story of how the statues got there is not in the art history books.

When Vasari designed the Uffizi in the mid-16th century, he placed graceful niches along the courtyard, solely for decoration. But in the early 19th century, a local printer named Vincenzo Batelli looked at them and decided they needed to be filled—with something—something celebrating the glory of the province, he thought. Unable to fund the project himself, he devised several schemes to get the residents of Tuscany to raise the money. They could either pay a monthly fee for three years or join a lottery. No surprise, the lottery won out and, with supplemental donations from a few wealthy patrons, Florence's celebrated citizens now overlook the summer crowds waiting to enter the museum.

We have two other great museums to visit. The Bargello is to sculpture what the Uffizi is to painting, and we linger undisturbed in the large ground-floor room in which four Michelangeos, three Cellinis, and several lesser stars are found. The statue of Mercury, so familiar from the FTD logo, is here, and I'm charmed by the *Fishing Boy*, who's clutching his wriggling catch.

At the Pitti Palace, there's an unusual exhibit: Stolen artifacts recovered by a special unit of the Italian *Caribinieri*. Most interesting is an enormous pulpit removed from a church. Over seven feet high and five feet across, it must weigh 2000 pounds. How and *why* would anyone decide to steal it? A question only the thief could answer.

In the evening, we don our rain gear once more and trek to Trattoria Andiolino for the Florentine classic *bistecca di florentine*, grilled, herb-dusted T-bone steak. When we enter, the unmistakable aroma fills our nostrils. Carved tableside and accompanied by the lightest *vedura fritto*, fried veggies, I've ever eaten, I linger over each scrumptious, meaty, and crunchy bite. We inhale the aroma and savor the flavors as much as we did the art of the past few days. All of it our ample, delicious reward for braving the rain.

Rome in December proves surprisingly warm. Meeting friends near the Trevi fountain, we snap some photos *senza i cappotti*, without coats. We've met up with our pal Suzanne from Philadelphia. Fearless and curious, Suzanne is a world traveler. She introduces us to her old buddies from Spoleto, Giorgio and Giusy, and their daughter Giorgia who now lives in Rome. We're off in their care to see the city and the Vatican Museums.

The path to our ultimate objective—the Sistine Chapel—meanders through one of the largest and richest collections in the world. The building goes on and on. Today the crowd is minimal, not at all like the pressing crush I remember from years ago. One of our favorite places is the Map room where a couple dozen hand-painted maps of the Old World line the walls. We find the one of Sicily and sure enough, there's the town of Petralia in the center. We plan to get there before our year is up.

In the *Pinoteca*, the painting gallery, we marvel at the scope and size of the collection. All the best Renaissance and Baroque painters are represented as are many later artists. From across the room I spot a Correggio, immediately drawn to his distinctive style. I really *am* getting to know my artists. Raphael is well represented, and not just his paintings. A busy guy, in the last four years of his short life, he frescoed the Pope's apartments, which we pass through.

After hours of walking and looking, we enter the Sistine. Last time I was here, it was just starting to be cleaned. Then, Michelangelo was considered the hands-down master of subtle, dark figures. Now that the whole room is rid of its years of grime, he's considered the master of color! I think I liked it better before. It looks a little flat to me now—the figures a bit too blocky. On the back wall, *The Last Judgement*, which I couldn't make out at all 30 years ago, is clearly visible in all its unsettling detail of martyrdom, glory, and damnation.

"*Silenzio*," hollers a guard from the opposite end of the room. Although there are signs posted at the chapel's entrance, requesting quiet, people are naturally talking about the masterpiece that surrounds them. "No photos!" comes another loud warning, this time in English. The room is massive, and the modest crowd mills back and forth to view each wall and ceiling section. Before long, the noise level has risen again.

"*Silenzio!*" The shouted order seems counterproductive.

When we exit into St. Peter's Square it's dusk. I search for the pointing heralds mentioned in *Angels and Demons*—with no luck. As we climb the stairs to the Cathedral something catches my eye. In the sky over the piazza, hundreds of birds are swarming, swirling in and out, up and down, making the most magnificent patterns overhead. I call our friends to look. Enthralled, we learn from Giusy that this phenomenon happens every night. No one knows why. Maybe they're migrating birds who've lost their GPS. But why do they circle just *here* in St. Peter's courtyard? Makes you wonder.

Inside the Pope's church, the world's largest, visitors at the opposite end are just specks. We wander from tomb to tomb admiring Bernini's handiwork, the golden throne of St. Peter, the canopy, and the dome. At five o'clock, a service starts. Chanting and quiet organ music float over the majestic space, and we drift off toward the distant door—and dinner.

The next day, we part from our friends to explore on our own. Our Colosseum guide explains that because Nero had taken land from the people, this public theater was a way of giving something back. Everyone was welcome to attend, even women and slaves. Using trap doors and elaborate scenery, spectacular bouts between men and animals, gladiators and the condemned were played out in grand, theatric style. Giant awnings that took four days to unfurl shaded the crowd 2000 years before our covered stadiums. They could even flood the enormous floor to re-enact sea battles. I remember the hundreds of cats that lurked around every pillar 30 years ago and search the steps and corners but manage to spy just two or three.

Afterward we amble across the huge Forum, imagining ourselves walking beside Caesar, Mark Anthony, Cicero, and Cato. The tourists scattered about the massive ruins could be citizens of classical Rome out for a day's stroll. By the time we reach the exit, we're weary from walking what seemed like miles. Time for a café, some proscecco, and people-watching.

In the evening, after a visit to Piazza Navonna and Bernini's famous fountains, we arrive at the Pantheon—the best preserved Roman building—its dome the largest built before the Renaissance. I would rather it had remained a Roman temple. But like many grand buildings, it has long ago been converted to a Catholic church. To me, the extra decoration, gilding, and saints detract from the simple beauty of its original design. The domed ceiling remains the same, however, its rows of recessed squares-within-squares smaller and smaller as they reach toward the massive, round opening at the top. Sunlight and rain water bathe the slanted floors in which the clever Romans had placed holes to drain the water away.

Our three days of walking over, we collapse on the train home. "My legs are exhausted, but it was worth it," I say, sliding into my first-class seat for the long ride back to Parma. "Not nearly as tiring, though, as trying to do all that in the summer heat."

"We'd never have been able to hike the Forum in July or August."

"I remember when Bonda and I did it. The temperature was 106."

"There were still lots of tourists, but not so many you couldn't see things." John twists back and forth in his seat trying to tease out a crack. "My back can't take all that standing in line."

"Remember our trip to Venice two weeks ago?" Venice is my absolute favorite place in the world. Actually, it's John's favorite too. We had discovered this nearly 20 years ago on our third date—another positive sign for our then budding relationship.

"Just the rain," he answers with a squeeze of my knee.

"Okay, the rain, but who cares. There was hardly anyone in the city. We were listening to Rick Steves' podcast for St. Mark's, and he's saying to try to work our way around the crowd to get a look at the Golden Altar. And I'm counting... ten...eleven...twelve people in the entire church. We spent about an hour there nearly all by ourselves."

"Not even any pigeons in the piazza." John turns to hand our tickets to the conductor. "My favorite, though, was stopping at the Danieli Hotel for a drink." We love tasting the rich and famous lifestyle by sipping Campari and soda in grand hotels.

"That was a great idea," I add. Why would anyone go to Harry's Bar and pay $26 for a martini in what looks like an average corner bar when they could go to the Danieli and, for less money, get a drink, a plate full of goodies, and enjoy the Christmas decorations in a Venetian palace?

"The rain in Venice is part of the charm," he says. "Slip-sliding down those twisting streets and ducking into a little *enoteca* to dry off."

"I'm probably crazy but I think the food in Venice tastes even better in winter. We have the tourist cities to ourselves now. Not a bad trade for wearing foul weather gear."

We slouch back in our seats to watch the Lazio countryside fly past. A few moments later, John leans over and squeezes my knee again.

"I think we're onto something," he teases. "Traveling in winter."

THE ECONOMICS LESSON

Italy has piled up huge public debt because successive governments were too close to the life of ordinary citizens, too willing to please the requests of everybody, thereby acting against the interests of future generations.

MARIO MONTI, PRIME MINISTER OF ITALY

Political parties are the cancer of politics.

GIANLUCA PERILLI, REPRESENTATIVE OF THE FIVE STAR MOVEMENT, ROME

WE'VE BEEN IN ATTIGLIANO NOW FOR FOUR DAYS. LOCATED 75 KILOMETERS north of Rome on the A-I Autostrada, it's been an excellent base for exploring Umbria's historical sites. We have been following Via Flaminia, the ancient Roman road that runs from Perugia, Spoleto, and Assisi in the North down to Narni. Yesterday we used the old road to get to the Roman ruins of Carsulae. Today we're planning to stop briefly in Foligno and Terni. From there, we'll take the Autostrada through the Martani mountain range all the way to Orvieto.

I'm about to have a morning coffee with Alberto, owner of the small hotel that has been our jumping off spot for this tour of Umbria. An amateur historian, Alberto has helped us navigate the wonders of Assisi, Perugia, and Spoleto. He steered us to lesser known wonders such as the Fossil Forest of Dunarobba, where two million years ago, waters coming down from the hills carried huge quantities of sediments that covered and preserved giant trees. Despite the name, the wood in these dead trees is not fossilized; it's actually wood that has been covered in mud for two million years.

Yesterday, when we went to Carsulae, we walked through ruins of Roman buildings constructed using three distinct masonry techniques that had evolved over a thousand years. Because my father was a stonemason, I've more than a passing interest in the evolution of the craft.

A handsome, white-haired bull of a man in his mid-seventies, with disproportionately large hands, Alberto is sitting at a table directly in front of the restaurant's 55-inch flat-screen TV; the sound is turned up to ear-break. Tipping the red Phillies cap I gave him yesterday, Alberto reminds me of someone but I can't quite place who it is. He smiles as he sees me and signals to Marla. "*Caffé per John.*" Motioning for me to sit, he has the look of a manager down by four runs in the 8th.

Shuffling a pile of official-looking documents, he turns and says, "Truly, John, if I were to pay all the taxes demanded of me by this government, I would have to close this place down. I have family and employees who depend on me. You know how it works here?" I shake my head. Fact is, I really *don't* know.

"Here's how it works. You employee somebody; for every euro you pay them, you have to give the government one euro for benefits." Because I still have not completely mastered the Italian language, when I hear something that doesn't sound quite right, I'm not as quick to question as I would be if we were speaking English. His claim gives me an odd, itchy, ill-fitting wool-sock feeling. It deserves to be challenged. But I'm too slow. Uncontested, Alberto barrels on.

"How can I afford to pay my wife and kids according to that formula? You know my daughter Laura. Officially, she works for an accountant here in town. But every evening she is here doing reservations, accounting, and more. My son Franco runs my engineering company, but he also works here part-time. So does his wife. My wife Anna does all the cooking. We all work very hard to maintain this little hotel."

I think to myself, there surely are a lot of hard workers here Alberto, but you're not one of them. The only work I've seen you do is change channels on the TV. He goes on. "We have only one official employee, Marla. She's Russian. Wonderful woman, excellent housekeeper, speaks good Italian. She has two small children, no husband. What would she do without this job?" He doesn't want an answer.

He stares at me with sky blue eyes that seem to say "you spoiled punk, do you have any idea how difficult my life is here in Italy?"

I suggest turning the sound down on the TV, but he simply waves at the screen and says, "The news. Politics and mafia. They're all the same. Bastards."

He's intent on his pitch. "Do you realize how the government hounds small businessmen like me? Our taxes are excessive. Not true for big business. Big companies like Fiat and ENI—the big employers—get special breaks. In Italy, everyone wants social programs—free education, free healthcare, unemployment benefits—but no one wants to pay for them. Do you know here in Italy, drug addicts are treated like the blind? They get financial support—and free drugs. Who pays for that? Not big business. Not the poor. No, I do. Do you understand?"

Oh, I understand his words but I'm still not entirely sure where all this is going. Is he looking for a loan? Does he think I have some clout with Berlusconi? He can't want me to pay our bill with cash; we've already prepaid with a credit card. Not sure what to do, I nod and say, "*Capisco*," I understand. Then, I add, "So, are you saying that the government is too large? You'd like smaller government? You know, many in our country say the same thing. Unfortunately, like you Italians, many of our people keep demanding more and more government services."

Alberto's stare is dismissive. Did he not appreciate my implication? His voice goes up a notch. "John, our government doesn't work for us like some other governments do. Look at China, Korea, and Japan. Their governments understand that without businesses, there is no economy. In Italy, small businesses like mine are persecuted. It's crazy. Stupid. Government is too large and too ineffective. We need incentives for businesses to create jobs—to bring back jobs that have been exported. We need to protect our jobs. Since joining the EU, we have lost millions of private sector jobs that aren't coming back. The Chinese and Koreans have already taken half our jobs. Without protection for us poor business owners, without tariffs, the Africans and Albanians will take the rest."

As a free-trader, I want to lecture Alberto about the dangers of protectionism. I wonder if he knows about Smoot-Hawley? Passed in 1930, it was the highest protective tariff in U.S. history. When 25 countries retaliated, the world was plunged into the Great Depression. But all I can think about is the scene in Ferris Bueller's Day Off. Faced with a totally disinterested class—Ferris Bueller is absent—the high school Economics teacher, played brilliantly by Ben Stein, drones through a lecture asking "Anyone, Anyone?" to which only *he* responds: "In 1930, the Republican-controlled House, in an effort to alleviate the effects of the...Anyone, Anyone?...the Great Depression, passed the... Anyone, Anyone? The tariff bill?...Anyone, Anyone? The Smoot-Hawley Tariff Act? Which...anyone? Raised or lowered?...raised tariffs in an effort to collect more revenue for the Federal government. Did it work?..Anyone?" I'm not sure what it says about the way my mind functions but whenever someone talks about protectionism, I immediately think of Ben Stein.

Screwing up my courage, I say "Alberto, times have changed. We live in a global economy. Anyway, restrictions rarely work. Besides, job creation is a two-way street. Restricting free trade can do more harm than good. The best way for Italy to protect its businesses is to become more efficient, more competitive."

Now I've done it. Alberto's face has become nearly as red as his Phillies cap. "More efficient. More productive. More competitive. Listen to me, John. I bought this land 20 years ago. First, we built the pizzeria and a small apartment for my family. We all worked in the pizzeria. When the A-I added an exit in Attigliano, our business started to grow. I added six hotel rooms and two more apartments—for my two children and their families. I have four grandchildren."

I complement him on having such a beautiful family. He goes on.

"Today, we have 12 guest rooms, the pizzeria, a restaurant, and the three apartments. I would add four more guest rooms but the state won't allow it. They say I'm in violation. That's the government for you: money for drug addicts but no help for a poor businessman trying to create jobs. You know why?" I shake my head.

"I'll tell you why," he says. "In Italy, we have more drug addicts than businesses. That's why. We have more government workers than business owners.

The best jobs are with the State. My daughter-in-law, the one who waited on you last night—yes, Francesca—she's an attorney. But she works for the library system as an administrator. She's very smart. Makes far more money than my son. You see how she dresses. Beautiful, eh? You think Franco could afford to buy her those expensive clothes she wears? No way."

Not wanting to anger him further, I pour myself another cup of coffee, select two biscotti (suitable for dunking) and say "We enjoyed chatting with Francesca last night. She's charming."

Seemingly mollified, he says "Thank you. You have to understand, John, Francesca is not your typical government employee. Francesca is competent. Most government workers are political appointees. Do you know how much the head of our social security system in Italy makes? I'll tell you. He makes nearly two million dollars a year—five times President Obama's salary. We have retired judges who have pensions exceeding your president's salary. They get these jobs, even the judges, because their fathers had them before—or they know the right politician."

"You need stronger regulations," I say.

"Regulations. Are you kidding? Here, the police are the worst offenders. You know the Guardia di Finanzia? They are the worst. Bastards. They hound small businesses like mine. In Italy, it's all about politics. Here, everyone looks to the government for jobs. Everyone wants a handout. Free drugs for addicts, more benefits for the unemployed. Government gets bigger. Sure, free education is great. But now we have millions of university graduates who can't find jobs. What are they going to do, become drug addicts? We already have too many teachers, too many lawyers, too many police, too many politicians."

Trying to sound helpful, I say, " What you need is more businesses and fewer politicians."

"*Punto*," he says. "The politicians sell us out for votes. It's a vicious cycle. As more and more people become dependent on big government, they represent a bigger and bigger portion of the voters. Politicians go where the votes are. Where does that leave someone like me? What they don't seem to realize is that without businesses like mine, there would be no taxes to support the drug addicts, the police, and all the lousy politicians in Rome. You know what our mayor told me? He told me that he pays taxes too. Imagine, John. He actually thinks that when he pays taxes, it's the same as when I pay taxes. He really believes it. You know, John, without my taxes and taxes from other businesses here in Attigliano, he would not have the income to even buy food for his babies."

I think to myself, our politicians are just as bad. Washington, D.C. has a household income that is 70 percent higher than the national average. Nine of the richest counties in the country surround Washington, including numbers 1, 3, 4, and 5. Per capita income in D.C. is more than twice that of Maine. All this explains why Gallop's Well-Being Index rates D.C. as the most satisfied, large metropolitan area in the U.S. For every dollar in taxes Washington, D.C. residents send to the Federal government, it receives five in return.

"John," he says, "you are so lucky to live in America. In Italy, the economy is dying because we have too many leeches. Too many immigrants. Too many politicians. It makes me sick."

I'm tempted to say, you sound like an American, but I don't. Yet, I know he's right about the political system. It's crazy. Currently, there are more than 40 political parties in Italy; the five major ones run the gamut from communist to conservative. No one party has ever had a majority. All governments since WWII have been coalitions. Keeping fragile alliances of diverse philosophies together has proven difficult. Since 1945, Italy has had 42 different governments. When a government flip-flops from one elite to another like that, you are going to get hatred, distrust, and stagnation. In the end, it's the masses who get screwed.

What scares me is that America seems to be following in Italy's footsteps. Our two-party system has always been America's bulwark of stability. But a two-party system only works if there's compromise. Today some want to do away with our Electoral College. But that would be a mistake. Direct election of the president sounds good, but our founding fathers knew better. Because it is very difficult for a fringe movement to win enough popular votes in enough States to have a chance of winning the presidency, the Electoral College has the practical effect of forcing fringe-party movements into one of the two major political parties. Thus, our coalitions tend to be found within our parties rather than within governments. Thank you Madison, Mason, and Jefferson.

Ironically, the two-party system started with the Romans. Indeed, when Caesar was making his bones as a politician and general, Rome had two parties. The Sulla faction, named after the former dictator, had been all-powerful since Sulla's death. The other faction, named for Sulla's predecessor, was the decided minority—at least until Caesar became its standard bearer. Unfortunately for Caesar, his all too successful reign caused him to want to make Rome a one-party town—his party. That's when Brutus, Cassius, and the others struck him down.

Because modern Italy is so regionalized, their parliamentary system has given rise to many different parties. Until 2006, all the parties were allowed to participate in national elections. Now to participate in an election, a party must have a minimum of five percent of the registered voters. Italians would do better for themselves and their country if they supported policies that a 19th-century Italian economist borrowed from our founding fathers. Vilfredo Pareto advocated systems that would maximize the greater good without harming any party. His optimization math is still used today by engineers and designers seeking to perfect process outcomes. I'm no expert, but I do know that it's easier to optimize two variables than 40.

Before I can say anything, Alberto is quoting another Italian, Niccolo Machiavelli. "Is it better to be loved than feared—or the reverse?" he asks.

I'm thinking: what's this have to do with our discussion? Nonetheless, I surprise him by answering in a way that I think Machiavelli would have approved of: "The answer, of course, is that it would be best to be both loved and feared. But since the two rarely come together, anyone compelled to choose will find greater security in being feared than in being loved."

Looking at me with a grin of approval, Alberto adds *"Bravo, John. Complimenti."* Congratulations. You know your Machiavelli.

Indeed, I do know my Machiavelli. When our book club read *The Prince* a couple of years back, Nancy and I hosted the discussion. In preparation, I typed out 34 Machiavellisms, printed them and cut them into strips. Our members each drew from a hat as discussion points. And I became the book club's resident expert on Machiavelli.

"OK, John," he says. "Would it not be better if politicians did not worry about being loved? All this love is ruining us. Wouldn't it be better if they taxed everyone equally instead of only taxing businesses?" He doesn't want an answer.

Alberto has probably never heard of the Pareto Optimum; it is also called the 80/20 rule or Pareto's Law. I'm reminded that in the U.S., 80 percent of Social Security recipients receive more in payments than they paid in. Put another way, 20 percent of Americans are supplementing payments for the other 80 percent.

Just then Nancy joins us. This is Alberto's cue to take his leave. Tipping his Phillies cap to Nancy, he says "Enjoy your trip to Orvieto, *signora.*"

Nancy asks him for a lunch recommendation. Alberto doesn't have to think about it. He says, "Go to La Palomba on Via Cipriano Menente. It's a little place, but good. *Buon prezzo,* modest prices. Be sure to try their *carbonara con tartufo*—a pasta dish with truffles. Would you like me to make a reservation for you?" Nancy looks at me. We both nod yes.

While my wife drives, I'm doodling in my spiral notebook. Alberto has me thinking. It's clear to me that when a government spends more than it takes in, there's a deficit. If debt gets so large that the government has insufficient revenue to pay interest and principal, that government is technically broke. Economists call this the Keynesian Endpoint. Is America at that point?

Kicking around numbers in my head creates a time warp. Before I know it, Nancy is carefully maneuvering the car through the streets of Orvieto, trying to get close to the cathedral. We can already see its gothic façade, but where to park? Nancy scoots our Ford Focus down a hill to a large parking area about 500 yards away. I put on my Philadelphia Eagles cap to complement Nancy's Parma Athletic Club cap, and we climb back up the hill to the cathedral.

The exterior architecture is striking, but it's the inside that really blows us away. The walls are constructed of layers of travertine and basalt that create a pattern of alternating three-feet-wide stripes throughout. Nancy, my art expert, says that the side chapel has several noteworthy paintings, done in 1447, that demonstrate the beginning of the use of perspective.

Click. "Math," I say.

Nancy gives me a quizzical look. "What about it? What about math?

The light bulb in my head is getting brighter. "These guys knew math. More accurately, they rediscovered Roman math, the math that allowed the Romans to build the Pantheon and the Via Flamina. By rediscovering Roman math 1000 years later, Brunelleschi helped create the Renaissance."

In preparation for our trip to Italy, we each read many books. Ross King's *Brunelleschi's Dome: How a Renaissance Genius Reinvented Architecture* was enlightening to me. Brunelleschi studied Roman methods of building aqueducts, arches, and domes like the Pantheon in Rome. He was able to rediscover the old methods and invent even better ones. Brunelleschi's optical experiments led to a mathematical theory of perspective.

As we tour the cathedral, I keep thinking that the Renaissance was much more than art. It was also math and science. The mathematical genius of artists such as Leonardo, Brunelleschi, Fra Angelico, and Signorelli was well established by the time Galileo began thinking about the geometry of space nearly a century later.

Renaissance. That's the answer. The Renaissance started in Italy. Because of their perfect location between western Europe and the eastern shore of the Mediterranean, Italian cities became important as trade centers and as commercial centers. The wealth this created helped sustain the political and social changes that were occurring at the time. Florence became the banking center of Italy during the 14th century. During the 15th century, the Medici bank began opening branches in major cities in the rest of Europe. In addition to lending money, the Medici bank operated mines, mills, and other commercial activities. Accumulating huge profits, it used them to finance cultural as well as political activities.

Italy's new wealth, however, proved too tempting to its neighbors. In 1494, the armies of French king Charles VIII marched into Italy. They were followed by the Spanish, who ultimately gained control of much of the Italian peninsula—starting in 1559. Just as the conquered Greeks had passed on their culture to the Romans, these wars had the effect of exposing the rest of Europe to the accomplishments and attitudes of the Italian Renaissance.

It's 7:10 by the time we return to the hotel. Nancy has done all the driving while I've been on her computer researching and writing. We both need a drink. Mama Anna is busy in the kitchen. Marla is setting the tables for dinner. Alberto is seated in front of the TV, watching "The Millionaire" with Gerry Scotti, our favorite Italian emcee.

He waves us over. "How was Orvieto? Lunch was good, eh?"

"Alberto, that was a great idea," Nancy says, "Thank you. The *carbonara alla truffa*, excellent. Here, I brought you a present. Salami. *Cinghali* salami."

His face broadens into a grin. "*Molto grazie, signora*. Sit, we'll have some wine with it right now. Marla, bring some glasses and some bread."

"Alberto," I say, "let me share some figures with you." I'm excited. "Parts of Europe are going through a Renaissance. Let me show you what I mean." I've prepared several spreadsheets from economic data I've gathered from the CIA's website. "Take a look at this chart I've labeled Makers. It includes Switzerland, Norway, Germany, Sweden, and Finland. They are socialist countries. Free healthcare. Free education. But here's the important difference: in Sweden the retirement age is 67. If you want all that free stuff—and apparently the Swedes do—you have to have a way to pay for it. The Swedes do.

Another thing about Sweden, Finland, Norway, and others on the list— they're all are net exporters. Italy and the U.S. are what I call Takers—net importers. The more the gap between imports and exports widens, the bigger the Takers' debt burden. The U.S. trade gap runs over $700 billion per year. About two-thirds of this can be accounted for by oil imports. Economists estimate that for every $120,000 in net exports, one new job is created. So, closing our trade gap to zero would create more than six million jobs. "

Just then, Franco exits the elevator with two of his boys who take off running for the garden while their dad chats with grandpa. Trying not to eavesdrop, I determine that Franco has worked all day with a new crew. "Yes, the Romanians worked out okay. All good workers. One can drive. So tomorrow they can stay in Narni while I take the other truck to Orvieto."

From their conversation, I gather that Alberto's company is among the contractors helping to remove the rockslides we saw yesterday along the Autostrada outside of Narni. That's why today we had to use the old road, Via Flamina, to go up to Orvieto. Slow but scenic.

Alberto removes his Phillies cap to wipe his brow—of course! He looks just like Charlie Manual, the Phil's manager doing a post-game press conference.

Alberto heaves a long sigh, "*Uffa*. Most of our work these days is for the government. It's the crisis. It's good work. Profitable. But they are so slow to pay. Bastards. I do have some good news though. Yesterday, Francesca got a promotion at the library. Not only does she earn more money, she's now in a position to put Laura in a good job. It would mean that Laura has to commute to Rome everyday, but we can all help with her baby. And we have Marla, the Russian. She helps with all the children."

I slowly close the lid on my computer allowing the spreadsheet to fade away—along with the economics lesson I was prepared to give.

Alberto pours me another glass of wine, slices off a bit of salami, and then turns up the sound on the TV. "For 3000 euros, what American president was known as the Great Emancipator?"

I think to myself: Is it better to fight the system or join it? *Qualcuno? Qualcuno?* Anyone, Anyone?

CHASING THE IDEAL

To become aware of the possibility of the search is to be onto something.

WALKER PERCY

I am an idealist. I don't know where I'm going but I'm on my way.

CARL SANDBURG

SOME COUPLES LISTEN TO THE RADIO OR BOOKS ON TAPE WHEN THEY TRAVEL. We talk. Ten or 12 years ago we started this conversation about the perfect place to live in America. It comes up over and over, the criteria changing with our situation and our age. We like fantasizing about living other places. Early on, the number one thing on the list was olives. Real Italian olives. The black crinkly kind for me and big green Sicilian ones for John. Who'd want to live in a town where all you can get are those spongy tasteless things in a can?

Next on the list was bread. Italian bread, like from South Philly. Not that stuff that passes for Italian in most of America. For years, we would stop at Cacia's bakery on a Thursday or Friday night—before heading to our shore house for the weekend—and pick up a big sack of their Best-in-Philly rolls, then tuck them in with our stash of Sicilian and oil-cured olives. Now the LBI stores get bread delivered daily from Brooklyn and even the local Shop-Rite carries oil-cured olives, though not good Sicilian ones.

An international airport was always on our list. It's good to have a quick escape route. Water was always important too—water for boating, maybe catching some fish, and for watching the reflected sun. For waterbirds and the ebb and flow, I need to be able to see water from my windows.

As we got older, top-notch healthcare moved up the list. We're spoiled— close to Philadelphia with several teaching hospitals and fine docs. A college or university for intellectual activities, and a youthful vibe are crucial. Culture, maybe a sports team. And parks for dogs to play. We talk and talk, change and shift the list. It's a fun game.

When we discovered Parma and moved here, the Ideal City conversation continued, and our Parma experience began to shape our ideal. This city is canvas for a weekly new palette of entertainment. City-wide festivals seduce residents into the Center, funneling them around tiny tables and tented booths laden with jewelry, puppets, and antiques, or goat cheeses, licorice, and warm chestnuts. On hot afternoons, we bike the ring road and along the river, always shaded by enormous trees, to picnic at the Cittadella, the old fort that's now a park. In October, we hear *Aida's* "Triumphal March" and "Va Pensero" drifting over Via Cavour's shops and cafés during the annual month-long glorification of Verdi. New Year's Eve, we join what feels like the entire town in Garibaldi Square for a pop concert and fireworks. We meet our friends in cafés instead of homes—living outdoors more than we had expected. Parma is flat. Even in winter we're on two wheels.

Now we compare every town we visit to Parma. Is its central square, often named Garibaldi, as welcoming? What kind of parks does it have? Does graffiti cover the walls? Is opera important? Do trees shade the residential areas? What's the traffic like? And how's the terrain? Is this latest city somewhere we could live...is it another ideal? The search for an ideal city is part of our adventure here—a way of exploring and connecting with each place we visit.

Our friend Tom, a Franciscan, urged a visit to Assisi, and when we arrive, we realize why. Approaching from the Umbrian countryside, the cathedral, perched atop the monastery's double row of arches, dominates the hilltop town. It's set apart by a wide stretch of verdant green lawn fronting the white facade. On the grass, an oversized sculpture of Francis, head down, shoulders slumped, even his horse's head drooping, rides home from a war in 1204. Inside, the cathedral is actually two churches, one on top of the other. The lower one, which contains the saint's tomb, feels intimate—each arch of its low ceilings flaunting a unique, intricate, colorful design. Upstairs, enormous Giotto frescos tell the story of the St. Francis's life. Staring at the expressive faces, it's hard for me to believe they were done 800 years ago. You can almost hear the screams of the mothers trying to protect their sons in the *Slaughter of the Innocents*. Even the horses are startled by the massacre. But I still prefer my Parma *duomo* with its Correggio dome of gold and flying angels.

Assisi is the prettiest town we've seen. Its buildings are uniform in size and all the same pink and taupe stone. The doors are polished wood, shutters are unpainted and well patinaed. Flowerpots tumble color down nearly every stoop or stair—or are bolted onto exterior walls. There's not a scrap of litter and no graffiti. It's an Umbrian Disneyland.

As we descend a steep street, I notice the handrail. Its delicately curved surface conforms to my palm. At the end, it curls back on itself and flares with four gentle ridges—like a gnocchi rolling fresh off a fork. I pull John back for a look. "Such a beautiful detail. And it's just here along an ordinary street." Everything in Assisi is primped for a photo.

We stop a passing man and tell him how lovely we think the town is, then ask if the Church helps keep it so beautiful. "The *Church* support the town?" he scoffs. "*We* have to support the Church."

One of Assisi's manicured streets is closed to traffic. Workmen have removed all the cobblestones, which are piled neatly along the sides. They've dug down several feet revealing blue, black, and red plastic pipes running across the open space. They're installing a large, white pipe. At the exposed base of the buildings lining the work area, you can see open conduit that takes the utility services inside.

"What a lot of work this is," I say, watching two men dig with shovels. "Not as easy as in the States where they'd have jackhammers and backhoes."

John nods. "Yeah, we usually have a nice wide berm to work with or, at worst, some asphalt to dig up. Not like the puzzle pieces here." Further along, the street is reassembled and we're taken back in time again.

We walk to where the Roman amphitheater has been turned into a tiny neighborhood and poke into a minuscule chapel built by simple stonemasons nearly a thousand years ago. We admire gracefully curved iron balconies, and huge stone archways. Along steep angled passageways, moss covers the edges of the bricks. Late in the afternoon, my legs are wobbly from climbing up and down, and attractive is now less important to me than horizontal. John suggests we rest at a gelato shop. He remembers one along the shopping street not far from the main square.

As usual, he's ready to order in a few moments, but I like to linger over my choices for at least three minutes, my imagination sampling all the flavors. "Do you want to sit down?" the scooper asks in Italian, nodding toward some tiny tables as she hands over our cones.

"*Sì*," we say together. John waits to pay while I flop into a chair.

"You better enjoy this," he says when he joins me.

"You bet. Coconut is my favorite."

"No, the chair. They charged us two euro *each*, just to sit here."

"You're kidding." We think we're pretty savvy then, boom, we get ripped off. "This isn't even a restaurant. Nothing to clean up when we're finished. She just about *told* us to sit down."

"Tourists. Lots of tourists and pilgrims come to Assisi. They must figure they can get away with it."

"I wonder how St. Francis would feel about that?" I say.

Renaissance artists, philosophers, and architects were obsessed with the concept of the Ideal City. Thomas More's *Utopia* describes it as a social framework, "fifty-four splendid towns on the island, all with the same language, laws, customs, and institutions." He certainly wasn't describing Italy where to this day, cities of every size defend their uniqueness with unwavering stubbornness.

For architects, thinking about the Ideal City was the beginning of urban planning. They began to build in an organized, logical fashion—for function and beauty—rather than just following a meandering cowpath from medieval times. Michelangelo envisioned a city with a sewage system and canals that served as commercial waterways. He designed multilevel streets for different kinds of transport—carriages, people, and unsavory goods. Sort of a layer of subways. But creating the Ideal City was much easier for painters. They could use perspective to execute wide boulevards and vistas leading out to the countryside.

Several Renaissance Italian cities were conceived to embody the aesthetic Ideal. Duke Frederico of Montefeltro built the city of Urbino on a hilltop in Umbria, inviting the finest artisans and architects to participate. Back then, hilltops were strategic defensive positions, and the duke was the Norman Swartzkopf of his time—a brilliant military leader. Because places mean more to me when I can connect them to a story that brings them to life, I like learning about who lived in a castle, who their contemporaries were, how they fit into what was happening at the time, and what intrigues might have happened there.

Duke Frederico has fascinated me since I first saw his portrait—one of Piero della Francesca's most famous. A close headshot, you may have seen it hung facing the one of his wife—in the Uffizi, in an art book, or on a poster. The duke is dressed in red—in a crimson cloak and a sort of pillbox hat. Painted in left-facing profile, della Francesca shows his warts, his gentle eye, and curly black hair. The most outstanding feature though is his prominent hooked nose. There are several other paintings of him that look like their artists pasted della Francesca's portrait onto the bodies they painted. In each setting the duke is in that same profile. It makes me wonder what he's hiding. In one painting, he is shown as a successful military leader, a dented helmet at his feet. Was there a battle wound, a slashed cheek, a drooping or missing eye? I ask a doctor friend from home if his nose was broken. No, he says, it's probably just genetic. The day I find the answer, I feel a sort of exhilaration, a tiny taste of what an art historian or paleontologist or CSI detective must feel when they confirm something they suspected to be true. It feels great.

"Honey, I solved the mystery!" I call, hurrying into the living room of our Parma apartment. "He *was* hiding something. In his youth, he lost an eye and sustained other injuries to the right side of his face during a jousting tournament." So he was a little vain, like most of us, and wanted the world to see his best side—the Renaissance Man side.

On our visit inside Urbino's ducal palace, I'm fascinated by Frederico's study. It's small, perhaps ten-feet square. To a height of about eight feet it's entirely *intarsia*, decorative or pictorial scenes made of inlaid woods. I have a small collection of inlaid wood boxes and I love their complex patterns. But this room is exemplary. An ideal Renaissance Man, the duke studied the classics, mathematics, music, art, ethics, and martial arts—all of which are portrayed here in intricate trompe d'oeil detail. Behind what appear to be open cabinet doors, you can see books with legible writing and scientific and musical instruments including a mandolin with a broken string. There are parrots in a cage, the workings of a clock, statues, and even a life-sized squirrel munching a nut. A faux drawn curtain reveals the duke's armor in a closet and, through a rendered window, you can glimpse the loggia and landscape beyond. These pictures, put together with such precision and authenticity from thousands of pieces of different colored wood, are an amazing example of *intarsia*.

In another part of the palace, we study Piero della Francesco's painting entitled *An Ideal City*. It portrays a wide piazza. In the center is a round, columned structure flanked on both sides by a street of porticoed buildings. Devoid of any life except for two tiny birds, it depicts perfect symmetry painted in perspective. Like a colorful architectural drawing, its precision is beautiful. But I find it cold. I agree with the ancient Greeks who said that people are what define a city, not buildings. When Plato imagined Greek democracy, he stressed that to be good, a city had to improve the physical and spiritual experience of its residents. Duke Frederico understood this and populated his court with the finest humanist thinkers and artists—to create an intellectual ideal.

Urbino today with its lively university *is* intellectually stimulating and architecturally beautiful, but its streets are steep and meandering. An elevator inside the mountain that it caps takes visitors from the roadside parking lot to the bottom of the old town. From there it's still many stairs to the Center. At the end of our day, my legs are aching and my spirits sapped. I'd like to think Plato had something else in mind when he spoke of improving the physical experience.

Searching for our rented Ford, John says, "That car seat is going to feel great. My legs are getting stiff. I couldn't live in a town where you need to take an elevator to get around."

"Right. That hilltop may have been ideal for Frederico, but *we* couldn't live in Urbino."

Growing up in Pittsburgh I never thought much about its hills. I rode my bike everywhere, pumping hard against the grades. If a hill was too tough, I'd simply hop off and push. Back on a bike nearly five decades later, I'm acutely aware of my thigh muscles. So when we approach Sabbioneta, situated between two rivers not far from Mantua, flatness is one of its best aspects.

Tiny Sabbionetta was built as an Ideal City in the late 16th century by the Gonzaga family of Mantua. Planned from scratch, it exemplifies architectural ideals for public spaces—with right-angled streets inside its defensive walls. Today rain is alternating between a fine drizzle and a blistering downpour. We maneuver the narrow streets, most barely wide enough for a single car, and weave back and forth inside the old ramparts—the grid pattern making it easy to get around. I'm realizing that for me, the organization of a city is as important as its culture. A good city needs to be easy to navigate—even though I love getting lost in Venice.

When we stop for coffee, we discover a rambling antique shop. Climbing to the third floor, we find ornate bedsteads, chests, and tables that I picture in castle towers. On the lower floors, we spend an hour picking through clusters of chairs, gilded mirrors, and Italian bric-a-brac. In the courtyard jumbled with artifacts, John is drawn to a marble fountain he thinks would look great in "our next apartment."

"Hard to take home on the plane," I say. But the idea of populating a small place back home with authentic Italian treasures tickles me. Will our "next place" be in Italy or America?

In the end, we find Sabbioneta little more than a village, not a place we would call ideal. And so we head to neighboring Mantua, home of the powerful

Gonzaga family for nearly 400 years. The city sits on a peninsula that juts into three lakes formed in the 13th century by the Mincio river. Parks run all around the perimeter next to the lakes, with tiny boats moored along the shoreline. And, yes, it's fairly flat.

That's probably not why Shakespeare banished Romeo here. In his time, it could hardly have been banishment. The Gonzaga court was populated with artists, musicians, and writers who flourished under their patronage. Opera as we know it today pretty much started here with Monteverdi's *L'Orfeo* in 1607. And my idol Correggio worked here before going to Parma. Mantua just might be an ideal place for us.

Because the 500 rooms of the ducal palace are too daunting for this visit, we walk through the enormous cobblestone piazza alongside the palace to explore the town. Wandering the streets, sometimes under a portico, we catch the nutty aroma of roasting chestnuts and stop to watch a mime near the vendor. Juggling three bowling pins, he's pantomiming for a crowd who laugh and cheer. Not far away we find Casa Rigoletto. Verdi's opera is set in northern Italy in the 16th century. In the Italian version it's set in Mantova under Gonzaga rule. Standing in a quiet garden, the sorrowful, bronze figure of Rigoletto dressed in drooping jester garb begs your pity.

We stroll to the cathedral on one end of Piazza del Erbe. Because it's under renovation, the front facade and altar area are completely shrouded. But the building is so enormous, you could probably fit the entire Gonzaga court or perhaps the population of the modern city inside. Pillars the size of a substantial room support six huge side chapels. But everything is covered in centuries worth of grime. It's too dark and dreary to appreciate the frescos that line the walls, chapels, and voluminous dome. The rounded ceiling of the nave is decorated in a pattern of squares that reminds me of the Pantheon. But it's not nearly as interesting as the leafy green and cameo portraits of Parma's *duomo* ceiling. Perhaps the church's beauty will emerge after the restoration.

On the way out of town through Piazza Sordello, we pass the church of St. Peter. "What a funny building," I say. "It looks like it was created in three different eras." In the rear, an unadorned brick-topped bell tower resembles the plain 12th-century towers of Bologna. Attached to it, the nave is also brick, but crowned with three narrow, pointy peaks and four slim, cylindric towers capped like a witch's hat. This part would be at home atop some of San Francisco's row houses. The white front is baroque. Topped with statues, the central portion is stuck on as a decorative facade with nothing behind it.

"That Gonzaga palace across the street is more my style," I observe. The red brick building has graceful checkerboard arches lining the portico, balconies overlooking the square, and Venetian-style Byzantine windows. "I'd like to live there."

"You'd just like to have all those rooms to decorate—and lots of servants," John teases.

"And what's wrong with that?"

At the edge of the square, I spy a crumbly-looking cake in the window of a bakery. It's about an inch and a half thick and dotted with whole almonds. "Oh, let's get one," I say, pulling John toward the doorway. We inhale aromas of toasted nuts and sugar and emerge with a large *sbrisolona* breaking off small chunks as we head home. It's seriously buttery, and I decide the crunch must be from polenta. As it dissolves on my tongue, I taste a hint of lemon. I wonder if we'll be able to get one in Parma? Probably not. Like so many things Italian, it may only be found locally.

Could Mantua be our ideal place? In 2005, it was named the Most Livable City in Italy—for its green space, air quality, good transportation, and traffic planning. Its streets, lined with buildings of different times and types, somehow work together. The lake gives it an island-like feel. It has culture and great art. So it fits our ideal profile. But I miss the bikes and tree-lined streets of Parma, and *our duomo* will always be better.

The question intrigues us. What makes a place ideal? It's not just what a city has to offer. It's how we *feel* when we're there. Carefree. That's how I feel in Parma. We walk out for a tiny adventure each day. Maybe it's just shopping at the Uns market a few blocks away or riding into the Center in midday to cruise the empty streets before the shops reopen—and then to join the strolling *passeggiata*. Parma feels comfortable, like I belong here. Its rhythm is steady, methodical in its daily repetition.

Struggling with the language means I pay more attention. I'm in the moment, not caught up in the next next thing. I think there's something of a nostalgic '50s feeling here. Not that there aren't problems. Italy has plenty of them. But they seem not to weigh down the simple pleasures of daily living. Life here feels authentic.

Is it all Parma, or is some of it us? Are we changing, learning another way of being? If so, can we take that back home when our year is up?

Every city we visit tries on the ill-fitting Ideal cloak. Sorogna and Fontanellato in Parma Province are our favorite small, castle towns. Quaint and tidy, their palaces define them. But they're really not much more than big villages—not enough to do and far from public transportation. When we were looking to leave Bologna, we read that Todi, in Umbria, had been voted Italy's Most Livable Town. It quickly fell off our list because it could only be reached by car.

Our year nearly up, we rent one to visit places beyond the train lines. Today it's Todi. Like in Urbino, we have to park below the town and take an elevator—this one to Todi's main square. The ample piazza is fronted by lovely buildings and a pink church. Stores, restaurants, cafés, and wine bars line the steep, narrow streets. All the artists' shops are closed though. Maybe they don't open until tourist season. Bundled against the chill, John and I are puffing up an incline when we see a window display with an enormous inlaid wood picture—a battle scene with horses and soldiers fighting and fallen—a wondrous *intarsia* picture. Inside, we see the woodworker.

"It's almost as good as the Duke's study," John says, and pushes the door open to investigate.

The tall man with close-cropped hair and dark-framed glasses is working on an inlaid version of della Francesca's *The Ideal City*. Behind him are life-size color photos of two cabinets in the Ducal Study and, next to them, an Escher drawing that he's using for another project.

"The men who worked on the Duke's Study were real *master* artisans," he tells us. "Each person had his specific role. Masters created the designs, and artisans executed them. Those fellows were the top of the craft. It's the same today. I use artwork created by others, sometimes taking liberties to make it my own." We admire his copies of Leonardo's geometric designs before stepping out to the street again. After the long walk down the hill, we agree that Todi is nice—for a visit.

Using the tiny village of Attigliano as our base, we take day trips to several Umbrian towns. Will any of them be our perfect place? Spoleto is deserted in late February, its artisan shops shuttered. I'm disappointed. I remember coming here with Bonda in the '80s and was hoping to poke through them again. In summer the town is overrun for the Opera Festival, but in early spring there's hardly a spot to get lunch. Our ideal city must be more than a summer place, so Spoleto doesn't qualify.

We started planning our year in Italy thinking we might live in Orvieto. About two hours north of Rome and off the tourist path, it would have been a good place to improve our language skills. Eventually we looked farther north, but we're eager to see the city that might have been our home. Atop a high hill, it's oddly flat and feels medieval—with a wonderful *duomo* of black-and-white striped marble.

The famous Signorelli Chapel is here. A graphic portrayal of the *End of Days* and *Final Judgement* goes all around the room. Some say the figure of the Anti-Christ has the face of Savonarola, the monk who had deposed Florence's Medici at the time the chapel was painted. Earthquakes, tsunami, falling stars, eclipses, and human strife foreshadow Christ's judgement. Rising Christian souls acquire new bodies for their life in heaven, while hideous devils surround the evil ones eager to torture them for eternity. For me, this room alone is worth the trip here.

"We ought to be able to get some great Orvieto wine here," John says late in the afternoon. "Let's look for a wine bar." We walk up and down the crowded merchant streets, poke through funky stores, cheese and pastry shops, and watch the children play in the main piazza. A stuffed *cingale* surprises me as he peeks around the corner of the entrance to a store featuring wild boar. At last, we find a modest wine bar and sample the local vintage. We decide we could have lived here, but easy access to train transport is missing. So this town isn't ideal.

To the north is Perugia, home to the Italian chocolate manufacturer and lately the Amanda Knox trial. While touring the chocolate factory, we meet a class from the *Universita` per Straneri*, the University for Foreigners, where Knox studied. Their immersion program is one of the best places in the country to study Italian. Although the class has a mix of ages and people from several countries, there are no Americans. The instructor, a cordial woman in her thirties with long, dark hair and a throaty voice encourages us to consider an extended class. "Let's think about coming here for a few months at the language school," John says after our tour.

"That's a good idea. The immersion would really help me." Thinking about a return trip has my wheels turning. Perugia is looking ideal.

Perugia's massive *duomo* is fairly plain inside with poor lighting. Only the ceiling is decorated. Here in the Center, the streets are wide and flat. To see the rest of the city, you need to climb. We descend to see an ancient well, then hike what seems like a million stairs up and down the medieval streets. After a downhill trek, we emerge through an Etruscan gate from 300 BC, then follow a winding stairway back up again. Just as we're about to leave in exhaustion, we stumble onto an escalator.

"Before we leave, we have to see where this goes," I say. Down, down, down we ride level by level, passing an exposed ancient ruin in one wall—until we emerge into an underground castle.

"This is pretty cool," John says, exploring a room not far from the landing. "It seems to be built right into the rock." Dramatically lit, the castle rambles on and on. It houses a museum, a school, and several exhibits. But we're still mid-mountain. More escalators descend to the street at the bottom of the mountain. When we emerge, we find just a few apartment buildings and a busy road. This escalator must be for commuters.

Perugia has a friendly feel and, if we had stronger, younger legs, we might just want to live here. At our age, however, a few months at the university is about all we could manage.

We drive through towns nearly a thousand years old. Towns perched on impossibly rocky hillsides. Towns lining dry riverbeds that swell to rushing torrents in the spring. Beautiful towns. One day it hits me: "I can't believe I've never noticed this before. There are no poles. No wires. That's why Italy is so beautiful. All their utilities are underground!"

John scans the landscape. "You know, you're right. I guess when we were walking in the towns, we just didn't notice. Now that we're driving...we can see more clearly."

"Sure, I get it. Clearly."

He's started to sing. "*I can see clearly now the poles are gone...*"

I don't get it. America could be poleless a lot more easily than Italy. And ultimately, it would cost less. On our tiny New Jersey island, storms routinely take down phone and electric service, and the repair crews are out on call for days. That has to be expensive. And yet, all they do is string more cables. Last summer, workers raised the poles and doubled the number of wires. It's deplorable. Our beautiful seashore resort has thick power lines lining both sides of the main road and huge transformers on every other block. "Why so many wires?" people say when they come to visit. "Why don't they put them underground?"

"Italians have a different aesthetic," John says when he finishes his little song. "Look at the highways here. No ugly billboards. Hardly any signs at all. And the ones they have are so small you almost can't read them until it's too late."

"Remember the woman at the B & B we stayed at who told us she wasn't allowed to put a sign at the roadside so people would know where to turn onto her driveway? Italians are crazy with their rules."

"But it does make for gorgeous drives."

Italians may not care much about providing directions, but they do care how their country looks. That's why everyone in America loves to come here— because it's *so* beautiful. Now that we've seen what a difference it makes, we're putting something new on our list. No poles. That would be ideal.

One city surprises us—Syracuse on the southern coast of Sicily. We weren't expecting much. The other cities we visited on this huge island—Palermo, Catania, Gela, and Enna were clogged with drivers who think that traffic signals are mere decoration. White-knuckling the steering wheel, my eyes are scanning every direction in fear of careening natives. I've never felt so terrified behind the wheel. Approaching Syracuse the traffic is quieter. We don't see the expected institutional apartment buildings with laundry hanging from the windows. Instead, the wash is dangling from little iron porches on lovely low-rise buildings, and flowers are abundant on the balconies even though it's barely spring.

We visit Syracuse's archeological park, its Greek theater carved into the hillside overlooking the Mediterranean. The park also contains Archimedes tomb and a huge grotto. In the well-curated museum, we find fossils, pottery, sculpture, and artifacts from prehistoric through classical Roman times. One statue of a man with straining muscles could have been carved by Michelangelo, but it was sculped 1800 years earlier—to me, proof of the reason Renaissance artists returned to the classics for inspiration.

The city Center sits on an island called Ortygia. Its buildings are creamy beige with ornate iron balconies and flowering vines. Their color warms the facades and our spirits. Dark turquoise water laps below the sea wall, and shops and restaurants line the street that tops it. In the vast main piazza, the pavement looks to be made of the same cream-colored stone as the buildings. At one end, the *duomo* is built over an old Greek temple. Instead of obliterating it, the Syracusians simply filled in between the columns. When you enter the baroque cream-white facade, you find another entrance—this one maybe a thousand years older. The interior is simple and serene—the old Greek elements retained. I can imagine coming here millennia ago, dressed in sandals and a flowing wrap, to make an offering to the ancient gods.

Why is it we so often want to erase the past and put our own imprimatur on the places we inhabit? Why the remake of the Pantheon and thousands of other ancient worship places into Catholic churches? On this tiny island where so much human history took place, they seem to have found a way to live with the past, even revere it. But then, like the Godfather, Sicilians *never* forget.

Walking all day—the island is flat—we find the city clean and inviting with charming shops, elegant apartments, and water sloshing at the docks near where we parked. "I never expected it to be so pretty," I say. "The people seem nice. Certainly those fellows where they made the *limoncello* were."

"The sea's wonderful," John replies, looking out over the aqua water. "I could live here and go sailing all the time." Yes, life here would be ideal. Except for the fact that it's too far from the rest of Italy.

One of our favorite movies is called The Golden Door. Felliniesque and visually gorgeous, it is about a Sicilian family who decide to emigrate to the United States around 1900. Shepherds, they come from a town that's just a big rock pile, and they're poor as pebbles. It's a terrible existence. They scrape together everything they can to buy passage to a better life. The town they leave is called Petralia. Sometime before anyone remembers, John's family must have left there too; they moved to Catania. It's very old, Petralia, as we know because we found it on the map of Sicily in the Vatican's 16th-century Map Room. Ever since, we've wanted to visit.

Today, driving towards it, we're looking for that big pile of rocks. We've passed hundreds of sheep on Sicily's rolling green hills. Now a road sign points us to a mountain. But rather than a rock pile, it's got two lovely towns tumbling down its sides—Petralia Sottana in the middle and Petralia Soprana at the top.

Arriving in the former, we're enchanted. It couldn't be prettier. John's father and probably all the folks who built this town were stonemasons, and their fine workmanship shows not just in the carefully pointed buildings but also in the sidewalks and streets. In shades of tan and gray, all the structures are set off with polished wooden shutters and doors in warm, reddish tones. Here and there, trees spring from the sidewalks and mountainside, adding a touch of green. I stop to snap a photo of a particularly appealing home with green French doors on its second-story balcony.

"That's my house," an Italian man's voice comes over my shoulder. "I live there." The speaker is a bit over five feet tall, with thick eyebrows. His eyes are set in dark recesses that make him look like he's wearing sunglasses. He has an impish grin and wears a crisp white butcher's coat over his clothes.

"Your house?" John asks. "Really? *E` bella.*" It's lovely.

"My name is Leonardo," the little man says in Italian. He tells us he owns the tiny market across the street and that he's 78 years old. He's very chatty and rattles on about the town and how he got his house—and points out his balcony in the framed tile picture on a nearby wall that depicts the town's best features. John tells him we're from America and that this town is special to him. Then he takes out his passport.

"*Guarda mia nome,*" he says. Look at my name.

Leonardo squints at the page. I think he needs his glasses. After a moment he gets it.

"*PETRALIA! Il nome della città.*"

"Yes, the same as the town. Maybe I'm the Prince of Petralia."

Leonardo laughs. He's getting more animated. He wants to make sure the Prince sees all the best places in Petralia. He'll take us to his favorite restaurant to meet the owners. They won't believe it. And we should stop at the museum. We can go there before lunch. We should walk up this street and out to the lookout for the best view. Wait, wait, he needs to get his cap.

And so we tour the museum, which is quite wonderful—with an installation of handmade geologic models of the terrain, an earthquake, and a volcano. You turn wheels to make them work—just like back in sixth grade. It was great. Because we're *Petralias*, Antonia from the museum staff gives us a personal tour.

We walk all around the tiny town enjoying its Italian picture-perfectness. Old men have gathered to gossip under a lamppost at a corner. Flowerpots decorate iron balconies and, in what appears to be the main square, there's a humble church with a bright red door and modest bell tower. At lunch, our host and hostess at Ristorante Petrae Lejum bring every patron over to our table to introduce us. Walking back to the car, we bump into Leonardo again. He's no longer wearing his white merchant's coat and invites us to have coffee. Inside a *bar* we share an espresso, and John chats with some of Leonardo's friends—before the three of us exit. Just down the street, three *ragazzi* of about twelve are sprinting toward the soccer field.

"My grandkids," says Leonardo, introducing them one by one. The boys pose for a photo, then hurry off to their game.

With a hug and *ciao grazie, grazie, ciao,* we part company and drive to the top of the mountain—to Petralia Soprana. It's still midday and the town is empty. But it looks just the same as its sister below—quite beautiful. In the center of a wide set of stairs, clay pots with budding flowers sit on every other step. We peek through the open iron gate of a house with a neat garden in front. "I could live *here,*" I say admiring the gracious facade. Just the place for the Prince and Princess of Petralia.

At the crest of the mountain is a large square with a war memorial at its edge. Seated around it are a dozen or so old fellows; this must be the "men's club" hangout. From this vantage point, we look out across the valley and see the road snaking back and forth up the hillside—the modern highway, straight and efficient just beyond it. On another hill, dozens of giant wind turbines spin like kinetic sculptures. "I wonder where that pile of rocks is," John says scanning the hillsides.

"Yeah, I can't see anything that looks like the movie. It all looks green from here." The old men are turning back toward town. Time for us to move on too.

On our way out, we can't stop noticing For Sale signs on local homes. There are plenty of places we could buy here—and at low prices. I guess people are still leaving. I wonder why? Probably there's not a lot of work here.

We laugh about meeting Leonardo, the "mayor" of Petralia. "I never thought we'd find such a nice place," John says, "much less get such a warm welcome. It was really special."

We *are* feeling special, welcomed into this community. We couldn't ride our bikes in the Petralias, but otherwise it was exactly ideal. We've been searching for months for our own kind of perfection. At first, we were looking for convenience, good transportation, and plenty to do. On our feet instead of driving everywhere, we've come to appreciate level streets. And bikes have reclaimed our youthful lightheartedness. That's something we want to hang onto. Music, culture, and learning are still really important to us, and now we're more aware of how the aesthetics of a place shapes how we feel about it. But maybe we've been looking for the wrong things. We still want the physical and cultural, but community, feeling part of a place, being embraced, that trumps all.

BEING GREEN

It is not the strongest species that survives, not the most intelligent that survives. It is the one that is most adaptable to change.

CHARLES DARWIN

It's not easy being green.

KERMIT THE FROG

THOUGH HIS MESSAGE MAY HAVE HAD AN ENTIRELY DIFFERENT MEANING, Kermit the Frog said it best: It's not easy being green.

Then again, Kermit did not live in Italy…or France, Denmark, Sweden, Germany, Switzerland, Norway…or Japan. Kermit, alas, lived in the least green of all the countries in the world—the United States.

According to statistics compiled by the Union of Concerned Scientists, in 2006 per capita CO_2 emissions in the U.S. were 19.8 tons—the highest in the world—compared to 9.6 tons in the U.K., 8.0 tons in Italy, and 6.6 tons in France. Compared to Americans, Europeans are paragons of greenness.

Some of the reasons for this are obvious—smaller cars, more mass transit, shorter distances—and there's that little matter of the price of gasoline. In Parma, we have to pay nearly $10 per gallon. No wonder people here drive small cars.

Based on our experience, it's a lot easier to be green here in Parma than it is in the U.S. For example, our apartment doesn't have a clothes dryer. Nancy hangs wet clothes on two drying racks. In summer, we put the racks outside; clothes dry in less than an hour. In winter, we keep the racks inside where it can take all day. But they do dry.

We have also noticed that the heat doesn't turn on in the fall until you've spent a couple of chilly weeks living in sweaters. The fridge is tiny. It has a small freezer but no ice maker. Because we live near the town center, we don't need a car. We have bikes. If we want to take the train to Rome or Florence, we pedal to the train station, park our bikes, and board a train. Elapsed time: twenty minutes. Back home on LBI, we also have bikes. But, they are for fun or exercise—not transportion. The nearest train station to LBI is 50 miles away. If we want to get to Philadelphia or New York, we have to drive. Both our cars are midsized; in Italy, they would be considered gigantic.

It's a lot easier being green here in Parma than it is back home—where we really, really work at it. Our house is heavily insulated and has three HVAC zones. Our appliances have the highest Energy Star ratings. We try to use air-conditioning sparingly. Our ceiling fans are on summer and winter. We use cleaning products that contain no phosphates or nitrates. We use native plants for landscaping. We don't use pesticides. And we live in a community where there is a fair bit of social pressure to behave in an environmentally responsible manner. We are members of the Sierra Club. And, Nancy and I have worked for years to promote awareness of environmental issues on LBI.

Unlike in America, there's a sort of environmental domino effect in Europe that helps you to be green. When you live in a town where nearly everyone gets around on a bike, for example, you can expect to have facilities to accommodate them. Parma's sidewalks are split into two lanes. The red lane is for bikes, the uncolored one is for pedestrians. Pity the pedestrian who meanders into the bike lane.

All bikes have bells to signal pedestrians. Nancy and I were cursed out more than once when, early in our stay, we made the mistake of walking into the bike lane while wandering and wondering. You haven't felt truly *stupido* until you've been screamed at in an archaic Emilian dialect by an 80-year-old *nonna* in a full length fur coat—barreling down on you at 20 miles per hour all the while *bizzinging* her bike bell. After a few such encounters, we literally fell in line. Now, when we are on our bikes, the shoe, as it were, is on the other pedal. Woe to the pedestrian who blocks our path.

In Parma, the Yellow Pages list 47 businesses that repair cars but 88 that repair bikes. There are also 23 places around town where you can rent a bike for a hour, a day, or several days.

Bet I know what you're thinking. Sure, if no one can afford a car, a bike or Vespa will have to do. Well get ready for another statistic. Not only do Italians have more bikes and more motorbikes per capita than Americans, they also have more cars. Yup, there are 541 cars per 1000 people in Italy. In the US, there are 487. Granted, gas is expensive, cars are smaller, and people drive less. But cars are not just beautifully made here, they're plentiful.

According to *The Economist*, the life expectancy of Italians exceeds that of Americans by about two years. I can't help wondering if part of the reason is that Italians walk more than Americans do. I do know this: it's not because Italians smoke less. That can't be possible. Because from my perspective—admittedly clouded by incessant smoke in my eyes, almost all Italians smoke. By law, they can no longer smoke inside restaurants but because everyone eats outside, the regulation has had little impact on cigarette consumption.

Nonetheless, Italians are healthier and slimmer than Americans. The obesity rate is about one-third that in the U.S. And there must be a law that says Italian women have to be slim as well as beautiful. Please understand, I'm talking Parma—where there's an unwritten law that half of all food consumed must be some combination of *prosciutto, Parmigiano, and gelato*.

When gas costs $10.00 per gallon, it really discourages shipping long distances. In Parma, 80 percent of the food we buy at the markets comes from within a 20-mile radius of the city. The other 20 percent comes from Sicily and other parts of the Mediterranean. There are no Chilean grapes or Maine lobsters to be found. While most Parma stores are small and specific, even the occasional supermarket carries mainly local meat, bread, and produce. Frozen foods, except for ice cream, are practically nonexistent.

High gasoline costs are one reason many people use public transportation. Buses run on natural gas. Clean, safe, accessible, and frequent, they cost one euro to ride. Intercity trains are fast and modern. From Parma, we can go almost anywhere in Italy at very reasonable fares.

Because most Italians live in cities, there is little in the way of urban sprawl. With the exception of Rome, Italy is composed of lots of small and midsized towns surrounded by farms. Parma, Modena, Bologna, Trieste, etc. all are between 150,000 and 300,000 inhabitants. All have similar town centers surrounded by greenery. Each town has its distinct food culture. And the surrounding farms thrive because they have a ready market.

City homes like ours in Parma are apartments. They are smaller than comparable homes in the U.S. Outside the city, you immediately encounter farms where people live in mini-villages composed of a big farmhouse and various outbuildings.

What's the impact on lifestyle? Anecdotally I would say small houses mean people spend more time outside. As a result, restaurants are mobbed until midnight. Lunch takes two to three hours. And, everyone has morning coffee at a *bar*. These are more than places to have espresso and pastry. They are where you go to read the newspapers—several of them—and to socialize, argue politics, gossip, and exchange ideas.

Parma also has something akin to Zip Car called *Io Guido* where cars can be rented by the hour. It's great for occasional shopping at IKEA or going to a late-night concert in one of the surrounding hill towns.

What's the government's role? Throughout most of Italy, the heating of buildings stops between April and October. It's the law. Tax on gasoline is astronomical. In addition, the government has major programs to encourage use of alternative energy, particularly wind energy. Bologna, for example, is spending $500 million on new wind farms.

In short, based on our experience here in Italy, higher gasoline prices in the U.S. may not be so terrible after all. As for us personally, we have managed pretty well without our two cars. We love the freedom of traveling by bikes which make us feel young again. We see much more of the city than we could driving or on foot. Moreover, we get to experience a certain smugness that comes with being green. Kermit would be proud.

MYTHS AND HEROES

Heroing is one of the shortest-lived professions there is.

WILL ROGERS

YOU CAN TELL SOMETHING ABOUT A COUNTRY BY ITS HEROES—AND something more from its myths and folktales. Americans revere sports figures. Italians lionize their musicians. Opera was born in Italy, and the kings of opera are still "rock stars" with annual fetes in their hometowns. August is the Rossini Festival in Pesaro, and July begins the Puccini Festival in Lucca.

October is Verdi Festival time in Parma, when the entire city dresses for the occasion. In nearly every store window stands a costume the opera company has lent. Rigoletto and Gilda can be seen in the COIN department store; an *Aida* prince, next to the elegant tablecloths of the linen shop; an *Il Travatore* soldier among the kids' clothes; a red-feathered hat next to custom shirts; and a yellow ball gown in the *salumeria*. Costumes stand among kitchen appliances, pastries, eyeglasses, even chocolates. Hanging from the arches of the town hall, giant posters announce this festival and in the covered loggia, huge photos of last year's performances, including a graphic rape scene, cover temporary panels. You won't see that at the Met. Verdi arias drift over Via Cavour in the afternoon, and there are concerts all over the city.

In Auditorium Paganini, behind the Barilla Center, we hurry to claim a seat for the free band concert on Saturday afternoon, then head home to change for tonight's opera. We bought the last two seats for *I Due Foscari*, which is based on a true story of the wrongful accusation of the son of the Foscari Doge in Venice. We know our seats are in the pigeon loft but when we sit down my head touches the ceiling. There's absolutely *no* view of the stage. Then again, it's all about the music. The dark story has only three principal characters plus the chorus, so fortunately we won't miss a lot of action.

"I wonder why they don't do this one in the States," I ask John at intermission.

"I think it's too much like Rigoletto. The music is very similar and one of the arias even uses the same words."

I don't know how he remembers that. "I'm glad we can see the supertitles even if they are in Italian. I can make out enough to get the gist of the story and even catch some of the rhymes." (Small victories over this complicated language are important to me.) When we return for the concluding tragic act, the singers are wonderful and the chorus, Verdi's specialty, makes even our cramped seats feel elevated. Verdi has done it again.

Nearly every choral concert in October, or any other time, closes with "Va Pensiero," the "Chorus of the Hebrew Slaves" from Verdi's *Nabucco*. Puccini wrote arias that make you cry. Verdi is master of the chorus, and his work is full of them. Along with *Aida's* "Triumphal March," this one is his most famous. It starts with strings that sound like buzzing bees—so soft you hardly notice. A lone flute twitters like the flutter of a butterfly. Then, *wham*, three full orchestral chords blast your ears. The flutter returns, this time with accompaniment that sounds like springtime. Then everything stops. Softly the chorus begins, a melodic song that in other circumstances could be a march. In the background the orchestra sounds like a beating heart. Rising and falling, the melody swells to full volume, an anthem, whose minor key pulls at your emotions. It ends quietly, repeating a single note six times. Sometimes translated as "Go, thoughts of the mind," the song speaks of a lost homeland with a longing that never fails to bring me to tears.

In Italy it's more than just a beautiful operatic piece. Every Italian can sing or hum "Va Pensiero." Like "God Bless America" is to us, it's the unofficial national anthem. If Giuseppe Verdi were alive today, Womanizer-in-Chief Berlusconi would be out of work and the composer would be Prime Minister.

Opera is often born of real life stories—tales so much a part of culture that they've become mythical. Paulo and Francesca's story is one of these. During our Cervia visit with Teresa and Giuliano we took a trip to Gradara, a castle begun in 1150 that eventually came into the Malatesta family who ruled Rimini. The castle is where their story of fated love takes place. A story known to all Italians—like George Washington and the cherry tree is in America.

In the late 1200s, Giovanni Malatesta, nicknamed Giangiotto, was the eldest son of the reigning family and a courageous soldier. Unfortunately, he was also an ugly hunchback. His father secured the hand of the lovely Francesca da Polenta for an arranged marriage, but Giangiotto knew she was certain to reject him. So his handsome younger brother Paulo was sent to court her. Francesca was well duped and only learned her husband's real identity on the morning after her marriage. She had fallen in love with Paulo and was horrified to find Giangiotto in her bed. Paulo was eventually forced into an politically advantageous marriage as well. Despite these minor obstacles, he continued to visit Francesca when Giangiotto was absent. A secret trapdoor in Francesca's bedroom allowed her lover to enter unseen.

Eventually Giangiotto became suspicious and one evening returned from a trip unannounced. He caught the lovers together and rushed to slay Paulo. But Francesca stepped in front of him and the sword felled both if them. In 1289, Giangiotto was within his rights to kill his adulterous wife and her lover, based on an Italian law that remained in force into the 20th century.

Such a romantic story couldn't die with the pair. Francesca's contemporary, Dante, immortalized the lovers in *The Inferno*'s Second Circle of Hell—the one reserved for the lustful. Like the Foscari tragedy, the lovers' story also inspired a two-act opera by Rachmaninoff, *Francesca da Rimini*, in which Dante meets the lovers in the Second Circle and they tell their fated tale.

Fated love, forbidden love has universal appeal. So does deceit and treachery. Not much has changed in 700 years. The opera's cautionary tale is as true today as when Paulo planted that first dangerous kiss.

Claudia and Silvano, our Thanksgiving dinner hosts, have invited us on a day's tour around Traversatolo. January snow covers the roads and fields as we set out to see some of Matilde di Cannosa's 40-odd castles. Set in a great defensive position, high on a hilltop, the fortress where Matilde brokered peace between the emperor and the pope a thousand years ago is our first stop.

"She was quite the gal," Claudia says as we wander through the information center below the castle. "Beautiful and powerful yet well loved by her people. She did a lot to help the poor and sick."

It's too snowy to climb up to the castle so we drive through the countryside where three or four more of her smaller castles remain. On the way back to our friends' home, the sky is orange and pink, and blue clouds mimic the shapes of the mountains below. It's hard to tell where terra stops and sky begins. When darkness falls, the lights of the villages and farms twinkle like a Christmas miniature railroad turning from day to night. As we drive through town, Silvano points out the Emergency Medical Station station where he volunteers and tells us how they've raised money for two new ambulances.

We pass the evening in front of a fire talking about Italy and America, culture and attitudes, how a thousand years ago a powerful yet kind Italian woman could bring an emperor to his knees but today the chance of a woman being elected Prime Minister is nil. We talk about how things are changing. Today young Italians rarely marry, choosing to live together instead, even after having children. Our hosts' younger son Stefano would like to marry, but too many girls just want to be waited on, he says. When his friends get together for dinner, it's the men who cook and clean up. It's a story we've heard from young men in Parma too.

Silvano shows us the plaque he received for his years of volunteer work with the EMS. "We have a strong tradition of helping our neighbors. It probably goes back to Matilde," he says. "I worked in the ambulance center for many years. Being part of it is very important to me. I don't go on calls anymore, but I still volunteer to work at events and fundraisers, especially ones about organ donation. That's where I met Reg Green. Do you know who he is?"

"No, never heard of him," John says.

"His California family is quite famous here," Claudia says and recounts their story.

In 1994, the Greens were driving in Calabria when their car was attacked by highway robbers. Reg was eventually able to outrun them—but not before the bandits shot several times into their auto, narrowly missing him and his wife. When they finally stopped, they realized their seven-year-old son Nicholas, sleeping in the back seat with his sister, had been shot. Police rushed him to a hospital. He died a few days later.

Random violence is rare in Italy, and the country was stunned. The Greens spoke to the media candidly. Rather than focusing on blaming the culprits, they said they wanted to donate Nicholas's organs and corneas. This second surprise brought the concept of organ donation to the country's attention. Italy's President and Prime Minister met privately with the family to offer condolences and thanks. Seven Italians received the transplants. A foundation created in the boy's name has sent what they call the "Nicholas Effect" around the globe, and Reg Green travels every year to educate people worldwide about organ donation. When he's in the Parma area, he stays with Silvano and Claudia.

"His family changed Italy," Silvano says. "Very few people donated organs before this tragedy. Today many, many people do. Reg and his family are heroes here."

Heroes. An American family turned their personal tragedy into a story and a movement that's saved thousands of lives. In Italy that's what a hero is—someone who touches lives, makes them better. It's the kind of libretto Giuseppe Verdi would have loved, one that would have a stirring chorus. Maybe someday a great Italian composer will write an opera called *The Nicholas Effect*.

ANZIO

Life is what happens to you while you are busy making other plans.

John Lennon

TODAY WE'RE DRIVING SOUTH OF ROME ON ROUTE 7 TOWARDS ANZIO. THE plan is to spend our last month exploring southern Italy. We left the bulk of our baggage at Alberto's hotel in Attigliano where we will return before we drop our rental car at Rome's airport. With two small suitcases, snacks, bottled water, maps, and guidebooks, we're ready to explore.

Our first stop is going to be Anzio-Nettuno—to visit the U.S. Military cemetery where a member of my family from Massachusetts is interred. But something's blocking my vision. "There's a big blind spot in this car," I say.

"How many fingers do you see?" Nancy asks me.

"Huh?" Now she knows there is a problem. I agree, I should not be driving, but in order to stop I have to find a place to pull over. Fortunately, there are emergency pullovers every three or four kilometers.

With our three good eyes working extra hard, I continue to drive while Nancy frantically searches for a vacant place to pull over. A truck blocks the first one we see. The next is blatantly occupied by a pretty, redheaded lady who beckons drivers to stop. She's wearing black fishnet stockings and the shortest yellow miniskirt, and lounging on a bright blue divan. Reluctantly, I drive on. In the next pullover, a woman wearing hot pants and six-inch stilettos is stepping down from a truck's cab. I drive on. Finally on the fourth try there's a vacant spot where we can safely deal with our emergency.

What to do? We agree quickly. We need expert help.

Nancy whips out the thick folder with all our travel papers and retrieves the phone number for my Medex insurance. Before leaving on our trip, we had discussed contingency plans for emergencies we might face. Because Nancy is under 65, she is covered by our regular health insurance in the U.S. Because I'm over 65, Medicare is my insurance, but it does not cover me outside the States. Knowing this, Nancy insisted that I buy supplementary medical insurance, and reluctantly I agreed. As in most things, Nancy was right.

Medex gave us the names and numbers of two ophthalmologists in Rome. The first number we call is out of service. The second is the office of Dr. De Arcangeles. Nancy tells the receptionist our problem. Lucky for us, the doctor has had a cancellation. We arrange to see him at 4:45.

Rather than fight the Rome traffic, we decide it best to continue to our hotel in Anzio, leave our car, and take a train back to Rome. But first we have to check the train schedules. Using her Mac and our handy Wind stick, Nancy checks the Rome train schedule online and determines that trains from Anzio run almost every hour. We have a plan.

Nancy takes over the driving while I try to navigate. Soon we pass a sign welcoming us to Anzio, "City of Nero." A few minutes later, we are at our hotel. Located steps from the Anzio beach where 7000 Allied soldiers lost their lives that horrific Spring of 1944, I know that I will want to explore the battlefield, but this is not the time. Right now, we have a battle of our own to fight. It's now 1:45; we're in unfamiliar territory, and we only have three hours to get to Rome to see Dr. De Arcangelis.

The hotel receptionist is a big help. There are two train stops in Anzio. To catch an express into Rome, we can go to the main terminal located about two miles away, or we can get the local at the stop just 100 yards up the street. Not wanting to chance leaving a car still loaded with luggage at the train station, we opt for the latter.

In less than an hour, we are in Rome where we hop into the metro. At the Colosseum stop we exit and walk several blocks up one of Rome's seven hills to the doctor's office on Via Alberto Sordi.

By 4:00 we're seated in a posh, crowded waiting room. At exactly 4:45, a receptionist escorts us into Dr. De Arcangelis' office. Tall, well built, with gray hair and a white beard, the doctor looks every bit the aristocratic Roman senator. I make a point of thanking him for seeing me on short notice. In English, he says "No problem," then goes on to apologize in Italian for not speaking English. To which I respond, "*No problema.*" The three of us laugh, then carry on in Italian. When he's ready to examine me, he asks Nancy to wait in the anteroom.

After he dialates my pupils, he implores me to look straight ahead and remain still, *firma e diretta.* Using an optical device with an intense light, he takes a close look at my retina. It does not take long for De Arcangelis to diagnose the problem. I already know what he is going to say. *Retina distacco,* detached retina.

As I was to learn, the retina is a layer of tissue at the back of the eye that collects light relayed through the lens. Special photoreceptor cells in the retina convert light into nerve impulses, which are transmitted to the brain. As with all living tissue, the retina is highly dependent on a constant supply of oxygen-carrying blood. When that supply is disrupted, vision is at risk.

Dr. De Arcangelis explains that unless the retina is surgically reattached, permanent vision loss can result. "I recommend you have the operation as soon as possible. There is a hospital here in Rome where it can be done. They have a fine surgeon, Dr. Rossi. If you wish, I can see if he is available."

What to do? This is all happening pretty fast. I tell him I want to talk it over with Nancy. He tells us to take our time, talk it over. Nancy and I conclude that we don't have too many choices. Either fly back to Philadelphia or have the operation here. We ask Dr De Arcangelis for his opinion. He says that a long flight might worsen my condition. He suggests that I meet with Dr. Rossi in the morning. We tell him to make the appointment. If Dr. Rossi agrees, I'll have the operation here. He gives me an eye patch and some eye drops with instructions on how to use them.

Dr. Scipione Rossi's office is located in the Hospital of San Carlo di Nancy (I view the name as a good omen) near Vatican City. Now familiar with the trains, I decide to make the early morning trip into Rome alone while Nancy unpacks the car and gets us organized in our Anzio hotel. Thankfully my eye does not hurt. And Dr. De Arcangelis has assured me that Rossi and his team are tops in the country. If I have any apprehension, it's that my eye patch may make me a target for pickpockets who operate on Rome's trains and in the stations.

From Roma Termini Stazione, I catch a taxi directly to the hospital, arriving at 7:45. I find Rossi's office and check in with a nurse. She already has my records from Dr. De Arcangelis. "Dr. Rossi will be arriving soon. Please have a seat," she says.

Outside Rossi's office, benches are filled with clusters of people. Four have eye patches. There is no place for me to sit, so I stand by a three-quarter life-size statue of the Virgin Mary. Around her neck hang several dozen rosaries of assorted sizes. At the far end of the hall, a woman about my age is sobbing; she does not want to go blind like her father. Her husband assures her that Dr. Rossi will be here soon and that everything will be fine. Another woman, attended by her middle-aged daughter, is quietly saying her rosary. Sitting next to me is a well-dressed man in his eighties; his impeccably groomed white hair contrasts with a black eyepatch. He whispers to me. "Dr. Rossi is the best. This is my third detached retina. He'll fix you up." Somehow, his comment is not reassuring.

No time to worry. As a tall man enters the office door, my white haired *consiglieri* smiles and announces: *eccolo*, here he is. Five minutes later, Dr Rossi emerges from his office. Thin, well groomed, early fifties, he is dressed in a white lab coat and holding a clipboard. He looks around and calls, "*Signor Petralia.*" I say, *ecco*, I am here. He responds, *Veni*, come. I am *first*. Others have been waiting longer. How can this be?

Dr. Rossi's examination is a repeat of Dr. De Arcangelis's. The diagnosis confirmed, he tells me that he can operate tomorrow if all goes well with my pre-op tests.

Dressed in a hospital gown, I am at my first stop: EKG. At least 20 people are waiting here. Most, I learn later, await their semiannual EKGs. Yes, semiannual! We Americans reserve such preventative maintenance only for our cars. My escort, nurse Melena, takes me to the head of the line. Again, for me, it's LIFO—last in, first out. No waiting. I guess Americans get special treatment in this hospital. Pretty nice.

With Melena running interference, we repeat the LIFO routine at the blood lab and again at Administration. In between I meet Dr. Leone, my anesthesiologist. A near double for actor Nicolas Cage, he immediately puts me at ease. Not only does he take time to carefully discuss the anesthesia procedures, he also wants to talk about movies. His favorite of all time? Same as mine. The Godfather. My second favorite, The Music Man, however, earns only a shrug. After a few minutes, it's clear that Leone knows way more about movies than I, especially Italian ones.

"Of course, I've seen The Bicycle Thief, Divorce Italian Style, La Dolce Vita." You know, the standards. But he is amazed that I do not know the works of comedian Alberto Sordi.

"Impossible!" That's when he plays the ring tone on his Blackberry. It's a guy singing an off-color ditty. I laugh but don't recognize it. "That's Alberto Sordi," he tells me.

"Oh," I say, "that explains why they named a street after him." Leone seems to enjoy my fractured Italian. But my comment befuddles him.

"There is a galleria called Alberto Sordi. Is that what you mean?"

That's when I tell him that yesterday, we were at Dr. De Arcangelis' office located on the other side of town—on via Alberto Sordi. Using his Blackberry, he's quickly in search mode. "You are right! Fantastic! Beautiful."

We both laugh. It's a nice moment. All smiles, he says, "I'll see you tomorrow. Remember, nothing to eat after 6:00. Ciao. Ciao. Ciao."

Nurse Melena scoots me back to Dr. Rossi's office. He tells me my preops are all okay. Then he explains the operation. He'll be performing what is known as a scleral buckling—the most common surgery for repairing retinal detachment. After I've had both local and general anesthesia, an inert gas will be injected into my eye—to help push the detached retina back into place. Then a piece of silicone plastic, buckle, will be inserted around the outside of my eye, the sclera, the white part. The buckle does not actually contact the retina but it does serve to deform the eye so that once the retina is pushed back into place by the inert gas, it will reattach. The silicone band is sewn to the eye to keep it in place. When the incision has healed, there will be little evidence of the operation, and the buckle will remain in place for the rest of my life. "I see," I say smiling.

Rossi, all business, does not react except to say that he anticipates that I will have to stay in the hospital for two days. Melena jumps in to add that she has arranged a private room with two beds, one for me and one for Nancy. Wow. This is a far cry from my Bologna experience—in a ward with 19 screaming men and no bathroom.

We arrive at the hospital at 8:00 the next morning, Saturday. A pretty nurse with curly, blond hair and a reassuring manner shows us to our room. Large, with two beds and a private bath, it is as nice as any hotel room we've had in Italy.

There's no time to dally. By 8:20, I am in a hallway surrounded by seven masks. Melena, Rossi, and Leone identify themselves, the latter by playing his Alberto Sordi ring tone, laughing pleasantly. Melena wheels me into the operating room where Leone hooks me up to his bottled sleep. Two hours later, I'm back in my room holding Nancy's hand. She smiles. It's a panacea. I don't need anything else.

I sleep most of the day while Nancy explores a bit of Rome with our local friend Georgina. The night is amazingly quiet for a hospital. A nurse looks in on us twice but otherwise Nancy and I are left undisturbed.

On Sunday morning, one of the surgeons who assisted Dr. Rossi comes in and checks my eye. Unmasked now, he seems awfully young. He speaks little English but reassures me. "The eye looks fine. You'll be released tomorrow." Periodically, a nurse hooks me to a drip of painkiller. My eye hurts.

Lunch comes at noon. Pasta lightly sauced with tomato, a roast chicken leg, salad with olive oil, bread, and a baked apple. Dinner, at around 6:30, reprises pasta—seemingly it's at every lunch and dinner—this time with fresh mushrooms, thin slices of veal, spinach, and a salad. For dessert, a kiwi. Nancy and I agree, it's the tastiest one we've ever had. Later we learn that kiwis are grown all over Italy. What a country!

On Monday morning, Melena escorts me to Dr. Rossi. He checks my eye and pronounces the surgery *perfetto*, perfect. I can go home today but I'll have to return on Wednesday to have my stitches lasered by his young assistant. I'll have to wear a patch, and I'll need two different types of eye drops administered four times a day for two weeks. By the weekend, we should be able to resume our travels, but he advises against my driving for a couple of weeks. Melena shows Nancy how to administer the medication. I thank them both. *Ciao, ciao, ciao.*

We take the train back to Anzio. I collapse for the rest of the day while Nancy works on rearranging our travel schedule.

After breakfast the next morning, we walk to the beach where the infamous WWII battle of Anzio was fought. General Mark Clark's Fifth Army landed here on January 22, 1944. By January 24, more than 30,000 Allied troops were on the beach. Their mission: Go around the Gustav Line, which extended from Tuscany all the way to Naples, and break Germany's grip on Italy. It was a bold plan. The initial landing caught the Nazis off guard, and the first day of the invasion saw only 13 Allies killed, 97 wounded. But instead of moving quickly inland to cut off the Germans as Clark wished, landing force commander General John Lucas opted to build up his strike force on the beaches. Meanwhile, Hitler ordered his generals to smash the offensive. By the end of January, Nazi troops there outnumbered the Allies 71,000 to 60,000.

The Allies eventually built up troop strength to more than 100,000, but for nearly five months the Germans, commanded by wily General Kesselring, held their positions. Entrenched in the Alban Hills, 13 miles away from Anzio, Kesselring's forces pounded the Allied positions with long-range 88-mm and 170-mm guns. Despite overwhelming air and naval superiority, the Allies sustained a casualty rate of 30 percent—the highest of any battle of WWII.

After months of intense fighting, on May 27, 1944, the Allies finally broke out from the beaches and penetrated deep into German lines. Finally on the offensive, the Allies fought with renewed vigor. Victory was at hand.

Unfortunately for the Petralia clan, this was also the day that a brave, American soldier, the son of Sicilian immigrants, winner of a Bronze Star and a Purple Heart, would be killed in the fierce action.

As the Fifth Army moved deliberately along the west coast, the adjacent British Eighth Army made notable gains up the valley of the Liri River, this route affording the most favorable terrain for encircling the German Tenth Army.

The commander of Allied forces in Italy, British General Sir Harold Alexander, wanted the Fifth and Eighth Armies to capitalize on the early successes. From his perspective, the German position was untenable. The Gustav Line was ready to break, and Clark had a clear shot at the vulnerable rear of the German Tenth Army. But General Clark had other ideas.

Instead of driving for the destruction of the enemy army, Clark elected to turn his entire force towards Rome, allowing Kesselring's troops to escape unimpeded into the northern hills. With the Germans gone, the Allies were able to enter Rome on June 4th without firing a shot. On June 5th, Roman citizens were celebrating in the streets and hailing General Mark Clark as their liberator. His moment in the limelight was short lived, however. On June 6th, the Allies landed in Normandy and the Italian campaign became a mere sideshow. Having learned from the Anzio fiasco, the commanders at Normandy knew they had to get their troops off the beaches fast.

Despite the controversy among the Allies about his behavior, Italians look upon Mark Clark as a hero. In the lobby of our hotel, there is a wall with photos from WWII. One shows General Clark entering Rome surrounded by cheering people.

I wonder about his motivations. Could he have easily crushed Kesselring? Is it unfair to call him a glory hound? Wasn't Rome the "prize" of the campaign? Didn't his troops—our boys—need a victory as much as he did? And what about the Italians? Didn't they need a liberator?

On Wednesday, we return to the hospital for the laser procedure that will seal the holes left by the stitches. Based on what Rossi told me, I do not expect much pain. I am wrong. Nonetheless, before we leave, we extend our gratitude to

Dr. Rossi and compliment him on his fine staff and facility. Obviously, proud of his work and the Italian medical system, he doesn't require much prodding to open up.

"You should tell President Obama about the Italian system. In America, you may have great doctors but you are not always practicing good medicine for all the people. You should adopt our form of healthcare. Unlike in America, in Italy everyone is covered—from cradle to grave. Everyone has a doctor. In Italy, the average lifespan for men is 80; for women, it's 84. Americans have life spans that are two to three years less."

I think to myself, it's not Obama who needs to be convinced. It's the average American. In America, we spend 40 percent more on healthcare per person than the next highest-spending countries—Switzerland, Japan, and Norway. Yet our outcomes are not as good. Even within the U.S., there is no clear link between higher spending on healthcare and longer life, less disability, or better quality of life. A 2003 study published in the Annals of Internal Medicine found that Medicare patients who live in areas with higher healthcare spending do not get better results. In some cases, more spending even appears to equate to poorer health. A 2004 study in Health Affairs found that there is actually worse care in states with higher Medicare spending.

Rossi is not finished. "The key difference in our systems," he says, "is that we practice preventive medicine and monitor compliance, not only regarding medicine but also food. Indeed, we consider food the most important type of medicine. We eat a Mediterranean diet. Low fat. Lots of fruits and vegetables. Lots of pasta. Very little meat. People at risk get frequent tests. No charge. Rich or poor, everyone is treated. Oh, sure, one might have to wait for procedures, but for a fee or with insurance such as you have, Mr. Petralia, you can trade up to a higher level of services and better doctors. Many people do."

Yes, I am beginning to see. With both eyes now, I see. Insurance. LIFO. Private Room. Top Doc. I see. I see.

That night in Anzio, we dine in one of their local fish restaurants. For starters, we share grilled calamari served with roasted red peppers and black olives. For the main course, I enjoy a local fish. Nancy has bronzino. Both are served with exquisite roasted potatoes, spinach, and grilled fennel. At the suggestion of our waiter, we enjoy a tasting of three wines—a Soave, a Pinot Grigio, and a Malvese—all very drinkable.

Friday is our last opportunity to visit the cemetery. Nancy wakes me smiling. "Ready to go to Nettuno?"

The WWII Sicily-Rome American Cemetery and Memorial is situated at the north edge of Nettuno on the west side of the Piazza J. F. Kennedy. Wearing a white patch on my eye and still in some discomfort, I follow Nancy into the one-story, brick office building to the right of the entrance. A well-groomed, middle-aged man in civilian dress greets us warmly in Italian. When we tell him we are Americans looking to find a specific gravesite, he switches to English.

"I'm Red Adick, retired Army; I have the high honor to work here." We tell him we are looking for the grave of John Petralia. He finds the name and location on his computer screen. "MIA", he says. "There are 2500 of them here. He will not have a specific gravesite; instead, MIAs are listed on the wall of the missing, at the memorial building." He points the way. Before we take the walk, he suggests we view a short film about U.S. military cemeteries. The film explains that the cemeteries are not maintained by the U.S. government, that most of the maintenance is done by volunteers. Although many are ex-military, most are locals.

The path from the office to the memorial building takes us across gently sloping fields of grass through the main part of the cemetery, where white marble crosses and Stars of David are ordered in the familiar diagonal pattern used by our military. We can see several workers in gray overalls carefully cleaning the markers. Each man has a white cleaning cloth, a bottle of cleaning solution, and a pair of shears. They use the shears to clip the grass close to the headstones where a mower cannot reach. Talking quietly among themselves in Italian, the men move slowly but deliberately from headstone to headstone. Touch. Look. Rub. Caress. Inspect. Caress. Move on. Gently. Gently. Gently. This is sacred ground.

Approaching the Palladio-style memorial building, I'm struck by the solemnity and beauty of the setting. As we pass the columns, we see a lighted circular wall with names of the Missing neatly carved into the stone. Adick had told us where to find cousin John's name, explaining that the names are alphabetical within service branch. And there it is Pfc. JOHN J. PETRALIA, Lawrence Massachusetts, KIA, May 27, 1944. Touching etched letters together, Nancy and I look at each other through watery eyes. We hug and shudder. I say nothing. I can't speak. All we can do is walk about and stare at the names and states of the other heroes.

The landing was led by an Oklahoma National Guard unit so, not surprising, many of the names are Okies. But there are also many from New Jersey, New York, and New England. I don't know why I'm interested in where the MIAs are from. Maybe it's because I feel their names deserve more than a casual perusal. Whatever the reason, I spend a long time looking. All so young. What a pity.

Outside, the sun is trying to break through the clouds. We're heading out the gate toward the parking lot when my phone buzzes. It's Dr. Leone, the anesthesiologist, calling to recommend a movie on TV tonight. *Un Italiano in America.* Alberto Sordi plays a son who travels to New York to visit his gangster father (played by Vittorio De Sica). "It's definitely one of Sordi's best. You have to see it." It will help you understand Italy and Italians. You'll love it."

We chat a bit about my recovery. I tell him that I'm feeling fine, using my drops, and not driving. I don't tell him that we're at the cemetery. We agree to connect again next time we're in Rome. He wishes us a safe journey to Sicily. I thank him profusely for the call. "*Ciao. Ciao. Ciao.*"

Leone's call lifts our mood. What a considerate thing to do. Nancy turns to me and says, "Don't you feel special?"

"You know what? I do. I really do. Special, proud, and very, very fortunate."

OLD DREAMS

Our truest life is when we are in dreams awake.

HENRY DAVID THOREAU

MY DREAMS OF ITALY BEGAN YEARS AGO. SINCE CHILDHOOD I'D WANTED to see Pompeii. In my teens I learned of Venice's *Carnevale*—the original Mardi Gras. When John introduced me to opera, I loved it. We've seen performances in Philadelphia, Wilmington, at New York's Met, and in Vienna. In Prague we saw *Aida*. But the *Aida* of my dreams would be done outdoors—in an ancient theater.

I remember being in sixth grade in a classroom shared with the seventh- and eighth-grade kids. Our teacher Miss Zeil would call each class separately for our English, math, or history lessons. If you didn't want to tune it out, you could eavesdrop on the other class's sessions instead of doing your homework. Because it was about the ancient world, I was always listening in on seventh-grade history. I even borrowed one of the textbooks so I could read about the dawn of man, the Egyptians, Etruscans, Greeks, and Romans. I read every book in the school library about the myths of Greece and Rome—and could name every god, hero, and tortured mortal. The textbook had a bit about Pompeii and Herculaneum—and the disaster that buried them for centuries. These places fascinated me, and I swore that someday I'd see them. Now, stepping off the

249

Circumvesuviana train from Sorrento at the Pompeii ruins, I'm remembering that sixth-grade girl and feeling her excitement again.

The sign at the train station says we're on Via Villa di Misteri, a street called the House of Mysteries. At the entrance to the ruins, we see a tall, red panel with a small photo of one of the many dog mosaics in the city—and a large one showing one of the mutts that lives here. "Adopt A Stray" it says in Italian and English. I'm always a sucker for dogs, but there'll be no taking one home from here.

It's a hot day and John's forgotten his baseball cap, so he folds our extra site map into a triangle and plops it on his head. I'll be walking the site with Tom Terrific, my favorite childhood cartoon whose "thinking cap" was a funnel on his head! Perfectly appropriate I guess as Tom was always with his best friend Manfred the Wonder Dog.

About one-tenth the size of New York's Central Park and as densely packed as Manhattan, a quarter of Pompeii has yet to be excavated. What surprises us is the reason so many buildings are in ruins. I always thought it was the eruption of Mt. Vesuvius, which we see to the west shrouded in clouds like the first puffs of a disaster. But we learn that 17 years before the volcano blew, a major earthquake flattened much of the town. Repairs began quickly, but many of the buildings were still in ruins when they were covered in ash. What remains carries us back to 79 AD. Because Pompeii was a working class town, the eruption preserved the style of ordinary living at that time. Walking here we learn about the first-century version of the life we lead each day in Italy.

We follow the ancient street from the entrance through an archway. Beyond it, the ancient town emerges all around us. Buildings, some completely in tact, bring the city to life. Others, their roofs destroyed in the fires that swept the city, have crumbled. Their heights undulate like waves.

The Forum, bordered by remnants of temples and an immense public administration building, was the city's public gathering space. It's three or four times the size of Piazza Garibaldi in Parma. Along one side under a loggia, stacks of pottery and cataloged boxes fill rows of shelves. Bits of friezes, cook stoves, and marble tables and basins cover the floor. A few eerie, plaster casts of the victims reside here too—two prone figures, a man sitting on a stool, his hand covering his nose, and a dog curled in agony.

The Romans designed their streets well—maybe because they wore sandals. Carts hauled commerce on streets made of enormous flat stones. High curbs kept animal residue off the sidewalks. Crosswalks of stepping stones, with channels cut to allow cart wheels to pass, also allowed pedestrians to cross the street without dirtying a toe or a toga.

Houses of the wealthy were designed with a central courtyard where a pool collected rainwater for the residents. Some of these homes had heated floors and indoor bathrooms. With rooms opening all around a porticoed courtyard, they're not too different from houses in Florida or Arizona today. John and I agree we'd be pretty comfortable in these spacious homes. Inside, Romans showed their love of color. Walls were tinted in tones of mustard, rust, beige, and dark turquoise—with elegant decorations of curlicues, faces, flora, and fauna. Many rooms retain the remnants of frescos showing landscape scenes drawn in *perfect perspective!* Like this buried city, that artistic ability was lost when the Romans fell—until it was "developed" in the early Renaissance.

Mosaics cover many of the floors. The most precious mosaics and frescos were often moved to palaces, sometimes destroying them in the process. But what remains is extraordinary. We see floors made of intricate geometric designs, sometimes with insets of birds or dogs. A few look just like paintings. The one depicting Alexander the Great's victory over Darius II—on the floor of the House of the Faun—is a copy. The original is in the Naples Museum. Its execution is of a style and quality seen in one of those huge 18th century battle scene masterpieces. Charging horses, fallen warriors, tilting spears, and a bareheaded Alexander leading the charge are all nearly life size.

In this middle class town were baths for men and women—with massage rooms and cold, warm, and hot pools. Food stands selling olives, roasted meats, bread and *foccacia*, wine, cakes, and fruit and cheeses lined the streets. Graffiti covered many walls like posters—telling jokes and announcing events. Much of it was political. Pompeiians attended the theater, gathered in the Forum to discuss important issues, and watched gladiatorial battles in the amphitheater.

Walking the streets, lunch in hand, we think the average Pompeiian lived much like the typical, modern Italian. They also lived better than half of the people alive today.

We spend the next day at Herculaneum. The sound of rippling water and fragrance of flowering bushes welcomes visitors to the place the Italians call *Ercolano*. During the eruption it was covered in volcanic mud, which filled the buildings and then solidified. Digging it out here is much more difficult than at Pompeii, and this is a much smaller excavation. The unearthed city sits in a pit 50 feet below ground level. From above we get an aerial view of the site and see the multilevel design with terraces, stone pergolas and gardens. Thanks to the mud, Herculaneum's frescos, mosaics, and building details are much better preserved than those at Pompeii. Even some wooden steps and window frames remain.

Here we get an even better impression of Roman life, this time in a wealthier city. We've stopped our self-guided tour to study our map when a man approaches and offers help. He explains that he works as a guide and he has a badge around his neck, but otherwise he doesn't look especially official. Dressed in dark blue pants and a blazer, a light blue shirt and baseball cap, he needs a shave. His hands have seen years of hard work. But his eyes crinkle when he speaks. Using a hand-drawn map, he offers explanations of what's before us.

He leads us to a house we would have missed and points out the toilet. Next he explains how the sewage system collected urine, which was used to treat wool before it was woven—and also to wash clothes. Imagine the odor. Maybe that's why these folks spent so much time at the baths.

"See these pipes," he says pointing to a few exposed ones along the sidewalk. "They're lead. Many were looted for munitions during the war, but you can see they moved water through the city. Most of the homes had hot and cold running water. Now, look here." He's lifting a No Entrance sign at the door of a partially excavated building and waving us under it. Walking back to the dark brown mountain of solidified lava that encases the rest of the building, he uses a knife to scrape some rubble off. "Here," he says. "A souvenir of the eruption." We know you aren't supposed to remove anything from the sites but a little rubble seems like it would actually help, so we pocket our private excavation. "Now come this way, I'll show you something special."

We follow him to a well preserved building where he again slips us into a "forbidden" door. "This is the Gladiator House," he tells us. "There's a body just inside this locked door—a man who died on a bed." We peek through the slit of the frame and can see a partial body in plaster. "Now, come over here next to these nice frescos and I'll take your picture." We pose beneath one of nude men exercising and again under one depicting the Hercules myth. When we part, he gladly accepts John's tip.

Although we've spent two long days exploring my longed-for cities, it would take years to see and appreciate all that's here. In my youth I considered becoming an archeologist, but the thought of a career dusting bones changed my mind. Perhaps the pursuit of Roman history would have brought me here to study. I'm happy to have finally seen these ancient treasures. More await us at the museum in Naples. As we depart, I already yearn to return for a longer visit.

Venice, city of water and fog, boats and backstreets, power and politics, remains the most mysterious place on earth. But never more so than in the two weeks before Lent when *Carnevale* spreads its bejeweled cloak over the city and everyone wears a mask. I've dreamed of going to *Carnevale* since I glimpsed my first photos of it as a girl. Now, surrounded by extravagant costumes and happy revelers, I'm in *sette cielo*, seventh heaven.

"Oh, look at that feather parasol," I say, pointing to the red and black plumes a crimson-clad woman carries. "And the green and purple one over there." Butterflies, ferns, and a bouquet of cattails are growing from the lily pad on the woman's head.

"I like the gal over there with all the puppets hanging from her hoop skirt. Take my picture with her," John answers, trotting in her direction.

On a back street, we pass an old lady dressed in her everyday attire—a white coat, black tights, and sensible, brown walking shoes. She's put some beads and hot pink plumes on her black hat. It's her partner who's dressed to the nines. Her little black terrier's mustard and brown costume with a ruffled, lace collar is covered in colored beads. The tiny, red hat that sits between his ears is decorated with more beads and purple pearls. I think he's smiling.

The *Carnevale* tradition began around the end of the 13th century when, during pre-Lent merrymaking, masked residents tossed eggs from their windows onto unsuspecting passersby. These simple pranks morphed into a chance for Venetians to disguise their identities for a few days, or weeks, of forbidden frivolity—what Lord Byron called "fiddling, feasting, dancing, drinking, masking, and other things which may be had for asking." The festivities died off after Napoleon conquered the city in 1797, and under Mussolini they were entirely banned. But since their revival in 1979, the celebration has become more elaborate and well attended.

Original costumes were black capes, tri-cornered hats, and pale, long-nosed masks. Today this guise is known to every Italian as *il doctore*, the doctor—the nose a reference to the physician's reluctance to get too near the plague patient. Some people wear half-masks, some carry a mask mounted on a short stick called a baton, and some wear no mask at all. But the classic is a full-face cover designed with no emotion, often white and sometimes decorated with gilt, embossing, or painted designs. When these pallid-faced creatures pose or slowly nod to John and me, it's like being acknowledged by some alien life form.

It's warm and sunny this February, and the Venetian streets are overrun. John and I, wearing paper masks in harlequin gold and black, slip in among the crowd. Along the narrow walkways float silent, costumed figures who stop politely for tourist snaps. None of these masked figures speak. As we near St. Mark's Square, the crowds get thicker and the costumes more "Ah" inspiring. There are tableaus. A group of five hefty men and women are dressed in 17th-century splendor of quilted, brocaded, beaded, embroidered, gathered, laced, and feathered designs—each in dozens of coordinated colors. Another group of five sporting capes, thigh-high boots, swords, and large feathered hats are Musketeers. Four young teens in similar dresses of alternating shades and hats that remind me of the cork on a genie bottle wave their six-inch golden fingernails and smile through their braces.

More typical, though, are the couples. A foppish lord in velvet, lace, and jeweled medallions has a tasseled walking stick in one hand, his lady's hand in the other. Her crimson dress is trimmed with tiny pearls and covered by a billowy coat embroidered with gold.

Another couple are in taupe and aqua floral print. A beauty is in brown velvet, a riot of flowers and dragonflies on the bodice. Her velvet-clad partner stares under a bright orange hat of feathers, beads, and bows. *Carnevale* is a photographer's fantasy. It's hard to avoid stepping in front of expensive long lenses, pocket cameras, and smart phones taking pictures. Along the waterfront beside the Doges Palace, the silent ones pose for the ideal shot—in front of bobbing black gondolas with San Giorgio in the background.

There are outfits that remind me of prickly sea creatures; others have headpieces so large and elaborate I don't know how they're anchored in place. A giant snail slides past us carrying a giggling man with hair piled nearly as high as the two-foot long legs that jiggle atop the snail. Some of these costumes cost tens of thousands of dollars, and I can imagine the fun the designers must have bringing crazy fantasies to life. The wearers peer around pillars and pose on banisters. Some carry costumed pooches. It's like falling down Alice's rabbit hole and finding all the characters in Wonderland.

We wander, mesmerized, snapping photos. Not everyone is wearing Venetian-style costumes. Clowns, rabbits, dogs, bears, and priests mingle through the crowd. Some visitors just wear the Chinese-made masks that are for sale everywhere. "Now *that* must be an American," John says of a stocky, young man in jeans and running shoes. Over his tight-fitting blue parka, he's sporting a huge, red tie with white polka dots and a stars-and-stripes hat.

I catch a shot of a trio of young women, faces white with greasepaint, who could have tumbled out of a tiny Ringling Brothers clown car. "Aren't they darling," I say, as they mug for the photographers. In elegant period costumes and simple homemade ones, everyone is reveling in the fun. Inside cafés lining the piazza's loggia, costumed players sip *caffè* or hot chocolate and smile through the windows for shutterbugs. It's simply magical.

For the afternoon's Best Costume Parade, we gather with hundreds of others in St. Mark's Square and watch a school of poofy jellyfish shaking hands with the crowd—and a tangerine-clad Marie Antoinette with what looks like Tinkerbell twirling in her foot-high ashen curls. "Each one's more fantastic than the last," I say to John, "and we haven't even seen the best yet." I'm jockeying to get my camera aloft among the dozens of others all around me. People are polite and when a few tire and leave, others edge into their places. I hope my one extra battery will be enough.

The big show is about to start so we all turn our attention to the stage where the emcee announces each entrant—in Italian, German, English, and French. First is a woman with a model of St. Marks on her head. Another, channelling Emilia Earhart, is wearing a pink-trimmed black airplane and aviator's cap. A droopy-eyed young man, the epitome of pear shaped, in a three-foot-wide plumed hat clutches his white purse and handkerchief. There's a creature, part architectural drawing, part sea life, with what looks like a shark's fin topping its head and shell coils for ears. A pumpkin-colored Sun King follows, curly red hair and five-foot feathers radiating from his face.

The crowd is packed tight now—talking, laughing, and waving cameras aloft. The square has no room for the famous pigeons. "Look, it's Madeline Kahn from Young Frankenstein," I say to John, about the woman with a silver thunderbolt emanating from her giant mat of black hair. Next a mother-daughter duo—mom driving a Roman chariot, the girl dressed as the Colosseum. The giant snail is here, and a 90-year-old woman who's once again made her own costume—this one a copy of a Klimt painting. When the emcee congratulates her and puts the mike to the costume, her voice is only a muffle.

"That fellow must be the Little Dutch Boy," John says, nudging me and pointing to the charming, red windmill on his head. A couple masquerading as the Trees of Life is one of my favorites. Their brown hair mimics upturned roots, and her green skirt traces her lineage with ribbons of photos. The best so far is a pair who look like Thai royalty—in shades of pink, aqua, green, and purple. I love all their pattern and color. He holds a parasol over the small city that rests on his head; she balances what looks like a temple on hers.

A quartet appears that's stellar—a riot of elaborate, Russian Faberge eggs. The women are wearing those 18th-century gowns that are flat in front and back but extend several feet on each side. The egg motif covers their dresses, hats, and purses. Large fabric egg halves even cap each oversized hip. A bouquet of flowers and eggs caps one man's head, and he carries a brocaded egg baton. The other man wears a turquoise coat trimmed in thick embroidery, rows of peacock feathers, and mink. The design and fabrics are exquisite. They've gotta win.

But no, it's not elegance but The Sewer Rats of Paris who take the prize. Looking more like plush toys than slimy rats, they're clever and there are a lot of them, but *come on*: there's not even one sequin!

Tired of standing for so long, we drift the narrow back streets until we find a local jazz bar. Its ceiling is decorated with the bras of former patrons. The crowd is largely American—or at least English-speaking. We fall into conversation with Mary, an Air Force nurse from Pittsburgh who's stationed nearby. She's in her fifties, single, and tells us she doesn't like Italy. "It's too lonely," she says.

"You've got to take some Italian lessons," John counsels her. "Not the ones on the base, though. There are great schools here in the city where you'll have a totally different experience. We have a single friend who comes here every year for three months to study and enjoy. In *our* Italian classes, we learned so much more than the language. You'd make local friends, and you'd start to feel more comfortable here." She doesn't look convinced.

"You're here in the most magical city in the world," I plead. "For three years! I'd kill to have that chance. You've gotta do it."

Her eyes drop to the wine glass she's absently turning back and forth. "Maybe."

"Mary, I grew up in Pittsburgh just like you. For me, going to New York City and the seashore was another world. As a kid, I thought I was a sophisticated east coaster. It wasn't until I'd moved to Philadelphia that I realized how midwestern Pittsburgh really is."

Our hometown is something she can agree with. "Pittsburgh's a great town. Always has been," she says with gusto.

I click her glass with mine. "I never got the chance to travel outside the States until I was in my thirties. But as you're finding out, living in a foreign country is really different from visiting it. You get a chance to see how people in other cultures spend their time, what's important to them, how different things are from home. Discovering differences is part of the fun. Every day is a little adventure, a new challenge to overcome. For me that's invigorating. We feel so lucky to be here." I'm on a roll now—can't help myself—so I push into tenuous territory. "One of the things we like best is learning what foreigners think of America. Getting our own impressions, not filtered or packaged by the media. I'd think that would be important to someone in the military." I can tell by how she's looking at me that she doesn't think about that.

"Italians love Americans," John adds, "especially when they try to speak the language."

She tells us half-heartedly that she'll look into it, but I think she just wants to find a new topic. I feel sorry for her. Here I am in my sixties trying to experience as much of the world as I can, wishing I'd started earlier. To be stationed abroad and not take advantage of that chance, *che peccata*, what a shame.

Our Venetian Chamber of Commerce duties over, it's now time to head back to St. Marks for the evening's Drag Queen Show. The most famous queens from all over Europe come to compete for the prize. The show is campy, gaudy, peacockish, and flamboyant. Each contestant, maybe 25 of them, parades up and down the stage, sometimes with a dancing or singing routine. Some come with escorts; others have entire entourages with props and breakaway costumes. It's a very funny show. In the end they declare two winners—one an opera-singing space alien and the other in red sequins and hair from Mad Max. What amazes me is how well-behaved the crowd is. They're patient and quiet, shouting only to ask the participants to turn toward their cameras. Back home, the cat-calls would be deafening and the audience full of rowdy queens. Not in Venice, the birthplace of extravagant dress up.

Taking a break from the costumed festivities the next day, we visit the tiny island of Burano—just a 30 minute *valporetto* ride from Venice. At breakfast, our B & B hostess recommended it. When the boat docks, it's a storybook sight. Small, colorful homes huddle around a small park where a seated, bronze nude leans longingly toward the sea. Once a thriving fishing village, the homes' owners painted their facades in pinks, greens, blues, yellows, and oranges, each different so the fishermen could identify them while out at sea. Today, they form the most vibrant and welcoming village we've seen in Italy.

We follow the crowd toward the central part of the village, down a narrow passageway lined with shops. Outside each hang gorgeous lace blouses, skirts, dresses, and table linens. More than for its colorful facades, Burano is known for lace. This is the first time I've wanted to buy everything in sight. The doors of a large shop are thrown open, revealing clothing arranged by color throughout the store. Seated prominently facing the doorway is an old woman dressed in black, working a lace pattern in her fingers.

"Oh, we have to come back here," I call to John who's already several steps ahead of me. Shopping will be later. Now we're off to explore. Like Venice proper, Burano has no motorized vehicles. Small canals slither through the village and pretty *ponti*, bridges, cross them here and there. Today the tide is high and on many of the wide sidewalks, water sloshes up from the canal and pedestrians pick their way on tip-toe.

Though the February weather is delightful, the crowd is minimal. We enjoy poking into the stores along the main canal but quickly move on to see the rest of the island village. Our hostess recommended a restaurant called *Gatto Nero*, Black Cat, and we want to locate it for lunch, later. Ambling down the streets, we think there must be some written or unwritten law that homeowners follow. First, all the shutters are painted the same shade of dark green, unifying an otherwise crazy quilt of color. Second, everyone hangs wash from the windows creating a stereotypic Italian photo op.

We happen into a large square where children are running in circles shrieking and giggling. On our left is the *Museo del Murletto*, the lace museum we want to visit. I'm disappointed that it's closed. For centuries, when the fishermen went to sea, the women of Burano passed their time making lace—the most beautiful lace in Italy. Now, with the remaining practitioners well into their seventies, the art is almost lost. So the government started a school here to teach the craft to young people. Too bad we can't see what it's all about.

Along one of the canals, a trench is being dug. We cross over the *ponto* and ask some locals what's going on. "We're installing a drainage system throughout the island," says a man wearing a woolen cap and tall yellow rubber boots. "When it's completed it'll prevent the water from swelling over the walkways. It can get pretty bad in winter." Venice's never ending battle with the sea. I wonder if they'll stay afloat.

"Can you tell us the way to *Gatto Nero*?" John asks.

His answer sends us in the opposite direction. Luckily, the entrance is well marked with a large awning sign and a marble black cat sitting on an outside table. Inside, it's casually elegant with lots of old wood, white linen tablecloths, and framed paintings covering all the walls. I'm intrigued by the unusual dishes on the table. We've now seen enough of the town to realize that the buildings painted all around the rim of the plates are the ones in Burano. At their base is the blue canal, and the same blue on the edge of the plate suggests the sky. They're quite beautiful.

"I bet they're made by a local artist," I say to John, "or maybe they're from Vietri or Deruta." I ask the owner.

"Each plate in the setting has a different design," he says with pride. "So many people have admired them that we sell them in the shop next door. They're made for us in Germany."

Germany? Aren't the Italians famous for ceramics? Yes, but not in the Veneto. And Venice was once part of the Austria-Hungary Empire.

Lunch is scrumptious, our fish just hours out of the water. Afterwards we head back towards the *valporetto* stop—and that great lace store. The old woman is still at work. She wears a gray wool jacket piped in red and a sort of soft top hat with a pink plume jutting out. She has a kind smile when I bend down beside her to take a better look at the piece she's working on. It looks to be eight- or nine-inches wide and less than two feet long.

"This is a very old pattern," she says in Italian, obviously used to explaining her work to visitors. "I'll work on this section for several days until it's finished.

Then I'll pass it on." She turns the piece slightly to start another part. Her needlework is tiny and elaborate. "It takes eight women to complete the pattern. Each of us specializes in a particular design stitch."

"And how long before the piece is finished?"

"About a month."

Eight women. A month of work. No wonder handmade lace is so pricey. I browse through the exquisite blouses around the store—each one unique. They're expensive but not outrageous.

"Is this lace made here?" I ask the clerk.

"This is machine lace," she replies. "It's still very beautiful but much less expensive to produce. It's more and more difficult to find people interested in the old art." I look back at the old woman and wonder who will want to perpetuate this tedious work.

"Try these on," John says, bringing over a few pieces he's picked out. So I spend the next hour reveling in magnificent, lace blouses and skirts—finally choosing a design in black and brown that I can pair with jeans or velvet.

Back in Venice on the way to our hotel, I spy a pair of shoes in a store window. Like most women, shoes are my weakness and I've restrained myself for months. "Oh wow, they're *so* gorgeous." Low-heeled and made of three colors of delicate suede, I can't wait to try them on. The store clerk, dressed as though for an office, patiently brings out pair after pair until I find the ones that fit just right. "They're amazingly comfortable," I tell him after pacing back and forth around the store. "I feel like I could walk in them all day."

"They're manufactured for us at a small factory not far from here. Their designs are beautiful and well made, and they understand good fit. You'll have no problem with these."

And so, we make a second expensive purchase. But this is Venice and, for us, the best values we've found for high-quality goods. You just have to be careful and buy from Italians. Heading back to our hotel to get ready for the evening's entertainment, we pass shop after shop of touristy glass and Chinese-made, "Venetian" masks. Inside, Asian faces greet the tourist trade. Like the rest of the world, Italy is changing. I wonder what it'll be like in 20 years.

We return to San Marco for the evening spectacle and somehow manage a spot right next to the stage. The night is black—no moon. The only light comes from the performers on the stage, *Ballo con Fuoco*, Dance with Fire. Bare-chested men hurl great flaming balls back and forth. Women dance, dishes burning with fire balanced on their heads, while twirling huge, fiery wheels. They pour a liquid onto the stage and light it...*whoosh!* Flames everywhere. Dancing together, pouring burning liquid all around them, the ovenlike heat bakes our faces. In the finale, the stage is ablaze with sparklers shooting along the sides. A 12-foot, bubbling sparkler fills the center, and all the dancers are twirling a half-dozen flaming batons. It's a scorching performance.

When the crowd disperses, we search for a place to sit and are drawn to a small café a few blocks from San Marco that looks especially welcoming. Behind the bar, a white-mitered pope is serving drinks and dancing to the pop tunes on the sound system. His assistant, dressed in black with a whip in her back pocket, struts her own stuff to the music. Three masked young women in a corner pucker up for a photo. We find a table near the wall and watch people drift in and out enjoying the spectacle. A big group comes in, one a skinny guy in flamboyant drag—long streaked hair, black stockings that end below his skirt, mascaraed eyes, and bright red lips. He hams it up draping an arm around an unsuspecting patron, whispering into his ear. While everyone laughs, he follows a bald-headed man towards the door, lips pouted. He plants a kiss on the back of the man's neck, then turns and makes a demure toast. *Salute!*

We chat for a few minutes with a young sales exec from Charlotte who's missing home and his wife. I understand. This is the kind of experience you want to share. The music rocks. We dance and sing with the crowd and toast with the other revelers. *Carnevale* is everything I'd hoped, a constant play of exotic and crazy characters, heaps of fun, but most of all, a fantasy shared with John. We've chuckled at the outrageous costumes, posed for photos, and relished the chance to speak with other revelers. In our silly paper masks, we've enjoyed ourselves as much as the wealthy, costumed merrymakers. My favorite memories won't be of Mummer-like costumes floating along canals but rather of foggy alleyways where two harlequin-masked seniors stole a kiss, and my *Carnevale* dreams came true.

Searching Google for opera performances in northern Italy, I find a listing for Verona...in an *amphitheater*. They're doing *Aida* in mid-August. That's my dream! I purchase tickets and start planning a two-day getaway.

At an important intersection of roads along the twisting Adige river, Verona became a Roman colony around 90 BC. Variously dominated by Goths, the Italian kings, Emperor Maximilian, and Napoleon before coming under Austrian rule, foreign control ended with Italy's unification in 1866. City architecture is a mongrel mix of this past. Entering the town we pass under the Porta Nuova, built by the Romans and updated by the Austrians. I wish the Austrians had left it alone. The Roman structure, white marble with columned pediment and three arches, has been topped with an incongruous Austrian coat of arms. Beyond it, a wide, tree-lined boulevard leads to the old Roman center. "It's like Paris," John says as we stroll in the shade.

We cross under two gigantic arches and enter Piazza Brà—Verona's central square. It's full of ambling visitors and only a few cars. On our left, restaurants curve gently around the enormous space—long, green awnings shading the patrons. We know the amphitheater is here, but we can't see it for the tall pines of a park in the piazza's center. Beyond the park, there it is—two stories of pink, marble arches echoed in the swirling cobblestone pavement. The 2000-year-old structure is the third largest amphitheater in Italy and the only one still in use. "It's fabulous, isn't it?" I say as we survey the massive walls. "If we lived here, we could go to every performance."

"Funny, isn't it," John replies. "This place is still in use but we had to build the Eagles a new stadium after only 30 years."

"So far, I love Verona. I just wonder how many tourists it attracts, what with the opera and Romeo and Juliet and all." For us, tourists mean too many English speakers, not enough chance to practice our Italian.

"Let's see how the city looks further on. We'll be back here tonight for the performance."

We find Verona nothing short of charming. Piazza Erbe, the old Roman forum with it's still functioning fountain, is surrounded by old palazzos. Casa Mazzanti, former home of the Della Scala family, is frescoed on the exterior. I can only imagine what the inside must look like. Set among the dozens of white tents shading vendor stalls that cram the square are bronze statues, an ornate stone column, a magnificent clock tower, and the Venetian lion atop a pillar. I pick out a wooden fan at a stand hoping it'll wave off some of the oppressive August heat.

Crossing under the archway into Piazza dei Signori, we look up at the whale bone suspended from the middle of the arch. Legend says it'll fall when an honest man passes beneath. When we walk through the bone doesn't even wobble. Kings, heroes and even popes have passed here, and it's still hanging. If it did fall, the Just Man would be unjustly clobbered.

Verona's most famous tourist attraction is Juliet's house. Shakespeare's fated teenagers may have been fictional but the the city isn't above cashing in. Someone thought this comely courtyard with its picturesque balcony would do the trick. Thousands traipse through every year leaving the arched entrance covered with amorous graffiti, notes, and letters. It's fun to watch folks wave from the balcony to cameras below or jostle for a snapshot next to Juliet's statue. John steps up on her platform and cups her right breast—the traditional "touch for luck"—and I manage one shot before another man steps into my frame.

We spend the rest of the afternoon wandering the residential streets, visiting several churches and the *duomo,* and taking a stroll beside the river. We poke into open garages with medieval wood ceilings and checkerboard archways, and stumble onto a simple dwelling with a bronze bust and plaque announcing Romeo's House. On another street, we pass under a three-tiered Roman arch and are surprised to find a huge, white statue of an acrobatic woman. Balanced on her elbows, her back is arched and her feet rest on her shoulders. It's a wonderful city.

As twilight settles over the amphitheater, the temperature is still in the high 80s and I'm glad for my fan. When we enter, we're given candles, the kind we light in church on Christmas Eve. People file into the 15,000 or so seats, and I congratulate myself for paying extra for real seats—not the ancient concrete. The orchestra begins and everyone lights their candles, pricking the darkening night with thousands of tiny flames. John reaches over and takes my hand, giving it a soft squeeze. "Happy?" he asks. I feel my eyes start to water and look quickly up to the sky, blinking fast. I'm beyond happy. I'm *here* living my dream. I'm still having a hard time believing it.

One end of the ancient stadium forms the stage. Egyptian hieroglyphics decorate three-story pillars and 40-foot obelisks. Sphinxes guard either side. Soldiers ring the amphitheater's crown and stand at attention on two lower levels. Among tall palm trees, hundreds of slaves, priests, more soldiers, and the royal court barely fill the space. The acoustics are perfect and we can hear the voices—some of the best in the world—with no trouble. I feel Verdi's music lift and pull on my heart as it floats through the night air.

At the beginning of the second act, the famous March includes a ballet—its star as lithe and graceful as a firefly lighting the stage. The March concludes, not with elephants, but with four prancing, white horses who bow before the king to a collective "awwh" from the audience. In the final act, in which Aida and her prince are entombed together, an enormous striped canopy unfurls over the massive stage. Their haunting duet, clear and plaintive, brings tears to both our eyes. Tonight is everything I had imagined.

On the way back to Parma, we chat about Verona's attributes. There's all the culture we could want, good food, shopping and, beyond the central tourist area, parks and charming, quiet places to live. The scale of the Center even minimizes the tourist impact, and the city feels welcoming. "I'm not ready to give up Parma," John says, "but Verona is someplace I could live."

"I agree. It's a lot bigger but it doesn't overwhelm you. It feels really livable. And there's the opera."

"But I still say there're too many tourists."

I'm drawn to the view of the countryside as we pass small, country homes where neat rows of vegetables and grapevines cover almost every lot. People are working in some, digging or weeding by hand. The train passes through villages and small towns with their familiar stucco or stone buildings and red tiled roofs—the church's bell tower always the tallest structure. The rootedness of this country appeals to me. I feel comfortable here. My dreams of Italy now realized, perhaps it's time for another dream.

WHAT'S THE DIFFERENCE?

French habits and manners have their roots in a civilization so profoundly unlike ours—so much older, richer, more elaborate and firmly crystallized—that French customs necessarily differ from ours more than do those of more primitive races.

EDITH WHARTON

WHAT SURPRISED YOU THE MOST? IT'S A QUESTION WE GET A LOT. BUT it wasn't until we nearly finished writing this book that I could formulate a reasonable response. Here it is: By living in a foreign culture for just one year, I learned more about America than I had in all my previous time on Earth.

It works like this: you're in a foreign land. It could be France, Germany, China, anywhere. For us, it was Italy. Things are different there. You realize early on that Italy is not going to adapt to you. If you're going to make the most of your time there, it's you who will have to change. Easier said than done.

It's not like throwing darts where you can see the bull's-eye. Before you can adapt, you have to understand the rules—the way things work—and you need a point of reference. That's when it happens. Click. You start making comparisons.

In Italy, gasoline costs three times what it does in America. At $10 per gallon, is it any wonder that so many people drive motor scooters? That's when you start to notice that what you drive impacts what you wear. If you're going to drive a motor scooter, by law, you have to wear a helmet. I don't know if driving motor scooters is the reason so many Italians wear tight-fitting clothing or if wearing helmets makes them favor short hair—even the women—but it makes sense. I wonder if Americans drive large cars because we are fat. Or, do we somehow grow into the size of our cars?

Facial hair is another thing. My guess is that 75 percent of adult Italian males have some sort of beard. Not a heavy Sigmund Freud beard. More like George Clooney between movies. You know, ruggedly casual. That's the typical Italian male look. Facial hair. Could it have something to do with having their faces exposed to elements while driving a Vespa? I don't know.

Along with their short hair, women wear little makeup. I'm not sure why, but somehow, it makes them seem less pampered, more self-assured, sexier. I like it.

In Italy, you notice that people seem to take a lot more time eating dinner, drinking wine, and arguing about politics. You observe a young mother at an outdoor café. She's smoking a cigarette and having a glass of wine; her toddler is exploring Garibaldi Square assiduously trying to catch pigeons as bicyclists zip by. In Philadelphia, there would be no square; the mother would not be smoking; the wine would be Starbuck's latte; and the child would be screaming to escape confinement from mom's clutches.

Indeed, time appears as a common denominator in much of what I see as differences between our cultures. Whereas Americans might speed up the production line to make things faster and thus cheaper, in Italy the focus is on quality. A new Ferrari is always faster, never cheaper. In medicine, we tend to put more resources into treating symptoms whereas the Italians are more concerned with prevention. We have drive-in movies, drive-in restaurants, drive-in banks, and even drive-in churches. In Italy, people may drive fast but never to a drive-in. America has two political parties. In Italy, where there are more than 40 parties, gridlock is cultural; change is glacial.

Walking the streets, you notice that Italians give themselves the permission and the time to notice you. I'm not saying they look you up and down—nothing that overt. Their gaze may last only milliseconds longer than an American's—but there it is. You not only see it, you feel it.

In Italy, when I look at a beautiful woman passing by, there is that magic moment when she steals a look back. In everyday transactions between men and women, sex lurks just below the surface. If you want to know why Italians live longer than Americans, it might just be that...that extra look, that extra bit of time.

In Italy, aesthetics and function are not viewed as separate concepts. Utility lines are buried. I know it costs a lot more to bury lines than to mount them on utility poles but, to an Italian, utility poles are ugly, unhealthy, and interfere with parking.

In America, our bananas come from South America and our lamb from New Zealand. We're all about world trade, globalization, commerce. In Italy, it's all about local and regional food. Italians are content with what's local and what's in season.

In Italy, churches are everywhere. Even small towns are divided into parishes. Church bells toll on the hour and half-hour. Italians like the sound, the symbolism. They like crucifixes in public buildings. They like Catholic schools, religious holidays, and statues. They like holy cards, long processions, and streets named after local saints. They like nuns and monks to wear traditional habits. They baptize their children. They like being the center of Roman Catholicism, and they like having their pope in Rome. What they don't like very much is going to church and receiving the sacraments. Save for Christmas and Easter, attendance at Sunday services is practically nonexistent. The Milan Cathedral, one of the largest and most beautiful edifices in the world, serves a total of 80 parishioners. The cathedral in Orvieto is so large, it is said to be able to hold all 40,000 of the town's residents. During a Sunday mass, we counted 23 worshipers including a Japanese family of four all wearing identical *Hello Kitty* caps. Isn't it curious that in a country where the lines between church and state are purposely blurred, the thing that suffers the most is faith?

In New Jersey, it's not uncommon to see a standard with Italian and American flags flying together. I'm not sure why, but in Italy, the Italian colors are rarely seen except on government buildings. I'm not saying Italians don't have national pride. Have you ever seen their behavior during the World Cup? Maybe it's because there are so many government buildings. Maybe it's because

Italians have other ways of demonstrating their nationalism—sports, movies, food, design—or maybe flags interfere with the way they hang laundry. I don't know. I can tell you this. I fly only an American flag. But I do have a variety of *futbol* shirts, including one that says *Italia, World Cup Campioni.*

I've always been a jazz fan. Unfortunately, in the States, jazz is pretty much dead. It's given way to Hip Hop and Rap. Kanye West, Beyonce, Lady Ga Ga, and Jay-Z may be your cup of tea. But, as they say in the song, they're *not for me.* Give me John Coltrane, Johnny Hartman, Mose Allison, Satchmo, Ella, and Nina Simone.

In Italy, jazz is thriving. If you hear someone refer to the Count and the Duke, they are more likely referring to Basie and Ellington than two guys in a painting by Raphael. In Parma's Piazza San Francesco, we heard concerts celebrating the likes of Monk, Armstrong, Kenton, and Dorsey. In Bologna, we frequented Club Chez Baker (in honor of Chet). In Roccobianco, we heard trumpeter Fabrizzo Bosso. When I closed my eyes, I heard Clifford Brown. How great is that!

For me, the comparisons are unavoidable. It's not that I'm looking for them. It's more like they're looking for me. For example, when we tell our American friends we love living in Italy because of the food, wine, art, music, museums, history, ambiance, and the people, they invariably bring up the E word. Isn't their economy in terrible shape? That's when the debater in me goes on the attack.

It depends on how you measure well-being. To me, it's not simply GNP. It's much more than that. On average, Italians live about two years longer than Americans. Healthcare in Italy is free; so is higher education. Italian workers get six weeks vacation. Their literacy rate is comparable to ours. Their income disparity is lower than ours—the ratio between the poorest 10 percent and the wealthiest is only 11:1. In the U.S., it's 16:1.

Italians are much more green than Americans. Solar and wind power, which already supply more than 10 percent of their electrical needs, is growing at 20 percent per year. At current rates of adoption, almost all of Italy's electrical power will come from renewable sources by 2025.

Green or otherwise, Italians use far less energy to produce each unit of GNP than we Americans. Of all the developed countries, the U.S. makes the least efficient use of energy. Every unit of GNP produced by an American is the energy equivalent of what is produced by two Europeans, four Chinese, 17 Indians, or 240 Ethiopians.

I'm not done. Only about 20 percent of Italians are obese. In America, the rate is closer to 60 percent. A recent study by the Center for Disease Control predicted that if current trends continue, 83 percent of men and 72 percent of women will be overweight or obese by 2020. As good as the science gets, we may not be able to make headway against related diseases without changing people's behavior.

Go to Italy to lose weight? No such luck. After living like Italians for one year, Nancy and I arrived home weighing exactly what we did when we left.

HOME AGAIN?

One's destination is never a place but rather a new way of looking at things.

HENRY MILLER

And one more thing...

STEVE JOBS

BEYOND THE PLANE'S TINY WINDOW, I WATCH THE NIGHTTIME LANDSCAPE change from black to glowing as neat rows of yellow-orange lights stretch far into the distance. Newark, New Jersey. My heart, along with the British Airliner, sinks towards the ground. Already I'm missing my adopted country.

"Well, we're home," John sighs when the wheels touch down.

Or are we? Nothing could have prepared us for how profoundly different we've become. Things we took for granted all our lives, now questioned, reexamined. Things we strove for all our lives, now less important. Living in another culture, not just visiting it, has reshaped our view of the world. Driving home with friends, we see our American landscape anew.

"Oh my God. Gas is really cheap here," I say as we cruise down the Garden State Parkway.

Imagine thinking that $10 petrol is a *good* thing. Now we understand how high-cost energy molds a country. Italians turn lights off—and heating too.

They embrace alternative energy. Their smaller homes mean less of everything. Less clutter. More focus on necessities and what's important. This means more time spent outdoors and in public places. People move about with a shared sense of living in a locale, a feeling of community. Great public transport makes it easy to get around in the city and inexpensive to travel. We lived happily without a car.

Our conversation with Susan and Sy, who met us at baggage claim, hasn't skipped a beat. "You'll come to dinner in a few days," Susan insists. "I'll make a leg of lamb for you."

Leg of lamb will be a treat. It's something we haven't eaten in a year. We ate lamb chops occasionally, but mostly pork—the most flavorful pork we've ever tasted. Lots of cheese. And all kinds of fresh fish. There's no hope of finding thin-sliced *polipo*, octopus, at our local ShopRite.

When we enter our home, we feel oddly profligate in its large, high-ceilinged great room. Our beloved Parma apartment, where we hosted a procession of visiting friends and relatives, would fit three times in our 3000-square-foot home. We've grown accustomed to living smaller and more simply.

At night we snuggle into our Tempurpedic, thankful that in America the heat isn't turned off in April. When I close my eyes, Renaissance portraits, hilly village streets, and softball-sized lemons float through my mind. I conjure our magnificent Parma cathedral, the tunes of the accordion man, and flying down Via Farini on our beloved *bicicletti*. Faces of the friends we've made, of John's Trieste family, and our favorite merchants smile through the darkness from across the ocean. Neither of us can sleep.

I reach for my iPod and start my favorite playlist. When the first familiar notes of Verdi's "Va Pensiero" begin, I hand John one of the earbuds. Lying together, listening to the now so familiar rise and fall of choral voices, I feel submerged in a pool of water, just under the clear surface, not sure whether to rise or sink. Tears fill my eyes as I listen to the Hebrew slaves..."*go, thoughts of the mind.*"

"I want to be back in Parma," I whisper.

"I know. I never expected to feel like this."

"I guess we have to wake up from our dream sometime, but I want us to stay in it."

He hugs me tighter to his chest. "It was a wonderful year."

Forcing a smile through my tears, I give him a kiss. "The *best* year."

Next morning, shopping for supplies, our Blazer feels gargantuan. No need to check our watches, the stores are open all day. The Jersey landscape is both familiar and odd. "Hey, no Vespas," John says as we drive along Route 72.

"And no buzzing motorcyclists weaving at 60 miles per hour."

The road is wide. No one blares a horn. No one careens in front of us. No one ignores the one-way signs or the traffic signals.

On the radio, we hear words in our native tongue. The news brings more updates on the healthcare legislation. The Public Option, which should have made healthcare available to everyone, has died. We'd followed the debate closely—both online and on TV. The vitriol was embarrassing. Our Italian friends couldn't understand what the fuss was about. "Everyone gets taken care of here," they said over and over. "Why doesn't *America* want to do the same?"

Our experiences with the Italian health system shaped our response to the debate back home—and not in the way we expected. We thought we'd be dismayed by Italian healthcare. Not so.

We pass the usual fast-food options along the way. KFC, Wendy's, Sonic, Burger King, and, of course, America's most ubiquitous export, McDonald's. Big box stores line the road, set amidst vast parking lots. There are no merchants in their shops (sometimes no bigger than a camping tent) filled with local produce, shoes, hand-made clothing, sweets, fresh roasting chickens, or bicycles. No cafés spill tables onto the streets where smoking patrons loll in conversation or stop to throw back an espresso before hurrying to work or school. Instead of sidewalks bustling with strolling men in soccer shoes, with woolen scarfs artfully knotted around their necks and young mothers with deep cleavage and stiletto heels pushing baby carriages, we see only curb-cut entrances to strip malls and shopping centers.

At the supermarket, we follow some super-sized Americans inside. "Looks like the *Esselunga*," I tell John, recalling the huge Parma supermarket I shopped in occasionally. Well, not exactly. Here there are oranges from Mexico, pineapples from Ecuador, asparagus, green beans, and tomatoes from Chile. Strawberries come from California, lamb from Australia, shrimp from Thailand, mussels from New Zealand, salmon from Alaska. Hundreds of cereals, some healthy and sugar-free, fill the shelves. And there's row after row of frozen stuff. Amazing!

"It's going to be hard to find local and unadulterated food," I say as we roam the aisles. "I'll sure miss my fresh-made pasta and Thursday's fresh-caught fish." We pick out some New York apples and pears, a big box of organic arugula, shiny zucchini and eggplant, frozen-on-the-boat cod, and a free-range chicken—plus several boxes of Barilla pasta.

Back home, I try an American version of a *piadini* on my stovetop grill using a whole-wheat wrap, some shredded fresh mozzarella, and a little mortadella. As it's warming, I look up from the cooktop, gaze around the great room and down the tranquil canal beyond our dock. "It feels so strange."

"Yeah," John says, stealing a slice of mortadella. "We're used to another way of life." So much has changed.

Most people say our island life is idyllic. Part of its charm is the Groundhog Day sameness of its summer events. Old friends return with the ospreys to nest for the season. Like a tight-wound toy that's suddenly let go, the social pace spins relentlessly until it slows and stops in early fall, when the nests are abandoned and we turn to quieter diversions. We've loved living here. It just doesn't fit anymore.

When the tennis season starts, John drops back into games with his old group. I still enjoy playing, but without my court buddy Rhoda, it's not so important to me. I miss the daily foray into some new aspect of foreign life— the sense of newness that every day brought. I miss walking in Parma; its ancient landmarks gave me a kind of comfort. Most of all, I miss the sense of community that doesn't exist here. Even though we were on the edge of Parma's community, we could meld with other residents for the evening *passaggiata* while the accordion man played folk tunes. At a festival or some special event, we were no different from the other Italians. Like other residents, we were always out in Parma—enjoying everyday activities. It *felt* communal. I don't feel that way here.

Italy aroused new energy in our lives. We wanted to take part in everything, sometimes planning three major activities in a day. We would cram as much stimulation into our hours as possible. We walked and walked to partake in all of it. We were like old sponges eagerly sopping up every drop of our environment's abundance.

Our relationship shifted. Living in a foreign place made us more protective of each other. The Parma apartment's smaller space brought us closer together. We were more in tune with each other's rhythms. A contented generosity governed us. In a whole year we had just one minor spat.

A division of labor evolved. I planned; John navigated the language challenges. At the train station ticket kiosk, he read off our "senior gray" discount numbers while I managed the touch-screen. I read the maps, remembered the routes, and read the road signs while he navigated the crazy drivers and precarious roads. I was always trying to understand the context of our environment, not only the history and art, but the mystifying rules of daily life and the latest, crazy advertising slogans. John was eagerly engaging the people around us, searching for *their* context. Together we assembled the puzzle, filled in the blanks, and deepened our appreciation of the country and each other. Can we keep those feelings here, where it's all too familiar?

Summer comes and with it Giuliano and Teresa. Their brief visit, part of their annual month in America, is a much anticipated delight. We connect every few weeks via Skype, and Giuliano and John keep up a running email conversation. We get occasional notes from Simona and the Trieste family. Nik sends chats. On Facebook, I stay current with Andrea, Miriam, Tony, and a few other Italian friends. Claudia posts regularly, and we visit her and Silvano in nearby Toms River when they come to stay with a friend. Yma and I exchange emails, and her handmade cards with photos of Sugar make me nostalgic. I'll always be grateful to that regal greyhound for bringing her and Livio into our lives.

We've been back to Italy twice since our "year" ended—once to explore new places and again to visit our friends. Each time the lightness in my heart returns with the Italian dawn. On our last visit, our Parma apartment was vacant for the exact time we needed it. After a nostalgic week in our comfortable, Parma lifestyle, including an evening with our landlords Andrea and Simona at their tennis club, closing the door to leave was as painful as before.

Now, when I turn the Blazer's key for the 15-mile drive to the ShopRite, I long for my *bici* and shopping on two wheels. We both yearn for the youthful thrill of riding, riding, riding along quiet city streets and through shady, residential neighborhoods. We have six municipalities on our island but no sense of community. We move in concentric societies defined by our interests with no common gathering-place and few shared experiences. We long to belong to a place.

The decision is easy, made almost before we returned. We need to move.

The cherry corner cupboard that holds my mother's flow blue china has been with me nearly 35 years. I've wrapped it carefully in movers' blankets at least seven times. It's my most cherished piece of furniture and, although it's uncomfortably out of place in our modern beach home, I've stubbornly refused to sell it. Now I stand admiring the well-patinaed exterior and hand-blown glass panes—and think how I've treasured it. A strange lightness overtakes me. "It's time for someone else to love you," I say as I stroke a burnished door. Letting go is surprisingly effortless. Nothing could be a clearer sign that our life needs to change.

Emancipating decades of accumulation feels great.

"I want to start fresh," John says, and I agree. We'll sell the house furnished and take just our personal things. We have a new Italian dream now.

On our last trip to Italy, we came home on a repositioning cruise—a boat moving from Rome to Fort Lauderdale. It was John's first time on a cruise ship and my second. He never had any interest in cruising, but traveling on a floating hotel, visiting three countries, with no airport hassles was easy to like. Then John met Ed. He was leisurely sipping a coffee as others scurried off for the day's land tours when John struck up a conversation.

"You're staying onboard?" John asked.

"I'm a veteran of repositioning cruises," Ed replied, "and I've done all these places before. I've got a home outside Lucca and a condo in Sarasota. I go back and forth each spring and fall between the two."

"Really? That's a pretty nice lifestyle. How long have you been doing it?"

Ed paused for a moment. "I guess about 30 years." A lifetime spent between Italy and America. *Che fortuna.* How lucky.

Our new dream is to do the same: cruise between Italy and America every April and October. Have a small place here and find something there—probably a rental. A nest in each culture. But where should our American place be? We've been searching for an ideal city for years. Life in Italy added new criteria to our list. But as we learned there, sharing the search is what matters. Another chance to share the quest is what we want.

It'll be part of a greater adventure—America. Both of us have traveled for work, and John's been in every state in the Union. But the airport-hotel-business-meeting view of a place isn't really being there. Giuliano and Teresa have trekked most of our national parks on their annual visits to the U.S. I've never even been to one. There are dozens of art museums, dinosaurs in Wyoming, and hillbilly bluegrass I want to know. Maine lobsters, crayfish, buffalo burgers, and lots of barbecue to eat. A multitude of cities and small towns to visit and learn about.

We want to spend a year on the road. Just the two of us again—together. Drive the backroads and scenic byways. Go to festivals and parades. Explore the waterways and seek out crazy American kitsch—Carhenge, pie-eating contests, the Bat Festival, and the Great Ball of Twine. I want to marvel at the Grand Canyon as I did Verona's amphitheater, follow the streets of small-town America like I did modest villages in Italy—and find what makes them special. Chase Paul Bunyan and Johnny Appleseed like we did Paulo and Francesca. We want to sit at diners and campgrounds, picnics and clambakes and talk to Americans.

I still long for Italy and the Italian way of life. When I think about why Parma has such a pull on my heart, I come back to this: I consciously appreciated every moment. Maybe because living in another language was so hard, I paid more attention. I treasured my conversations with people, even the simple every-day ones. Deliberately observing how others live, really listening to what they say about their lives gave me a satisfaction that's hard to describe. I wanted so much to know them, I engaged with everyone, not just my friends.

I'd like to know America the same way. Not just to see the great sights, but to listen to the people. To know what they think about our country and our future. To hear their stories, their myths, and what shapes their lives. I want to recapture that thing we felt in Italy, that thrill of discovery, the authentic *now*.

Acknowledgements

We must start by thanking Bonda Garrison and Donna Sudak for their exuberant commitment to our project from day one.

Were it not for the Writers' Group at the LBI library we would never have completed this book. Margaret Hawke, Richard Morgan, Kim and Jim Trotto, Beth Mann, Laura Maschel, Nancy Gallagher, Iris Culhane, Barbara Blank, Jackie Ostberg, Jeanne Sutton, Helen Gallo, Cindi Graham, and Dotti Turkot provided constant encouragement and unnerving, insightful advice on style and format. We are grateful to the LBI Branch of the Ocean County Library, especially Linda Feaster, for providing our weekly meeting space. The folks at Peter Murphy's Winter Poetry & Prose Getaway, especially Tom Peele and Barbara Hurd, gave us invaluable feedback and encouragement.

Our heartfelt appreciation to our early readers Michele Fabrizio, Sandy Silverman, Bob Quinn and Tom Scangarello for their responsiveness and suggestions.

Ginny Green provided careful, intelligent editing, and Toby Schmidt Meyer gave us a brilliant cover design. Together you made us look better than we thought possible.

We are indebted to the members of our book club, Jack and Barb Benson, Linda Waddell, Phyllis Swain, Steve and Nancy Talis, Mary Ann Koller, Ruth Wilf, Bob and Patti Block, Bill and Peg Felix, Kay Binetsky, Burt and Barbara Nemroff, Dorie Green, Bonnie Clarke, and Dorothy Lurie, for elevating our reading skills.

Our gratitude to the friends who constantly encouraged us: Enrico and Lydia Marini, John Mastronardo, Sy and Susan Koslowsky, Winnie Jo Wilson, Susan Vitale, Dottie Pfohl, Bernie and Harriet Rothman, Tim and Phyllis Beck, Christine Rooney, Ron and Barbara Sorvino, Susanne Root, Bob and Cathy Holland, Sybilla Zeldin, and Linda and Bob White.

Un grandissimo grazie to our Italian friends, most of all Teresa and Giuliano Vitali who adopted us, chauffeured us, fed us and taught us. Without them our experience of Italy would have been much poorer. Thanks also to our Madrelingua teachers Stefi and Lucia, and to friends Claudia Salati and Silvano Sarti, Andrea Chiari and Emanuele Rotelli, Andrea Gambetti and Simona Porta, Yma Marconi and Livio Consigli, Umberto and Patricia Marconi, Miriam Sadlakova and Giuseppi Lodi, and Nicola Bortolini for teaching us more about Italy and the Italians than we could ever have hoped to learn in English.

To Petralia family members in both the United States and Italy we owe a special debt for their thoughtful advice, warm hospitality and help with our family tree.

And to the writers of all the books and poems we have read and hope to read we send our appreciation for your amazing talent, generosity, and inspiration.

ABOUT THE AUTHORS

John and Nancy Petralia are currently out in the world living their next adventure.

Visit the authors' website, NotInATuscanVilla.com.

Join the email list for a free reading group discussion guide for *Not in a Tuscan Villa*.

Made in the USA
Las Vegas, NV
18 January 2023